D1359552

LIONS CLUBS in the 21st CENTURY

Paul Martin
&
Robert Kleinfelder

authorHOUSE®

AuthorHouse™
1663 Liberty Drive, Suite 200
Bloomington, IN 47403
www.authorhouse.com
Phone: 1-800-839-8640

First published by AuthorHouse 4/8/2009

ISBN: 978-1-4343-9411-8 (sc)
ISBN: 978-1-4343-9412-5 (hc)

Library of Congress Control Number: 2008905381

Printed in the United States of America
Bloomington, Indiana

This book is printed on acid-free paper.

Cover design by Lisa Smith, Graphic Arts Department

This book is dedicated to the Lions, Lionesses, Leos, and their families throughout the world who have worked with cheerful persistence to provide hope, opportunity and healing to those who might otherwise have had none of these.

Table Of Contents

Foreword

Mahendra Amarasuriya
International President – 2007-2008

The year 1917 was, indeed, one of historic significance. The "Great War" was unleashing its terrible carnage. The Russian czar was overthrown, eventually leading to the Bolsheviks coming to power. Science and technology continued their inexorable rise to redefine how we live and communicate. In Chicago, Illinois, and Dallas, Texas, of that year, yet another momentous event was taking place, one that would have an impact of communities across the earth.

A new organization was being given structure and direction, and it would grow into the largest, most active, service club association in the world. This is the story of The International Association of Lions Clubs, a story of commitment and selfless dedication on the part of millions of men and women who, since 1917, would proudly call themselves Lions. The authors, both Lions, have shown how Lions clubs have for more than nine decades now given personal testimony to the ideals proclaimed by the association's motto, "We Serve."

This commitment is demonstrated in the manner in which Lions have answered the call to assist people in greatest need, partner with young people to give them hope and confidence for a fulfilling future, rally to the aid of communities struck by natural disasters, provide funding and hands-on involvement in cases whenever and wherever the situation warrants, and, of course, the focal point of Lions Clubs International, to promote sight preservation and restoration.

Only a few of the countless projects of Lions clubs and districts could be accommodated in this book; space permitting there could be thousands of pages more. All have established and reinforced the foundation and vision of the association from the second decade of the 20th Century into the new millennium.

It is a story of growth, of accepting challenges to adapt to new courses of involvement when change was required, and of giving service-minded individuals opportunities to experience the priceless joy and satisfaction of making lives better, healthier and happier for others. Through it all, the family of Lions Clubs International has achieved remarkable success in enhancing global peace, harmony and understanding.

This is the history of the Lions clubs. For our membership, it will fill them with greater pride in knowing what Lions worldwide have accomplished and are presently doing on behalf of human needs. For others, it will demonstrate all that groups of men, women and young people can make possible when motivated to be of voluntary service.

Chapter One
An Ideal Triumphant

It began as an idea, a feeling that if individuals who were successful in business and the professions devoted a portion of their time and energy to community service they could be a positive force for building not only their own communities, but also the world community. They could also be a positive force in helping people in greatest need by enabling them to enjoy healthier, happier, more productive lives. The idea evolved into the International Association of Lions Clubs, today, with more than 1.3 million members, the largest service club organization in the world. How has it impacted the lives of those most in need of a helping hand? Let Juanita Hernandez explain what the Lions' motto *We Serve* has meant to her. She is a grateful example of the hugely successful project of the Lions Eye Bank in Mexico City that has provided more than 3,000 free cataract operations and makes available corneal transplants and regular glaucoma screenings for local residents.

"I didn't realize I had cataracts and just thought my eyesight was dimming because of aging," she says. "The Lions offered a free cataract screening which I attended, and the doctor discovered the cataracts and scheduled me for an operation one week later. He operated on one eye and implanted an intraocular lens. Then, a month later, he operated on the other eye and planted a lens. I'm 60 years old, a school teacher, and would have not been able to work much longer. How my life has been renewed! I never understood much about the Lions before this experience, but now I am aware that they are good people who help others."

Still another example of the many ways Lions reach out to help people in need is witnessed at the 440-acre Lions Youth Haven in Kambah, located in the Australian Capital Territory. Supported by local Lions clubs, it has, for more than a decade assisted well over 2,000 young Australians who live in the capital city of Canberra or within an hour's drive. Most of these young people are considered "chronically unemployed," some are school dropouts and others have a degree of brain damage. Others are homeless or facing homelessness due to unfavorable or abusive home environments. The rules at Lions Youth Haven are simple: no violence, no alcohol and no drugs. One critical demand is that of acquiring skills or an education. It is expected that they become involved with projects on the farm, attend the local technical school and other educational institutes in order to gain skills. The opportunities for training abound. Options include horticulture, textiles, crafts, glass sculpture, carpentry, metalwork and video production, in addition to more traditional classroom instruction.

As one Lion involved in Youth Haven observed, "This project gives young people, who probably haven't had the opportunity we had when we were younger, some confidence and skills to help them get on with their lives."

Helping others enjoy healthier, more productive lives, has been a goal of Lions since the second decade of the 20th Century.

First Steps

The site was the LaSalle Hotel in the heart of Chicago's downtown; the date, June 7, 1917. A successful insurance man named Melvin Jones, at the time the secretary of The Business Circle in Chicago, essentially a professional men's luncheon club, called together a group of community leaders representing various service organizations, including a number of Lions clubs scattered across the United States, for the purpose of bringing them together to form one strong association. The Business Circle, which Jones joined in 1913, was no different from similar luncheon groups which, for the most part, were devoted to advancing the business interests of their members. He was concerned with more than promoting such interests and reaping the resulting financial rewards.

"What if these men," Jones asked himself, "who are successful because of their drive, intelligence and ambition, were put to work helping improve their own communities?" With this relatively new concept in mind, he invited men of various clubs to Chicago to investigate such a possibility. Among those participating in the meeting at the LaSalle Hotel were the International Association of

Lions Clubs based in Evansville, Indiana, the Vortex Club of St. Louis, Missouri, and the Business and Professional Men's Association of St. Paul, Minnesota. Jones also invited representatives of the Optimist and Exchange Clubs, but the Exchange Clubs opted not to attend.

Evansville physician Dr. William Woods is listed in the minutes of the Chicago meeting as "President, International Association of Lions," and representing 27 lions clubs listed under this name. The corporate records of the State of Indiana show that on October 24, 1916, Dr. Woods, Carmi Hicks and C.R. Conan filed Articles of Incorporation for a non-profit organization titled The International Association of Lions Clubs. Consequently, all Lions clubs chartered after August 30, 1916, were organized under that name and by June 1, 1917, there were 35 clubs that had received charters from the association. On May 16, 1917, Melvin Jones asked Dr. Woods to attend the meeting at the LaSalle Hotel "with a view to lining up our organization with yours."

The minutes of the meeting show that Edwin J. Raber and W.J. Livingston introduced the following resolution:

"That the Board of Directors of the Business Circle of Chicago enter into negotiations with Dr. W.P. Woods of The International Association of Lions Clubs, and with other clubs with reference to the affiliation of these clubs and that said Board of Directors have full power to make and complete all arrangements for said affiliation and any act they do on the premises shall be an act of this club and binding thereon," and that "the motion was seconded by A.F. Sheahan and unanimously adopted by the Business Circle."

The minutes also show that Dr. Woods invited the various clubs to join the International Association of Lions. He is quoted as stating:

"Whereas all clubs represented here today have different names, and whereas the Lions clubs have an international organization, with approximately 30 clubs in different parts of the United States, and whereas the Lions clubs are not now represented in any other cities represented by the other clubs; therefore, as president of The International Association of Lions Clubs, I hereby extend an invitation to these clubs to accept charters in The International Association of Lions Clubs and become part and parcel of our organization. If you accept this invitation, there will be no membership charged, and all we ask is to adopt our name and pay dues to The International Association, which are at the rate of $1.00 per member, payable semi-annually in advance."

The St. Louis club accepted the offer and received its Lions Club charter on July 25, 1917 and the Chicago Central club on August 2 of that year.

Determined to make an informed decision, Melvin Jones wrote a letter on June 19, 1917, to J.T. Coleman, secretary of the Ardmore, Oklahoma, Lions Club, saying, "Dr. W.P. Woods, your international president, has extended to our organization an invitation to accept a charter and the name of The Lions Club. We have about decided to do so, and our decision will no doubt be influential in getting other clubs in other cities to do the same thing.

"Before making a final decision we would like to have you tell us about your organization in Ardmore. How many members have you? How often do you meet and any other information you care to write to help us in our decision."

J.T. Coleman replied that in his judgment, "The Lions club is a very valuable organization for any city. I know it is a success in other cities. I have given the matter considerable thought and say without hesitation that I can recommend it to the business and professional men of any city."

The association kicked into high gear. On July 21, 1917, Dr. Woods notified all clubs, "The first convention of the Lions clubs will be held in the city of Dallas, Texas, on the 8-9-10 of October of this year."

Millions of lives were eventually transformed because of what happened during those three days. Countless human beings were able to see, hear, walk, work and are alive because of the extraordinary association that was organized at that gathering. It began on Monday morning, October 8, and today men, women and children the world over benefit from that legacy.

The headline in *The Dallas Morning News* that day declared: "Lions' International Meeting Opens Today." The delegates were welcomed by Dallas Mayor Joe E. Lawther in the Palm Garden of the Adolphus Hotel at ten o'clock in the morning. With a prophetic look to the future, Mayor Lawther said, "Your organization is made up of men who accomplish things; men who recognize no obstacles."

In addition to Dr. Woods, 36 delegates and eight alternates took part in the meeting. Twenty-two Lions clubs were represented at the Dallas convention and six others clubs were still in existence or being formed at the time. Twenty-two of these clubs have functioned continuously since then and in 1951 each was officially designated a "Founder Club of Lions." They are: Little Rock Founder and Texarkana, Arkansas; Colorado Springs Downtown and Denver, Colorado; Chicago Central, Illinois; Shreveport Downtown, Louisiana; St. Louis Downtown, Missouri; Ardmore, Chickasha, Muskogee, Oklahoma City Downtown and Tulsa Downtown Oklahoma; Memphis Downtown, Tennessee; Abilene Founder, Austin Founder, Beaumont Founder, Dallas Founder, Fort Worth, Houston Central, Paris, Port Arthur Founder and Waco Founder, Texas.

The delegates elected officers on the first day. L.H. Lewis, president of the Dallas Lions Club, was elected international president by acclamation, but he refused the post and asked delegates to name Dr. Woods to the position. This was done, and they proceeded to elect the other officers by acclamation: L.H. Lewis, first vice president; E.N. Kaercher, St. Louis, Missouri, second vice president; Melvin Jones, Chicago, Illinois, secretary-treasurer. R.A. Kleinschmidt, Oklahoma City, Oklahoma, and James L. McRee, Memphis, Tennessee, were named directors for three years. H.F. Endsley, Texarkana, Arkansas, and Roger Wheles, Shreveport, Louisiana, were chosen directors for two-year terms.

There were two directorships for one-year terms and these were filled by ballot, with A.V. Davenport of Tulsa, Oklahoma, and C.J. Kirk of Houston, Texas, being elected to these posts. Nine states were represented at that first convention: Arkansas, Colorado, Illinois, Indiana, Louisiana, Missouri, Oklahoma, Tennessee and Texas. Texas and Oklahoma brought the largest delegations and received two seats each on the Board of Directors.

At the time of the convention, Lions clubs were also operating in Pueblo, Colorado, and El Reno and Okmulgee, Oklahoma. Clubs in

Oakland, California, and Temple, Texas, were being organized and began functioning soon after.

The delegates voted to open membership to women and retained the Lions' emblem, the head of a lion holding a club in its mouth marked "International." The convention chose purple and gold as the association's colors and Melvin Jones was authorized to open a headquarters in Chicago.

Votes, however, were not unanimous. W.J. Power of St. Louis spoke in favor of changing the name of the organization from Lions to Vortex. E.N. Calvin of Waco, Grant Richardson of Shreveport, and others contended that the name of Lions should be kept. The motion to retain the name was passed by a vote of 24 to six.

The interpretation of the association's name was stated in a 1931 issue of THE LION Magazine: "Our name was not elected at random, neither was it a coined name. From time immemorial, the lion has been the symbol of all that was good, and because of the symbolism that name was chosen. Four outstanding qualities—Courage, Strength, Activity and Fidelity—had largely to do with the adoption of the name. The last mentioned of these qualities, Fidelity, has a deep and peculiar significance for all Lions. The lion symbol has been symbol of fidelity through the ages and among all nations, ancient and modern. It stands for loyalty to a friend, loyalty to a principle, loyalty to a duty, loyalty to a trust."

The report of the committee on constitution and by-laws was received with little debate, and most of the provisions were adopted without difficulty. However, there was a heated argument about an amendment to the constitution offered by W.A. Lybrand and J.C. Leonard of Oklahoma City. A principle that has become a guiding precept in the association's program of international service, the amendment stated: "No club shall by its by-laws, constitution or otherwise hold out the financial betterment of it members as its objects." After a stormy session, the amendment passed.

The United States had entered World War I six months before the Dallas convention and the delegates voted to support the war effort and the Liberty Loan. The secretary was instructed to transmit a copy of the motion to President Woodrow Wilson.

Austin and St. Louis asked to be the site for the 1918 convention and the delegates chose St. Louis.

The first convention of Lions Clubs International closed on October 10, 1917. The structure was in place, with Dr. Woods having been elected international president. The Lions Objects and Code of Ethics began the process of being drafted and were altered only a little over the years. For more than nine decades they have been viewed as embodying the moral strength and spirit of Lions Clubs International. At the conclusion of the Dallas Convention, Dr. Woods reported that the association had a grand total of $72.05 in the bank.

Lions were now able to prepare for the future. That small gathering of inspired community leaders in Dallas provided a basic form that in a few years would make the fledgling organization a force for voluntary service, goodwill and mutual assistance throughout the world. Had these men been able to foresee decades beyond, they would have been astounded, pleasantly so, at the personal impact Lions were having on the lives of others, people who desperately needed the helping hands of caring and concern.

As an example, in Karachi, Pakistan, the professional Lions Club organized a medical camp during which more than 250 residents were examined and in Turkey, the Bursa Hisar Lions Club constructed a primary school in the village. Zamboanga City La Bella Lions in the Philippines distributed food packages to leprosy patients at a sanitarium and in India, members of the Patiala Samrat Lions Club brought food to leprosy patients. The Kansas City, Kansas, South Lions joined with Guatemalan Lions and 40 physicians, dentists and nurses on a medical mission to treat children in Honduras and Texas Lions sponsored a summer camp for insulin-dependent diabetic children.

In 1999, Indiana Lions traveled to Tulancingo, Mexico, to bring sight services to people in need. Eyeglasses were distributed, many to children, and during the week-long mission nearly 5,000 individuals received care. This was, in fact, one of many such missions that Indiana Lions have led to Mexico and Central America. More than 2,000 books for children in Nepal were collected and sent by Colorado Lions and distributed by the Lions Club of Kathmandu Downtown. In the state of Washington, Lions held their first fishing derby for special needs children in 2005, making it possible for these youngsters to enjoy the refreshing sport for the very first time. "Within seconds," said Federal Way Lion Bob Darrigan, "shouts of joy and encouragement would be heard throughout the Ashburn Mill Pond."

Whether the projects be large or small, they all were conducted on the important one-to-one basis and encouraged the participating Lions not to forget their oath to assist in humanitarian endeavors wherever needed. These and countless other activities worldwide, gave substance to the ideals envisioned at that first convention back in 1917.

During 1917 and the following year, however, services were confined to the United States with Lions greatly concentrating on projects to support the nation's war effort, ranging from bond drives, collections of books and magazines, entertaining servicemen, helping war orphans and widows and fundraising for the Red Cross. Now step two in the march of Lions to enhancing their pledge to service was upon them and they grasped the opportunity.

St. Louis, 1918—The Future Beckoned

Despite the spreading influenza epidemic, a total of 79 delegates and alternates from 24 cities participated in the 1918 Convention in St. Louis, Missouri, October 19-21 in the Marquette Hotel. Twenty St. Louis members were there and 20 from Oklahoma's seven clubs. There were 17 Texas Lions in attendance, seven from Chicago and six from Arkansas. They immediately got down to business.

As the convention opened, R.A. Kleinschmidt of Oklahoma City moved to declare all offices vacant and to permit the nominating committee to fill all offices. The motion passed, thus unseating several directors who had one or two years remaining to serve. Also, it placed elective power in the hands of a few rather than the majority. A nominating committee was elected and then resigned immediately. The chairman reported "two or three committee members, I believe, should be elected as officers and directors and the committee does not want to nominate any of its members." Following an understanding that members could nominate from their own numbers, the committee was re-elected.

8

The officers nominated by the committee were elected: L.H Lewis, Dallas, Texas, president; Jesse Robinson, Oakland, California, first vice president; Dr. C.C. Reid, Denver, Colorado, second vice president; F.C. Brinkman, Jr., Shreveport, Louisiana, third vice president and Melvin Jones, Chicago, Illinois, secretary-treasurer.

The Constitution and By-Laws Committee proposed an amendment to the constitution eliminating women from membership in Lions clubs. It was passed by the delegates. This would subsequently be reversed nearly 70 years later at the 1987 International Convention in Taipei Multiple District 300 Taiwan.

To the delight of the officers, the delegates applauded news of the association's solvency. The secretary-treasurer reported receipts of $2,360.83 and expenditures of $1,944.68 between October 9, 1917, and August 15, 1918. The bank balance at The Northern Trust Company in Chicago showed $488.40.

The Oakland Lions Club asked for the 1919 Convention but then withdrew in favor of Chicago, which thus became the site of the third gathering of Lions. Momentum was growing with each convention.

New clubs were continually being chartered. At the St. Louis Convention, for example, some of Melvin Jones' earlier efforts were rewarded when the Cirgonian Club of Los Angeles, California, with which Jones had corresponded during 1916-17, wired the convention: "Cirgonian Club of Los Angeles expresses its desire to affiliate with the Lions Clubs. Please instruct us what to do. Send us the constitution, by-laws, literature, etc. Sorry we cannot send delegate to convention. We rely upon you to represent us." The governor for the Pacific Coast was immediately authorized to induct the new Lions club.

Melvin Jones had been working in a small office in the Insurance Exchange Building in downtown Chicago. The rent was $12.50 a month and a stenographer received $40. The convention voted to increase Jones' salary from $400 a year to $750 and authorized him to find a larger office in the same building.

The Board of Directors voted to purchase 1,000 lapel pins bearing the association's emblem. It also voted in favor of a motion to raise dues from $1.00 to $2.00 effective January 1, 1919 and to keep the charter fee at $10.00 until September 1, 1919.

Author's Note: Unless otherwise stated, all funds reported in this book are in United States dollars.

G.M. Cunningham was given the post of national organizer. He was to receive a stipulated sum per member and pay his travel and organization expenses from that sum. The first district officers were also appointed. G.M. Cunningham became district governor of Texas; Jesse Robinson of California, Nevada, Oregon and Washington and Leon T. Kahn of Louisiana. Furthermore, the Finance Committee recommended publishing a magazine with all of the association's income above office expenses and the secretary's salary used for the publication. Melvin Jones was authorized to handle this responsibility as he thought best.

In closing the convention, President Lewis announced his plans to visit every Lions club in existence, at his own expense. He declared the convention adjourned at 1:00 p.m. on August 21, 1918.

The first issue of THE LION Magazine was published in November 1918. It appeared in 28 pages plus cover, with dimensions of 6 ½" x 9" and summarized the St. Louis Convention, listed new clubs and reported on the activities of existing clubs. This initial issue also included an expanded list of district governors, rather than the three named by the Board of Directors during the convention. These governors included: T.J. Parker of Little Rock for Arkansas; Louis K. Cameron of Denver for Colorado and Wyoming; G.W. Milligan of Chicago for Illinois; E.J. Wenner of Waterloo for Iowa; William J. Repke of St. Paul for Minnesota; A.V. Davenport of Tulsa for Oklahoma and John E. Lippett of Memphis for Tennessee. Robinson and Davenport had been appointed at the board meeting and Louisiana had a new district governor, F.C. Brinkman who replaced Leon Kahn.

Melvin Jones was invariably cheerful about the present and optimistic about the future, but even he might well have had difficulty envisioning the magazine's eventual growth. It was destined to be published in 21 languages and would become the multilingual voice of Lions Clubs International.

Lions clubs continued to expand. Lion Cunningham was joined by S.A. Hicks and they worked primarily in the western United States. By the end of the first fiscal year they had organized new clubs in Colorado, Wyoming, Missouri, Oklahoma and Texas. Club extension then met a roadblock.

Influenza was spreading and about 548,000 American died during the 1919 epidemic, including Lion Cunningham's son. Few clubs were holding meetings and many were delinquent in their dues. President Lewis had an appendectomy, his wife became seriously ill and he was unable to visit all clubs and promote new ones. Momentum slowed and then ground to a halt. But just when the future looked gloomiest, a large Lions club that had owed dues for a full year, paid in full and several others that had been on the verge of expiring returned to life. Lion Cunningham resumed work and organized 11 Lions clubs in four states in less than five months. The association was again on the move.

Club activities during the first two years provided a preview of the value Lions clubs would be to their communities in the years and decades ahead. World War I had ended, but famine, sickness and misery remained. Early in 1919, the Lions Club of Houston, Texas, sponsored a concert featuring Belgian musicians from the Brussels Conservatory. The performance raised more than $1,000 for the Belgian Relief Committee to help suffering children in that country. This concert was, in fact, only the latest in the projects conducted by the Houston Club to reduce pain in war-ravaged Europe.

Another Texas Lions club, the Corsicana Club, voted in 1918 to furnish a drinking fountain for each school building in the city. Although a small project, it signaled the beginning of cooperation between Lions and educators. By the 21st Century, the beginning recorded in Corsicana had grown to hundreds of schools constructed by Lions worldwide. The Lions of Mexico have especially been recognized for their leadership in building and equipping schools. The Oklahoma City Lions Club established a summer camp for children in the area that included a "swimming home," all amid trees and country land where, the club members said, they could be taken away from the city for a month to live in a dreamland made possible by the Lions clubs.

The association was now charged with energy and growing commitment and was en route to Chicago to celebrate the 1919 Convention. The founders had fashioned a bold blueprint dedicated to helping the less fortunate, working meticulously to design a practical approach that was soon to be reflected throughout the world.

The majestic Adolphus Hotel where Lions Clubs International became an operational unit still stands as a centerpiece in downtown Dallas. The La Salle Hotel in Chicago that witnessed the first gathering of community leaders determined to build an organization devoted to the cause of humanity, however, fell victim a number of years ago to the wrecking ball, surrendering to a new generation of hotels that now dot the landscapes of cities the world over. When it was torn down and its furnishings disposed of, one very important item was rescued; a plaque testifying to an event that occurred there so many years before, one that has been of supreme importance to communities, the blind and visually impaired and less fortunate people the world over. It reads: Lions International Founded here at LaSalle Hotel, June 7, 1917. "We Serve."

Both hotels earned their place in the history of what is now the world's largest service club organization. Thus it was with an air of expectancy that Lions converged on Chicago for their third convention, poised to soon move onto the international stage.

The first steps had been taken…the future beckoned.

Chapter Two
The Objects and Ethics:
The Backbone of Lions Clubs
International

Every organization, be it in the private or public sector, business or service, requires a set of guidelines, a path along which it can proceed toward its goals of growth and accomplishment. Such is the case for Lions Clubs International, and its framework has been the heralded Objects and Ethics, recognized as a resounding exclamation point of individual commitment to community service and assistance to those in greatest need. Drafted during the association's first year of existence, the Code of Ethics was officially adopted at the 1918 International Convention in St. Louis. It proved to be a document that, since the second decade of the 20th Century, has motivated millions of men and women to set aside their personal lives to answer the needs of others.

Much of the work on the Code was performed by G.M. Cunningham, secretary of the Houston Lions Club. The original draft was sent to Melvin Jones who, after considering its points, forwarded it to Oklahoma City Lions R.E. Kleinschmidt and Walter Lybrand for review. Jones, himself, had exhaustively studied similar codes drawn up in human history. He had examined the thoughts of Hammurabi of Babylon (2250BC), the Napoleonic Code, the Mosaic Commandments and the Justinian Codex and had been struck by one feature common to all. "They were," observed Jones, "all legal codes filled with negative commands. That was not what we were looking for. What we finally drafted was what you might call a *leadership code* and there isn't a 'Thou shalt not' in it."

The code presented in St. Louis reflected his thoughts. The chairman of the committee charged with examining the historic proposal was Lion J. Hirsch and was assisted by committee members K.H. Warren, D.F. Hurst, Arlie J. Cripe and H.H. Endsley. Following close consideration, they agreed to its substance and challenges to individual conscience and proposed their adoption.

The association's Objects were also debated, considered, explored and examined at length and in depth by the time they came up for vote at the 1919 Convention in Chicago. Each representative had an opportunity to declare his views and following a spirited discussion voted their approval. Both the Objects and Ethics have served as standards of individual conduct and operation ever since.

"They are," said Past International President Lloyd Morgan of New Zealand, "a practical guide to behavior enriched by the fact that there is a warm feeling of satisfaction in knowing that you are associated with others who believe as you do."

They read as follows:

Objects

To create and foster a spirit of understanding among the peoples of the world.

To promote the principles of good government and good citizenship.

To take an active interest in the civic, cultural, social and moral welfare of the community.

To unite the clubs in the bonds of friendship, good fellowship and mutual understanding.

To provide a forum for open discussion of all matters of public interest; provided, however, that partisan politics and sectarian religion shall not be debated by club members.

To encourage service-minded men to serve their community without personal financial reward, and to encourage efficiency and promote high ethical standards in commerce, industry, professions, public works and private endeavors.

Code of Ethics

To show my faith in the worthiness of my vocation by industrious application to the end that I may merit a reputation for quality of service.

To seek success and to demand all fair remuneration or profit as my just due, but to accept no profit or success at the price of my own self-respect lost because of an unfair advantage taken or because of questionable acts on my part.

To remember that in building up my business it is not necessary to tear down another's; to be loyal to my clients or customers and true to myself.

Whenever a doubt arises as to the right or ethics of my position or action toward my fellow men, to resolve such doubt against myself.

To hold friendship as an end and not a means. To hold that true friendship exists not on account of the service performed by one to another, but that true friendship demands nothing but accepts service in the spirit in which it is given.

Always to bear in mind my obligations as a citizen to my nation, my state and my community, and to give to them my unswerving loyalty in word, act and deed. To give freely of my time, labor and means.

To aid my fellow men by giving my sympathy to those in distress, my aid to the weak and my substance to the needy.

To be careful with my criticism and liberal with my praise; to build up and not destroy.

These challenges to the integrity and dedication of Lions has been witnessed for more than nine decades. Compared with the concepts and goals of most private organizations in 1917, they were unusual. It was instantly evident to new members that Lions placed a priority on meeting community needs and demonstrating high ethical standards in their personal lives. The results of adhering to these points of behavior and commitment are reflected thousands of times over. To cite one example:

In Canada, the British Columbia Lions Society for Children with Disabilities also owns the provincial franchise for Easter Seals and is recognized as the Easter Seal Society for British Columbia. As reported in an issue of THE LION Magazine, the society's mandate is to enhance the lives of children with disabilities and thousands have benefited from the program since 1947 when some Vancouver East Lions Club members volunteered to use their own vehicles to transport children and adults with polio and tuberculosis to hospital appointments. In 1949, other Vancouver clubs joined to purchase three buses to serve the city, and in 1952 the British Columbia Society for Children with Disabilities was officially registered as a nonprofit charitable organization.

The society is among the largest nonprofit organizations in Canada and raises approximately $8 million annually, employing a full-time staff of 40. The society's board of directors is made up almost totally of Lions. Its primary objective is to focus on the abilities of special-needs children and to enrich their lives by emphasizing those abilities. The society is committed to introducing these youngsters to new experiences that will help them achieve greater independence and self-esteem. Most of the services are provided at minimal or no cost to the families.

Through the years, the Lions Society has helped thousands of youngsters whose disabilities included cerebral palsy, Down's syndrome, spina bifida, muscular dystrophy, autism, mental health disorders, cardio-pulmonary diseases, hearing and vision impairments and cystic fibrosis.

The purpose functions on the belief that special-needs children should be able to enjoy the same recreational pursuits as others their age. The Lions Easter Seals camps enable the children to hike, swim, canoe, perform skits, sing songs around a campfire and sleep overnight in tents. "We do everything here," enthused one child who relies on crutches to get around the camp. "If I fall down, it doesn't matter. I just get up and keep going."

The Lions Society also provides a fleet of more than 70 specially equipped Easter Seal buses in 56 communities that take children to and from school, medical appointments and recreational activities. Without this program, some of these youngsters would be unable to attend school and required to learn through home study. They would have fewer opportunities to socialize with other children and develop new skills such as swimming and even wheelchair basketball. The end result is the development of a priceless degree of independence.

The society also provides low-cost accommodations for 55 families every night while their children receive medical treatment in Vancouver or Prince George. Each year, more than 9,000 guests use the facility. "I always feel welcome here," said one 17-year-old patient. "It's like my second home."

Lion Barry Evans, who has served as the society's president, proudly explained, "The Lions Society has become a way of life for Lions in this province. A mother's warm words of gratitude, a father choking back tears as he thanks us, hundreds of smiling young faces—these people touch our hearts. We try in every way we can to reach out and help them."

Could anything be clearer evidence of the Code of Ethics at work?

Still another example of how Lions worldwide are bound to the ethical standards set forth in 1918 and 1919 and to work with other community leaders is witnessed in South Africa where Lions have committed themselves to putting children first.

The Ilitha Care Centre, founded in 1995, is located on the outskirts of Port Elizabeth, next to the main airport. The area is home to thousands of poor people with an extremely low employment rate. The centre was developed to relieve the effects of poverty and provide crucially needed child care and food distribution, relying on donations from local businesses and churches because parents could not provide financial assistance for the more than 20 children, ages three to five, who were sheltered there.

Port Elizabeth Cape Recife Lions Sue Kinnell and Tom Pittaway visited the centre to learn how Lions could become involved. They discovered that the facility was in desperate need of maintenance to improve the shelter and security of the children. One of the outside classrooms offered little protection from the weather and the entire centre needed a boundary wall to shield the youngsters from passing traffic and dust thrown into the air by vehicles.

The Cape Recife Lions soon assembled a team of businesses and individuals from Port Elizabeth who were willing to provide building expertise and services to improve living conditions. A local job creation center produced "vibacrete" walls, bringing about two productive services: employing craftsmen to create the walls and then put them in place to help protect the Iliatha children. The 45-foot walls were erected with two wide gates and fitted with a metal trellis to improve security.

To assist financially, an export company contributed one South African Rand (US$6.13 at the time) for each rand spent by the Lions, and as one Cape Recife member explained, "This was a great way to double the funds and get more mileage for our efforts." The Lions also commissioned a local construction crew to assemble the wall and perform the necessary upgrades to the outside classroom. This had only consisted of a cement floor and a shade for a roof. The roof was replaced with a waterproof metal sheeting and the old shade was used to provide wind protection on the sides of the classroom.

This revamped centre proved to be a tremendous cooperative effort between the Lions and local businesses, one that has improved the lives of the township's children in immeasurable ways because the Lions were dedicated to reflect their concept of the Code of Ethics to put children first.

These feelings can easily be repeated at Lions-supported camps and other projects around the world, all reflective of a code of Objects and Ethics adopted more than 90 years ago.

Past International President H.C. Petry Jr. observed upon his first reading of the document, "I could not help but become personally interested in Lionism and recognize it as an organization of tremendous value and integrity. Following these documents in one's personal life develops character and integrity in ways which might not happen otherwise. I thank the Lions for bringing my own personal commitment of time and resources for the benefit of those less fortunate than myself."

The commitment of time and resources on the part of Lions from different lands and in cooperation with other community leaders, for example, can be attested to by all who have benefited from a new healthy water supply system in the town of Bandipur, Nepal. Truly, it exemplifies the first Object of the association and was reported in THE LION Magazine by Lion Hank Hoekstra, a member of the Edmonton, Alberta, Canada, Lions Club. The project was initiated by the twinned Lions clubs of Edmonton South and Funabashi Higashi, Japan. In June, 1994, on the occasion of the Edmonton Club's 40th Charter Anniversary celebration, Funabashi Lions who were visiting the club determined to celebrate the event with a service project that would benefit an area of the world not normally served by Lions. But where to begin their search?

Both clubs consulted Dr. Drake Hocking, an expert in plant pathology, forestry and water conservation, and he strongly suggested improvements in the water supply system of the Bandipur District in far-away Nepal. The 30-year-old system currently in use was built to serve 5,000 people, but suffered from rusted pipes, leaking joints and unauthorized tapping by private lines. The result was that water was available for only one hour each day and the growing population made improvements critical.

It was determined that with the donation of materials and equipment by the Lions clubs and the help of local workers, the system could be refurbished to provide cleaner and more plentiful water to Bandipur residents and those in several other villages—a total in excess of 22,000 people. In order to help this population so far removed, the Lions requested and were granted the cooperation of the Bandipur Social Development Committee, comprised of Bandipur natives who had migrated to the capital city of Kathmandu and subsequently prospered in business and government service. They were interested in improving living conditions in their home district while still maintaining its unique character as much as possible. A comprehensive plan was developed and presented to the two Lions clubs. They enthusiastically endorsed it and each club contributed US$8,500 in the spring of 1996.

Upon approval, the Bandipur Social Development Committee formed several water committees to coordinate that project in each of the smaller hamlets and developed policies for water distribution and access. These local groups met with residents of the affected areas for their input and participation, and worked with commercial enterprises, schools and hospitals in order to maximize benefits. Through their roles in the decision-making process and by providing much of the labor, the inhabitants made the project their own. This is essential because the long-term success of the improved water supply system was dependent upon community-wide participation and support. This type of commitment is true not only in Bandipur, but in any area of the world where Lions help to improve health and living conditions.

The rewards for the Edmonton and Funabashi Lions were exactly what were envisioned: a more consistent and plentiful clean water supply system available to more than four times the number of people previously served, and now available several hours a day for more locations throughout the area. Furthermore, impressed by the careful use of resources in Bandipur, the two Lions clubs authorized the Social Development Committee to use surplus funds from the project to initiate other improvements in the area, such as upgrading the road to the lowlands and coordinating efforts to cultivate economic, educational, health and tourist services.

What occurred in Bandipur, Nepal, was, indeed, taking a challenge straight out of the heralded Objects and Ethics of Lions Clubs International.

The rise and fall of civilizations is often marked by the rise and fall of values—and the documents which express those values—observed 1971-72 International President Robert J. Uplinger. "As history moved on, the world received the English Magna Carta, the Mayflower Compact, the Declaration of Independence and other landmark documents," he said. "When American culture changed from rural to urban at the time of World War I, Lions Clubs International adopted the Objects and Ethics as we have them today. They proved to exercise a profound effect on all of our leadership and serve as a rule and guide for Lions everywhere."

The impact which the ideals of Lions Clubs International have had in the business community are evident in the first three Ethics and the final Object. However, in designing these standards the founders made it clear that this new service club was, in fact, separating itself from the business community. They emphasized that a Lions club was not just another quasi-social arm of private business and the professions. Leaving absolutely no room for confusion, they declared that it was to be a private, non-political, non-sectarian association. This is demonstrated clearly in the fifth Object: "To provide a forum for the open discussion of all matters of public interest; provided, however, that partisan politics and sectarian religion shall not be debated by club members."

Over the years, the Objects and Ethics have served as guidelines for members; a set of principles for private and professional life and standards by which a person can become a better citizen. They stimulate thoughtful action and cooperation with other Lions and community leaders in improving conditions on the local, national and international levels. Indeed, they encourage Lions to become citizens of the world.

"Working as a Lion," said Past International President Edward M. Lindsey, "made me more acutely aware of my fellow man and his plight, gave me a higher understanding of my citizenship obligations, a more sensitive compassion for those in need and a desire to live up to the almost spiritual aspects of the Lions Code of Ethics and Objects."

Although the delegates to the early conventions were exclusively from Lions clubs in the United States, clubs not having been chartered outside the country until the 1920s, the founders envisioned a global mission. They foresaw the international goals of the new organization and realized that Lions in the future would be concerned with providing help where it was needed. They were confident that although Lions Clubs International was born in the United States, it would eventually take root and flourish on every continent.

Hence, the significance of the very First Object: "To create and foster a spirit of understanding among the peoples of the world."

"There were no national borders to confine Lionism," observed Past International President Joao Fernando Sobral of Sao Paulo, Brazil. "It finds a home wherever people are willing to give of themselves for the benefit of others."

For 90 years now, history has attested to the wisdom of the delegates who wrote and approved the Objects and Ethics. Where there is a need, local Lions find a way to answer it. Take the Lions of Morioka, Iwate, Japan, for instance. In 1973, they became increasingly concerned about a seemingly epidemic of deaths among young children in their nation. The annual mortality rate was more than 60,000 and growing each year.

"Among all traffic fatalities," wrote one newspaper editor, "the most serious problem we face is that of pre-schoolers. During every spring and fall, Traffic Safety Weeks, geared to protecting young children from traffic accidents, is always listed as one of the goals. But for the past two years, the number of victims has been on the rise…We ought to determine what we are doing wrong and hasten to solve the problem."

The Morioka Lions voted to change this situation and made it a major service activity. By the end of 1973 they had developed a program called the "Leo Safety Method."

When the Morioka Lions began implementing the program they found that simply supplying informational literature to families was inadequate. They instead discovered that elementary school children could be taught to understand and obey traffic rules learned in school. Pre-schoolers, however, were not able to comprehend the rules. The Lions found that when young children dart into a busy street they are acting instinctively, not intellectually. So, the Morioka Lions designed a technique that appealed to a pre-schooler's instinct. The final method was engineered especially for pre-schoolers who would then be instructed by their mothers at home.

The Leo Safety Method includes instructional materials and two instruments used in training the little boy or girl. The Leo Pendant is a necklace that helps the child tell the difference between a "safe zone" and a "danger zone." When the child is told to wear the pendant, he or she knows they are about to enter an area of heavy traffic. When the necklace is removed, the danger is no longer there. The child comes to understand this through repetition.

Another device employed in the program is a belt leash worn by a child when crossing the street. When coming to a crosswalk the mother pulls the belt and calls out "stop." The child learns to stop on his own after this is repeated again and again.

Major Japanese newspapers, along with radio and television stations, publicized the program. Highly effective, it spread to many others sections of Japan. Unquestionably, countless lives have been saved and injuries prevented because of what the Morioka Lions began as a response to a serious problem.

Most assuredly, the Objects and Ethics are a call to moral excellence and far from easy. It smoothes personal relations by basing them on truth and consideration for others. Stunning in their power and undeniable in results, these words offer fresh and positive visions in the midst of a world often seething with tension, confusion and uncertainty. The ideals spotlighted by these twin documents provide a framework for harmonious action. They dissolve boundaries of nationality, culture, religion and economics. A case in point is the successful project of the Pecs-Normandia Lions Club in Hungary that brought parents close to their hospitalized children.

Initiated in 1994, the idea for the project was raised by the Pecs Medical School Children's Pediatric clinic Oncology Department. The Lions club had been sponsoring an annual charity ball to help fund cures for children with leukemia and tumors. The new goal was to provide a home that would enable parents of hospitalized children to be beside their children who were undergoing treatment. Parents would no longer have to worry about the expense and hassle of finding somewhere to stay close to the hospital. The local government granted the club the right to rent a building free of charge for its new Parents' Accommodation program. Initially, space was available for two and during the first year parents took advantage of the accommodations for a total of 67 nights.

The space proved to be insufficient and the Lions acquired another part of the building, renovating the facility so there were eight beds. Kitchens were added making it possible for parents to prepare favorite dishes of their sick children. Doctors ascribe considerable importance to the fact that parents stay beside their children during the period of treatment. More than 50 percent of those with tumors and 80 percent with leukemia are able to return home.

In 1998, Hungarian President Arpad Goncz visited the facility and asked heads of the self-government to support its enlargement and another building was provided for restoration. The Backnang Lions Club of Germany even assisted financially in the renovation by providing US$29,000. Total renovation costs were nearly US$98,000. The buildings now have 12 beds, two full kitchens and two bathrooms and guests have spent in excess of 2,300 nights at the home and entire families can stay close to their children.

The Pecs-Normandia Lions Club financially supports the home, paying all utility bills and providing all furnishings. The necessary funding comes from its charity balls and concerts, second hand clothing sales and grants. Keys to the two facilities are given to the Children's Clinic so that doctors may decide which families truly need the free accommodations. The hostel also serves a dual purpose because the Lions club utilizes it for its monthly meetings. Thus, the project has not only fulfilled a community need, it has also been a bonding point for all members of the club.

Mahatma Gandhi once remarked, "Knowledge is useless unless we use it to experience a change within ourselves." Indeed, the *experience* of millions of Lions throughout the world for nine decades has been reflected in countless service projects that have changed the lives of men, women and children everywhere.

"We best meet our Objects if we serve in an unselfish manner," suggests Past International President Everett J. "Ebb" Grindstaff. "We are on earth to be of service to our fellow man. We are asked to grow into a mountain, not shrink into a grain of sand." Lions have been so successful in implanting the spirit of the Objects and Ethics, he continued, that "there is no question that the thousands of projects that our local clubs, districts or multiple districts are involved in add up to more service than any other civic or social organization in the world."

Communication is a key and is usually looked upon as written or verbal messages: books, newspapers, magazines, radio, TV and personal conversations. But there is another type of communication that has nothing to do with words. It is the result of what a person is…or what a club is. Ralph Waldo Emerson described it perfectly: "What you are speaks so loudly I can't hear what you say."

Past International President John L. Stickley drove home the same point when he wrote that he was more influenced by the way Lions lived the Code and Objects than he was by the Code itself. "I came to realize that Lionism is one great ecumenical movement, binding together in a common cause people of all races, creeds, nationalities and colors."

The Objects and Ethics have beyond a doubt played an expanding role in the growth of the association. In the spirit of fellowship, Lions work tirelessly to improve the human condition. The first Object, for example, is witnessed in such global programs as LCIF, youth exchange and youth camps, the eye bank network, sight-restoring missions, Lions Day with the United Nations and myriad projects involving members from different nations. The language spoken by all Lions is the universal tongue of voluntary service.

Far-sighted individuals of good will composed and adopted the Objects and Ethics, providing a moral foundation for people the world over to work together to bring about a healthier, more peaceful world, one in which integrity, mutual respect and compassion can become a way of life.

Chapter Three
Helen Keller and the
Knights of the Blind

When setting guidelines and standards to achieve its goals, it is undoubtedly true that every government, every association, be it voluntary, social, business or professional, can point to one moment in time, one document or decision that defined its course, that established itself as a force for progress and growth. For Lions Clubs International it occurred in 1925 in Cedar Point, Ohio, the site of the Ninth International Convention. The source was a woman who was already revered for her personal accomplishments despite tremendous odds that had stood in her path, one who had endeared herself to the general public for her leadership on behalf of both the sight and hearing impaired and for her many other humanitarian endeavors which for years had inspired people throughout the world.

Her name was Helen Keller and her ideals, courage and enthusiasm proved to be a beacon that challenged millions of men and women who proudly have worn the lapel pin identifying them as Lions. Her will and determination became a vision for Lions and all people of good will to live by and reach out to others in desperate need of caring and hope.

"Many persons have a wrong idea of what constitutes true happiness," she said. "It is not attained through self-gratification, but through fidelity to a worthy purpose."

It was in Cedar Point, however, that Helen Keller made her lasting impression for what she was confident would be a "worthy purpose" for the growing service club association to adopt. But first, who was this remarkable woman whose commitment and legacy would reward her with an admiration reserved for so few individuals in the course of history?

Helen Keller was born on June 27, 1880, in Tuscumbia, Alabama, to well-to-do parents. Her father, Arthur Keller, was a former officer

27

in the Confederate army and her mother, Kate Adams, was related to Robert E. Lee. An unusually bright and alert child, she contracted an illness when she was 18 months old that was diagnosed as congestion of the brain and stomach. It left her with neither sight nor hearing. Very soon, she forgot the few words she knew and became completely speechless. Angered when her parents or family servants failed to understand her signs she lashed out with kicks, screams and tantrums.

In the 1880s, the law in the United States still labeled deaf and blind persons as *idiots*—even though writing through raised dots read by touch had been invented by Louis Braille, a blind Frenchman in 1826. Teaching the deaf and blind had, in fact, started in Scotland as far back as 1793.

However, an enlightened physician who knew Helen sensed the spark within. He believed her intelligence could be developed once communication was established with her dark and soundless world. He imparted his feelings to the child's parents and Arthur and Kate Keller soon contacted Alexander Graham Bell who, after inventing the telephone, had turned to teaching deaf children. He suggested they hire a teacher from the Perkins Institution for the Blind in Boston. Not long after they discussed their daughter's condition, the staff promptly recommended nineteen-year-old Anne Sullivan, later Mrs. John Macy, as a personal teacher. She soon arrived in Tuscumbia…and Helen's life bloomed.

In her autobiography, *The Story of My Life*, Helen Keller wrote: "The most important day I remember in all my life is the one on which my teacher, Anne Sullivan, came to me. I am filled with wonder when I consider the immeasurable contrast between the two lives which it connects. It was the third of March, 1887, three months before I was seven years old."

As reported in the January 2007 issue of THE LION Magazine, by Senior Editor Jay Copp, "Anne set to work with Helen. After weeks of slow progress and terrible tantrums, the well-known 'miracle' of recognition occurred. Anne led Helen to a water pump and held her hand there. She spelled out the word 'water' on Helen's hand. At last, she understood the mystery of language. Within a few hours she learned the spelling of 30 new words and her ability to read and write rapidly blossomed. After the director of Perkins publicized her accomplishments, she became world famous.

"It's hard to appreciate today the public esteem in which Helen was held. She didn't cross the ocean like Lindbergh or swat mammoth home runs like Ruth. She was famous not because of what she did but who she was. She was revered not just for her ample intelligence but also for her dignity and serenity. She had not merely triumphed over her disabilities but seemed to stretch the boundaries of human possibility. People who met her walked away convinced they had touched greatness. Mark Twain, a friend and fervent admirer, praised her as 'fellow to Caesar, Alexander, Napoleon, Homer, Shakespeare and the rest of the immortals. She will be as famous a thousands years from now as she is today.'

"The fact that Helen Keller, whose moral force derived from her transcendence over blindness, would meet with the Lions precisely when they were poised to commit to a service mission was a minor miracle in itself. But the appearance that Lion leaders had been begging from her for a year nearly didn't happen."

Before that occurred, however, Helen and her teacher were on the campaign trail for another cause. "In 1924," it was stated in THE LION, "the American Foundation for the Blind hired them to raise funds. The foundation began operations in 1921 to serve as a national clearinghouse for information about vision loss. Concern for the blind, if not actual services and opportunities, was growing. The blinded veterans from World War I were a strong impetus for change. They had arrived home from Europe and found themselves unable to work or continue their education.

"The goal for the Helen Keller Endowment—American Foundation for the Blind was $2 million, a huge sum then. The foundation planned to use the money to prevent blindness among children and for other related purposes. Helen and Anne took to the road for three years, eventually speaking to 250,000 people at 249 meetings in 123 cities from coast to coast. Helen had mixed motives about the tour. She was adept at raising funds, but both she and her teacher disliked it. *Beggars* was how she described it and the foundation questioned whether the $2 million was realistic, and although most stops produced a steady stream of donations, the ultimate goal seemed far distant. 'We set out to raise that large sum in six months, and now it seems a thousand years ahead,' Helen complained to a family member.

"Her irritation with the campaign was also partly connected to her clashes with the foundation which preferred that the two spend the bulk of their time calling on the wealthy in their homes. Helen was extraordinarily effective in soliciting funds through these home visits, but she was a socialist who privately seethed at the extravagances of the rich and humiliation washed over her when she made her pitch for support. She argued that the middle class could be counted to back their cause and typically asked her audiences to pledge 25 cents a month for a year, and most nights the crowds responded with generous pledges.

"Weighing on Helen, too, was the precarious health of her teacher who had lost most of her own vision at age five. The time on the road had aggravated her health and when they reached California in the late spring of 1925, Helen decided they should spend the summer there in its mild climate. Coincidentally, the foundation determined to halt the tour until fall and asked the two to return to New York no later than June 15.

"That was like a match thrown into oil. Anne and Helen, whose exterior placidity masked a fiery core, reminded their employer that the Lions had invited them east for their convention and they would honor that commitment."

"We were in San Francisco in 1925," said Anne, "when letters began to come in from secretaries and representatives of Lions clubs begging us to attend the convention in Cedar Point, Ohio, that summer. At first we refused, as we were planning to spend the summer in California for my health. But the requests became so urgent that we decided to attend the convention, whatever the personal inconvenience might be."

It was in Cedar Point that Helen Keller herself became the spark that lit the Lions' mission for the blind. Lion leaders did not promote her speech prior to Cedar Point. A detailed preview article in the magazine one month before the convention did not even mention her. But the hall was full by the time Helen and Anne arrived.

On that Tuesday morning at the convention hall in the Breakers Hotel, International President Harry A. Newman, of Toronto, Ontario, Canada, introduced Helen Keller and her remarkable teacher. They were greeted by a standing ovation. Helen sat down and Anne began speaking movingly to the hushed audience about Helen's journey from the beginning in 1887 to the convention in Cedar Point. Upon conclusion, the Lions showered her with applause and then a five-member blind band from Joplin, Missouri, played several tunes.

Now it was time for Helen Keller to address the audience. "She had, of course, overcome tremendous adversity in her life," said Copp in THE LION, "but despite strenuous voice lessons had never learned to speak clearly. Her voice was tinny, robotic, almost other-worldly. So, as was her custom, Anne stood by Helen's side, ready to repeat each sentence for the audience, Helen braced herself, for she knew that this audience was quite unlike any other. Her regular plea was for financial support. But here was a unique opportunity to marshal the resources of the civic minded.

"As usual, Helen's voice was not pretty but her words poured forth with power and precision. She spoke directly to the concerns and interests of the Lions. If the first rule of speechmaking is to understand your audience, Helen fulfilled that directive splendidly. In less than 10 minutes, in a scant 500 words, she changed the course of Lions history and ultimately the personal histories of untold millions without vision or threatened by blindness."

Her voice filled the hall:

"I suppose you have heard the legend that represents opportunity as a capricious lady, who knocks at every door but once, and if the door isn't opened quickly, she passes on, never to return. And that is as it should be. Lovely, desirable ladies won't wait. You have to go out and grab them. I am your opportunity. I am knocking at your door. I want to be adopted. The legend doesn't say what you are to do when several beautiful opportunities present themselves at the same door. I guess you have to choose the one you love best. I hope you will adopt me. I am the youngest here, and what I offer you is full of splendid opportunities for service.

"The American Foundation for the Blind is only four years old. It grew out of the imperative needs of the blind, and was called into existence by the sightless themselves. It is national and international in scope and in importance. It represents the best and most enlightened thought on our subject that has been reached so far. Its object is to make the lives of the blind more worthwhile everywhere by increasing their economic value and giving them the joy of normal activity.

"Try to imagine how you would feel if you were suddenly stricken blind today. Picture yourself stumbling and groping at noonday as in the night; your work, your independence, gone. In that dark world wouldn't you be glad if a friend took you by the hand and said, 'Come with me and I will teach you how to do some of the things you used to do when you could see.'? That is just the kind of friend the American Foundation is going to be to all the blind in this country if seeing people give it the support it must have.

"You have heard how through a little word dropped from the fingers of another, a ray of light from another soul touched the darkness of my mind and I found myself, found the world, found God. It is because my teacher learned about me and broke through the dark, silent imprisonment which held me that I am able to work for myself and for others. It is the caring we want more than money. The gift without the sympathy and interest of the giver is empty. If you care, if we can make the people of this great country care, the blind will indeed triumph over blindness.

"The opportunity I bring to you, Lions, is this: To foster and sponsor the work of the American Foundation for the Blind. Will you not help me hasten the day when there shall be no preventable blindness; no little deaf, blind child untaught; no blind man or woman unaided? I appeal to you Lions, you who have your sight, your hearing, you who are strong and brave and kind. Will you not constitute yourselves Knights of the Blind in this crusade against darkness? I thank you."

Sitting in rapt attention, the Lions had heard every word. Applauding wildly, they stood en masse as Helen finished. On most stops, Helen touched people's wallets; here she touched the soul of an organization. Caught up in the excitement, Lion Ben Ruffin from West Virginia proposed that Helen Keller be given an honorary membership in Lions Clubs International. The motion was seconded exactly 100 times. Anne Sullivan-Macy was accorded the same honor. "I am happy and proud to be a Lion," Helen told the crowd. Still buzzing. The die was cast. Before the delegates left Cedar Point, they voted to adopt sight conservation and work for the blind as a major service activity. The rest, as they say, is history.

"Helen's speech galvanized Lions," stated THE LION Magazine's article. "Individual clubs had been working on behalf of the blind through health camps, milk funds and scouting. Helen's plea intensified their efforts. Prior to Cedar Point, 58 clubs assisted the blind in some way. A year later, that number had soared to 143. Given an overarching mission, clubs fulfilled their charge in numerous ways. The Hollywood, California, Lions purchased a press for a Braille publishing house. The St. Augustine, Florida, Lions set up a blind Girl Scout camp. The Sudbury, Ontario, Canada, Lions Club paid for a sight-restoring operation for a child.

"The greatest assistance which can be rendered to a blind person," proclaimed an article in THE LION in a 1927 issue, "is to make him find his way to a fitting employment, thus making him self-respecting and self-supporting." The involvement of Lions in sight-related activities did, indeed, move forward with increasing speed after her famous challenge. For example: During George A. Bonham's term as president of the Peoria, Illinois, Lions Club in 1930, he witnessed a problem. Soon after, he devised the solution. Bonham watched a blind man trying to cross a street, left helpless as traffic whirled about him. Futilely tapping his black cane on the pavement, the man was isolated in the center of drivers who did not understand his handicap.

Bonham pored over the problem. Suddenly he had the answer. Paint the cane white and put a wide band of red around it. When the blind person crosses a street let him extend it so that everyone can see and be aware of his blindness. George Bonham presented the idea to the Peoria Lions Club and the members voted unanimously in favor of it. Canes were painted and given to the blind in the city. The Peoria City Council passed an ordinance giving the right-of-way to a blind person using a white cane.

The 1931 International Convention in Toronto, Ontario, Canada, saw the introduction of a resolution describing the Peoria Club's white cane program. It read in part: "The adoption of this plan is recommended to our clubs as part of our major activity, Blind Work. Full information as to this plan, including copies of the ordinances which have been adopted, may be obtained through our activities department."

By 1956, every state in the United States had passed White Cane Safety Laws giving any person using a white cane the right-of-way at crossings. These laws include protection for blind individuals who travel with dog guides, as well.

During World War II, the Veterans Administration set up a rehabilitation center for blind war veterans. Techniques for using white canes were refined at these facilities. The extended cane is moved in a semi-circle in rhythm with the user's footsteps and a light touch on the ground at the end of each arc. This enables the blind person to feel such obstacles as gratings, steps, posts, walls and other objects. State and private agencies have adopted these techniques for their own training centers.

An offshoot of these mobility devices has been that many Lions clubs use miniature white canes as part of fundraising programs for the visually disabled. A lapel pin in the form of a white cane is given to each contributor.

A number of electronic devices have been developed to assist the blind in traveling. The Beltone Ultra Sonic Aid was invented by Dr. Leslie Kay of New Zealand and has been called a "seeing ear for the blind." Operating like a tiny loudspeaker, the transmitter sends out sounds that bounce off objects in the user's path. They are picked up on the receiver as *beeps, chirps* or *twitters*. After learning how to interpret the sounds, the blind person identifies the object and acts accordingly.

"The Nurion Laser Cane is another electronic aid for the blind," explained Lee Farmer, who worked as a technology transfer specialist at Hines Veterans Administration Hospital near Chicago. "The Laser Cane emits three invisible light beams when the cane is activated. These consist of an upper beam, straight-ahead beam and a downward beam. There are three audible signals which correspond with the light beams; the tones are high, middle and low pitched. These alert the user to objects which are either directly in front, or above or below, such as a curb. While they work very well for some individuals," Farmer cautioned, "they are not for everyone."

On occasion, Lions have persuaded their legislators to assist in helping the blind. President Franklin D. Roosevelt signed the Randolph-Sheppard Bill on June 20, 1936, "whereby blind people are to operate vending stands inside government buildings." The co-authors of the bill, Representative (and later Senator) Jennings Randolph of West Virginia and Senator Morris Sheppard of Texas were both Lions.

In 1964, President Lyndon Johnson issued a proclamation that marked the climax of the campaign by the blind to gain endorsement of their rights as pedestrians. With Johnson's proclamation, the white cane became officially recognized.

"A white cane in our society has become one of the symbols of a blind person's ability to come and go on his own. Its use has promoted courtesy and opportunity for mobility for the blind on our streets and highways. To make the American people more fully aware of the meaning of the white cane, and of the need for motorists to exercise special care for the blind persons who carry it, Congress, by a joint resolution approved October 6, 1964, authorized the President to proclaim October 15, 1964, as White Cane Safety Day.

"Now, therefore, I, Lyndon B. Johnson, President of the United States of America, do proclaim October 15, 1964, as White Cane Safety Day."

The flame lit by Helen Keller has, most assuredly, burned brightly down the decades.

It sparked invention, such as the Banks Pocket Braille-Writer which allowed blind people to type messages to one another. Invented by a Lion, a physician blinded in World War I, its manufacture was accomplished by the Lions club in San Diego, California. The Lions talked with Thomas J. Watson, president of IBM, to see if he would cooperate in its manufacture. Eager to help, Watson offered to produce the first thousand machines free for distribution by the Lions to blinded World War II veterans.

The machine uses a keyboard with six keys and a space bar. The cover lifts to show a roll of narrow paper tape on which Braille characters are printed by striking the keys. Dr. Banks produced the writer after 12 years of experimentation and development. Users sometimes say they can now "talk by the yard rather than the hour."

Helen Keller's flame kindles the imagination of extraordinary people who accomplished extraordinary things. To cite another example:

There was the high school teacher who became totally blind at age 55. He founded what amounted to a national correspondence university for the blind, teaching courses he designed on the basis of his experience as a successful teacher and blind person. And there were the members of Illinois Lions clubs whose support helped the fledgling correspondence school grow. How did this come about?

The influenza epidemic of 1915 marked the beginning of this, one of the most fascinating chapters in the history of Lions working with the blind. A pre-Christmas cold turned to influenza for teacher William Allen Hadley, who headed the commercial department of Chicago's Lakeview High School. Two days later, he suffered a detached retina in one eye. Hadley has already lost the sight in his other eye when he was very young. His doctor and close neighbor, E.V.L. Brown, knew that Hadley was a voracious reader and shrewdly played on Hadley's pain at being deprived of his books. "Learn Braille and you can read again," was Brown's counsel. Hadley followed it.

Soon Hadley was tutoring high school students in his home in Winnetka, a north Chicago suburb, and also typing manuscripts for an author friend. In 1919, a minister from Oklahoma who was visiting another Winnetka neighbor of Hadley made a startling suggestion on a summer evening as the two men were chatting on Hadley's front porch.

"You have proven you are a brilliant educator," he told Hadley. "There are thousands of students who you could teach. And you are no further than your own mailbox. Why don't you teach other blind adults through correspondence courses?"

Hadley's subsequent letters to people working with the blind brought much encouragement and hundreds of letters from blind people eager to sign up. One came from a farmer's wife in Kansas who, like Hadley, had been an avid reader until she lost her sight. Hadley created his Braille correspondence course for this book-starved woman, using the Braille-Writer which was invented by Frank H. Hull of the Illinois School for the Blind in Jacksonville. Founded in 1949, the school's name was changed to Illinois School for the Visually Impaired in 1977 and Lions have been deeply involved in its teachings.

"Through the years the support of Lions has played a key role in our school's ability to help the blind," said Dr. Richard Ulmsted, former superintendent of the school and past president of the Jacksonville Lions Club. "There are Lions clubs in the state that donate year after year to help keep us operating."

The farmer's wife from Kansas is just one of thousands who have benefited from the expertise offered by the school and from William Hadley's dream. Between November 1920 and June 1921, her Braille typed exercises were mailed to Hadley who corrected them and sent them back, usually with a word of encouragement.

With his first student's successful completion of the course, Hadley knew that he could teach by mail. He put an ad in a Braille periodical which brought more than 100 inquiries. Hadley found himself in the correspondence school business, and in a big way. By 1932, his school was incorporated as the Hadley School for the Blind. The curriculum catalog of that year listed 14 courses, including English grammar, psychology, salesmanship, typewriting and Bible studies.

Hadley liked to refer to his school as the "University of Courage." When one applicant wrote on his application that his prior schooling was with the "University of Adversity," Hadley shot a note back, "We are making arrangements from the University of Adversity to the University of Courage." In 1929, Elmer Selby, a member of the newly chartered Winnetka Lions Club and a reporter for the town's weekly newspaper, dropped in to see Hadley. Selby had written a number of articles on the school for the paper and the two chatted amiably. The talk led Selby to suggest that the Winnetka Lions Club make Hadley's school its main project. His fellow Lions eagerly accepted and their enthusiasm quickly spread to other Lions clubs in the state. By 1936, more than 4,000 students had enrolled at Hadley since its founding.

Lions throughout the United States and other nations also became generous contributors to the school with totals today exceeding

$20,000 annually. In its early years, Hadley had satellite schools in other countries, but today only operates a school in Fujhou, China.

The Hadley School for the Blind remains the largest distance educator of the blind and visually impaired in the world. By the year 2007 it was teaching more than 10,000 students each year in all 50 U.S. states and more than 100 countries, offering in excess of 100 home study courses in a variety of formats. In all, hundreds of thousands of blind individuals who are 14 years of age and older, their families and blindness service professionals have benefited from the initiative of William Hadley and the inspiration of Helen Keller. This ongoing accomplishment was testified to in 1975 at the association's international convention in Dallas, Texas, the 50th Anniversary of Helen Keller's speech in Cedar Point.

During the third plenary session, actress Carolyn Jones read Miss Keller's challenge to the Lions. This was followed by an address by Dr. Richard Kinney, at the time director of the Hadley School for the Blind. "Lions," said Dr. Kinney, deaf and blind himself, "you are playing a tremendous role in attacking the most terrible blindness of all—the blindness of ignorance and prejudice that sets one man against another, one race against another, one nation against another…. It was once said, 'Live and let live,' but Lionism has raised this principle to that nobler, 'Live and help live.' "

Helen Keller's challenge was to be transmitted and amplified by Lions clubs the world over. There was the girl stricken in the late 20s with polio which blinded her and paralyzed her right side. Adopted by the Lions Club of Redondo Beach, California, she was educated at the University of Redlands. The Lions club also underwrote several eye operations. She went on to use her education, she says, "to do my little bit in helping free those without sight from the shackles of darkness and bring them light and truth. Without the generous-hearted Lions I would never have realized my dream."

About the same time, a young women in Winnipeg, Manitoba, Canada, was thrown from her horse while riding to school. According to a report written by John Sturrock, secretary of the Winnipeg Club, two physicians who treated her over a two-year period believed her injuries had left her "hopelessly" blind. The Moosejaw, Saskatchewan, Lions Club didn't give up so easily. One of its own members, Dr.

Frank McElrea, a chiropractor, treated the girl so successfully that 60 percent of her sight was restored.

Vision tests for school children became commonplace projects for Lions. In the 1940s, for instance, the New Lexington, Ohio, Lions Club sponsored tests for more than 1,000 high school and grade school children. Such a service has been emulated countless times by Lions throughout the world. During the 1930s and 1940s, Berkeley, California, was perhaps prouder of its Lions club-sponsored blind Boy Scout troop than of anything else in town. The troop met in quarters built for them by the Lions and every nail was personally driven by a club member. The Lions took troop members on mountain hikes, taught them to swim and became their friends.

In the mid 1940s, the Naples, Florida, Club carried out projects that were then and are today identified with Lions when they examined hundreds of children at its eye clinic. One member, Dr. Goodrich T. Smith, a retired eye, ear, nose and throat specialist, spearheaded the effort, donating his time and necessary equipment. The club donated the facilities and picked up the expenses for children who needed but could not afford treatment.

Among the largest and most comprehensive Lions-supported rehabilitation centers for the blind is located in Little Rock, Arkansas. Known as Arkansas Enterprises for the Blind for many years, it is now called Lions World Services for the Blind for it does, indeed, meet the needs of the blind worldwide. It was established in 1946 by the Little Rock Downtown Lions Club (later renamed the Little Rock Founders Club) and over the years dynamic programs have been developed by professional staff members. It began when the governor of Arkansas appointed visually impaired Little Rock Lion Roy Kumpke to find and train blind individuals in the community to set up vending stand businesses in federal buildings, an outgrowth of the Randolph-Sheppard Act. This he did, but quickly realized they required additional training in communication and independent living skills.

"The idea seized my imagination as nothing before," he recalled. "As I pursued my daily tasks, I understood that blind persons needed to be trained psychologically and socially before they were trained for a vocation. From that realization came a dream that would shape the next 40 years of my life." It was this dream that he presented to his fellow Lions, and the rehabilitation center was born.

"Opportunities for the blind have greatly expanded since 1947," reported Elise White, the center's Community Relations Specialist, in a 1998 article in THE LION Magazine. "Several occurrences are responsible for this change," she elaborated, "and include computer technology for Braille, voice output and large print display; medical advancements to save more vision and passage of the Americans with Disabilities Act for job rights. Specialized services were developed to meet these new opportunities, and today, Lions World Services has 13 vocational programs from which to choose, the largest array in the country."

One unique program was initiated in 1967 in a cooperative agreement with the Internal Revenue Service that eventually resulted in the placement of hundreds of blind people in career jobs across the United States. In 1992, a state-of-the-art greenhouse was opened to complement the new horticulture vocational course. It now serves blind individuals from throughout the country.

Examples of how Lions enhanced their image as Knights of the Blind cover decades since that seminal message on a bright morning in Cedar Point. Building on this image had become a way of life for Lions in lands spanning the earth.

In 2004, the San Juan-Petit Juan Lions Club in the Republic of Trinidad and Tobago provided two cornea grafts and 30 cataract surgeries for residents throughout the Caribbean nation. It was one of the largest sight saving projects ever held there. How did this come about? Selwyn Skinner was president of the Fort Lauderdale, Florida, Lions Club, a native of Trinidad and an active Lions before moving to Florida. When the Trinidad Lions notified him that a local ophthalmologist had agreed to perform two corneal transplants at no charge if Lions could obtain the corneas, Skinner immediately contacted the Florida Lions Eye Bank and was told the corneas would be available in a month. When they became available, he and his wife, Huldah, also a Fort Lauderdale Lion picked up the corneas, boarded a plane and hand-carried them to Trinidad. The transplants were a success and news coverage was widespread with articles appearing in Trinidad and Florida newspapers.

In the spirit of international cooperation, the Florida Lions Eye Bank has made possible more than 30,000 corneal transplants and sends quantities of tissue to countries in the Caribbean and Central and South America. It is the dream of the Trinidad Club that one day all citizens of Trinidad and Tobago in need of sight-saving surgery or other specialized treatment will receive it, regardless of their financial situation.

Lions from half way around the world joined with local Lions and others to construct and equip a facility that is having a major impact on reducing preventable blindness and eye disease. Fairfax Host, Virginia, Lion Dennis Brining and his wife, Linda, attended a special ceremony in 2002—the dedication of the Rugarama Health Center in Kabale, Uganda. An eye center there that was opened in 1991 was not able to provide adequate care for the people living in that area. Said Lion Brining, "It's estimated that there are 4,000 blind people in the Kabale District alone and most suffer from preventable blindness. About 2,000 are blind because of cataracts. Also," he added, "the Uganda Ministry of Health reported that 100,000 children needed eyeglasses and there was no eye screening system for school children in place."

Action was needed and it began in the form of an anonymous donation of $70,000 from a TOUCH (Treasure One Uganda Child) sponsor at the Truro Episcopal Church in Fairfax to initiate the building of an expanded eye clinic in Kabale. The project was led by a donation from LCIF, the Fairfax Lions, the diocese of Kigazi, the Lions of Kabale and the Ministry of Health, resulting in the expansion of the Rugarama Health Center. The involvement of the Fairfax Lions had actually begun earlier with the shipment of 3,000 pairs of used eyeglasses from the District 14-A Eyeglass Recycling Center of Northern Virginia. "As a result of this initial involvement," says Brining, "we became aware of the desperate need for a modern facility. This fit perfectly with the mission of Lions clubs." Brining, a TOUCH sponsor, was named to oversee the building of a new health center. As a result of this international endeavor, the new center serves nearly 1.8 million people, not only in Uganda, but in parts of Rwanda and Congo, thus having a major impact on reducing preventable blindness in these areas of Africa.

Because of its altitude and exposure to ultraviolet radiation, Tibet has a high rate of cataract. Each year, statistics point out, 7,000 people there are newly blinded, but because of poor medical access few receive surgical care. The Lions of China, however, are working to make Tibet a cataract-free zone explained Yoky Chen, a member of the Shenzhen Lions Club which sponsored a massive project in 2003 to bring clear vision to citizens of Tibet suffering from cataract.

To fund the project, Shenzhen Lions and the Yantian municipal government organized a giant sale of sunglasses donated by a local Lion who manages the Doctors Eyeglass Corporation. More than 750 Lions from 12 clubs in China's District 380 participated, selling 1,250 pairs of the sunglasses and raising $7,500 from shoppers. The Lions also personally donated $1,500. People continued their generosity and when the medical team left for Tibet, an additional $10,600 had been raised. All donations were used to purchase equipment for cataract surgeries. "About $60 can help one cataract patient receive an operation," said Lion Chen.

The first medical team left in September 2003 for Lhasa, Tibet's capital city. "A total of 98 people received free cataract operations," said Chen and team members were praised as "ambassadors of light." A second team left shortly for another area of Tibet and brought 2,000 pairs of eyeglasses and surgical equipment. A total of 198 patients received cataract surgery, the oldest being 96 years old and the youngest four. Helen Keller's vision had reached the heights of the Himalayas and, said Chen, "Cataract patients of all ages walked from far and away just to see a light of hope when our teams arrived in Tibet."

Again from THE LION, January 2007, "Helen Keller maintained a close relationship with Lions the rest of her life. She spoke at gatherings and lent her support to official activities. She was the perfect vehicle to send Lions toward their destiny. She was not a do-gooder per se. Her power lay in her message and her message was herself. She embodied the inherent dignity and capabilities of those with disabilities. She didn't ask Lions to be 'do-gooders.' She wanted them to recognize and unleash the full humanity of those with disabilities.

"Helen participated in the 1927 Lions' International Week for the Blind in Washington, D.C. Her speech gave her stamp of approval to their enlightened attitude toward the blind. According to her, Lions rejected the current view of society that blind people were miserable creatures incapable of advancement and self-enrichment. 'The Lions attitude toward the blind is something new in the world,' she said. 'What I mean is that Lions are trying to help the blind as they would help one of their own number who had met with misfortune and not as people different from everyone else. That is why the Lions are going to be a power for good in the work for the sightless. Keep the blind before your mind's eye as people just like yourself and you will avoid the mistakes that are so often made by those who started out to assist the blind.'

"Then in an eerily prescient remark, akin to her friend Mark Twain's prediction that he would exit life with Haley's Comet just as he entered it, Helen Keller concluded: 'Some day you will come together again in this beautiful capital of our country and look over the fields of your endeavors. If I am alive then, I will stand before you with glad confidence and say to you, *Well done, good and faithful Knights of the Blind,* and you will say with equal joy, *We have received as richly as we have given.*'

"She made her last public appearance in 1961 at a Lions club meeting in Washington. She received the Lions Humanitarian Award and effusively thanked the Lions for their decades of stellar service to the blind. She then slowly ambled off the stage, as Lions stood and showered her with thunderous applause one final time."

Her wisdom and keen insight into human relationships were always sought and she has remained one of the most quotable individuals to have ever lived among us. Consider these heartwarming words, especially as they well relate to the work of Lions: "Walking with a friend in the dark is better than walking alone in the light."

Helen Keller died in 1968.

Her legacy and optimism has been witnessed in countless programs and innovations sponsored and supported by Lions clubs worldwide, expanding since the final decade of the 20th Century in the remarkable success of SightFirst.

Chapter Four
Sight Services: Helen Keller's Global Legacy

The year 1925 stands as a monument to arousing the commitment of Lions around the world to reach out and help the blind and visually impaired who are in desperate need of a helping hand. Helen Keller's speech at Cedar Point was a challenge to the fidelity of Lions to the Objects and Code of Ethics to which they had so solemnly pledged. The ensuing record of Lions over decades has demonstrated this vow to answer the needs of the blind and to work with them to enable them to live fulfilling lives. Lions have made it possible for those who lived in darkness to nonetheless have a positive vision for the future, most assuredly a testament to the dedication of caring men and women to the spirit of volunteerism. When this spirit is allowed to flourish, it recognizes no limits.

Lions have been and continue to be involved in myriad activities that exemplify the title Helen Keller so romantically bestowed upon them: "Knights of the Blind in the Crusade Against Darkness." Hands on involvement in projects has, beyond a doubt, been a hallmark of the activities Lions have conducted around the world on behalf of the blind and visually impaired. But efforts of a less personal kind, have proved to be of equal importance in fighting blindness. These are witnessed in the magnanimous generosity of Lions in building and equipping research centers; establishing eye banks with the resultant corneal transplants; eyeglass recycling; education; vocational training and other ventures that give hope and prospects for new lives to the blind.

Research, Restoration, Recycling

Research into the causes and prevention of blindness has been a key point in the commitment of Lions to give substance to the challenge offered by that courageous woman to answer one of the most demanding needs facing people the world over. Three models serve to demonstrate the impact of numerous Lions-sponsored research facilities around the world.

The Aravind Hospital in India stands as a shining example. Officially, it is designated the Lions Aravind Institute of Community Ophthalmology (LAICO), located in the southern Indian city of Madurai. Established through a SightFirst grant of US$1.3 million in 1995, it is the largest institution of its kind in the world and was hailed by the *Harvard Business Review* as a model of efficiency.

LAICO has provided training and management skills to eye care programs throughout South Asia. Teams from more than 125 eye hospitals have learned to increase their surgical capacities by improving everything from staffing patterns to patient recruitment. By the year 2001, the results were undeniably impressive. Of the 36 Lions-operated eye hospitals that chose to be involved in the program, the average increase in cataract surgeries was 116 percent in their surgical volume after completing the program.

"The impact of LAICO is now being seen throughout India, as hospitals from every hinterland hear about the miraculous results and want to hear how to do it," said Past International Director M. Nagarajan. "We are really teaching these institutes how to do it for themselves, or as the old saying goes, teaching them how to fish rather than giving them the fish." The LAICO training center has reached beyond India with hospitals from as far away as Kenya and Indonesia enrolling to learn firsthand that sustainable solutions to blindness are within reach. Depressing conditions of blindness continue to exist around the world, but the expertise provided at Aravind has resulted in many successes and provide hope for the future.

In yet another example, the Lions Research Unit of the Royal Victorian Eye and Ear Hospital in Melbourne, Australia, began spearheading studies to exterminate trachoma which has been severely affecting that nation's desert aborigines. Extremely contagious, the trachoma virus attacks the lining of the inner surface of the eyelids and the outer coat of the eye. The mucous membrane covering the inner surface of the eyelids in front of the eyeball become severely inflamed. They develop a "sandy" surface that leads to scarring and deformity of the lids. The eventual result may be total blindness.

After exhaustive investigation, the western Australian form of the virus was isolated in Perth in the early 1960s by Professor Ira Mann, who had done previous work at Oxford. The virus was brought to the Lions National Research Unit and introduced into the blind eye of a volunteer. It was then studied by Dr. H. Courtney Greer, a pathologist who had come to Australia from London. The experiment produced an effective form of treatment with antibiotics with the result that countless residents of Australia's desert areas have been saved from blindness.

All this was able to come about because, in 1955, the hospital had no eye research institute unit and the Lions determined to fill the need. A suitable building was found near the hospital, but to buy and renovate the structure would cost an estimated $55,000. Moving quickly, the Melbourne Lions Club provided $11,000 to enable the hospital to begin the work and hire Dr. Greer, at the time only one of five ophthalmologists in the world specializing in pathology. The project was presented to the District 201 Convention in 1956 and was adopted. The Lions raised the necessary funds in three years to purchase and remodel the building for $40,000. The surplus of $15,000 was invested to create scholarships for medical research into the causes of blindness and to refine techniques for treatment.

Another example of such sweeping success is found in Chicago, Illinois, at the Lions of Illinois Eye Research Institute. In 1977, the Lions of Illinois Foundation adopted the objective of establishing such an institute and selected as its site the West Side Medical Center of the University of Illinois at Chicago. The Lions correctly determined that it was a convenient location with access to eminent eye researchers at the university's modern facilities. Figuring large in their calculations was UIC's excellent Ophthalmology Department and its history of working with Illinois Lions.

A blue ribbon committee was established to plan and direct the fundraising campaign to establish the institute. At the beginning of the drive, a popular button worn by Lions read, "I feel good, let's make it happen." And make it happen they did. In 1981, the Lions of Illinois Foundation assumed direction of the campaign and by September 1982 more than $4.1 million had been subscribed in outright pledges and contributions.

The campaign maintained its pace and went on to raise $5 million to erect a new building for the institute. At the 1985 dedication, International President Joseph L. Wroblewski delivered the keynote address and asked the Lions of Illinois about the buttons. "What do you feel good about?" he asked. Hundreds of voices responded: "We're doing something good for humanity."

Presently, a team of more than 30 researchers, clinicians and teachers are seeking to unlock some of the secrets which will lead to better diagnosis and treatment of such major and debilitating eye conditions as diabetic retinopathy, glaucoma, macular degeneration and cataracts.

"We believe that discoveries made at the Lions of Illinois Eye Research Institute will be of tremendous value, not just to the people of Illinois, but to people at risk of blindness wherever they are on this earth," said Dr. Morton I. Goldberg, former head of the university's Department of Ophthalmology. "The institute will hopefully do away with much of the blindness that now exists. We believe our team of outstanding scientists and eye doctors, working together, will conquer many of the eye diseases affecting our families, friends and people across the earth."

Corneal transplants have been a large part of the work of Lions in sight restoration, and the association's eye bank network has paved the way. Corneal transplants, however, are not new. The first successful transplant was performed December 7, 1905, by Dr. Eduard Zirm at Olomouc University in the present-day Czech Republic. Shortly thereafter, surgeons around the world began to replicate Dr. Zirm's sight-restoring procedure.

Located in the front of the eye, the cornea is the clear window through which light passes. It may become clouded through injury, disease, infection or congenital defects and varying degrees of blindness can occur. A corneal transplant replaces the damaged cornea with a new cornea taken from a donated eye. This process restores sight in more than 90 percent of the cases in which it is performed. In every instance it transforms the life of a person who had been living in darkness.

Corneal transplantation, as a routine procedure, is a relatively recent development. Back in the mid 1940s, some 500,000 people in the United States suffered from blindness, and it was estimated that at least 30,000 of them could be helped with a corneal transplant. Unfortunately, only a limited number of corneas were available. In 1944, a New York City eye doctor, R. Townley Paton, established the world's first eye bank, a system for recovering, processing and distributing corneas. The Staten Island Central Lions Club immediately began to support Dr. Paton's non-profit facility, the Eye Bank for Sight Restoration. The following year, the Buffalo, New York, Lions Eye Bank and Research Society became the second eye bank. It was a challenge soon accepted by Lions worldwide. Today, there are more than 60 Lions eye banks in 11 countries with Lions supporting them through financial donations and volunteering as eye bank guides and corneal tissue transporters.

To observe the history and humanitarian achievements of eye banks, Lions Eye Bank Week was celebrated December 4-10, 2005. It was commemorated in many ways. For example, in New York, the Lions Blind & Charity Fund presented a check in the amount of $22,000 to the Upstate New York Transplant Services. Financial contributions from Lions fund "technical innovations, such as incubators for research," according to Sarah Golembek-Peltier, manager of center's Eye and Tissue Services. "The research facility" she continued, "hopes to grow more corneal tissue from fewer cells and thus be able to cure more patients with corneal transplants and other diseases of the eye."

In March 1986, the International Board of Directors adopted The Lions Clubs International Eye Bank Program. It was designed to standardize policy and assure that all Lions Eye Banks operate in harmony with the policies of the association. The program helps in establishing new Lions Eye Banks the world over. The primary objectives are to extend Lions eye banking internationally in order that quality eye tissue will be available for corneal transplants, research and other medical purposes. Throughout the world, local Lions are the starting point in most eye bank programs. With eye donor drives and public information projects, the Lions secure pledges for donation of eyes after death.

When people sign the pledge card they help assure the success of sight restoration or preservation. Tissue is issued by the bank to investigate glaucoma, cataracts and other eye diseases, procedures that are often implemented with state-of-the-art equipment donated by Lions. Since many eye diseases are hereditary, research may ultimately benefit unborn generations. The special card declares the individual's decision to be a donor. A file is maintained at a central location (the eye bank) and upon the donor's death the attending physician or next of kin notifies the eye bank. The eye bank then sends a member of its technical team to perform the procedure. It the tissue is suitable for transplant, the cornea is carefully remove and placed in a solution that allows it to be stored for up to five days.

The eye bank then calls the surgeon next on the waiting list and it is his or her responsibility to inform the patient that the gift of sight is now available. Transportation of the tissue to the location where the operation will be performed is handled by the eye bank. Oftentimes, individual Lions club members handle this transportation, and, if necessary, state patrols, helicopters and airlines all cooperate to guarantee that the transport will be as expeditious as possible. Corneal tissue is even taken from one nation to another when necessary.

Testimony to the success of corneal transplants through Lions eye banks are, as one would expect, quite extensive. The Georgia Lions Eye Bank, located at Emory University in Atlanta, has given new hope and life to hundreds of people. In the early 1980s, Eric Jones, who lived on a nearby farm in northern Georgia, received this gift of sight. "Eric had a corneal transplant on his right eye when he was only four months old," said his father, Clyde Jones. "We were a little bit afraid of the first operation, but everything went just fine and his recovery was excellent. He never had any problems and everything went so well that when he was 14 months old he had a corneal transplant on his left eye, and we didn't have any problems with that either.

"You can't put a price on sight, especially with a little fellow as small as he is who's never seen anything. To have the windows opened in his eyes so that he can see things that we take for granted is really something. If it hadn't been for the work of the Lions and the Lions Eye Bank our son would be blind today."

Another Georgian, Jerry Hall, a local businessman is also the recipient of two transplants. "I didn't realize that I had become a person who was not competing in life anymore. Through my corneal transplants and being able to see again, I can see not only visually, but also where my life had gone. As a result, I was able to become a competitor. Once again, I can participate in staff meetings because I can see the visuals that are used. I can take part in my family life again because I can become enthusiastic about games and others things they are interested in. Receiving a corneal transplant not only renews your sight, it gives you a whole new life."

Recipient Shirley Blankenship of Joplin, Missouri, a homemaker with three children, exclaimed, "I'm a new person! I received the transplant for my right eye in April 1961, and one for my left eye in 1965. I was able to pass my driver's test, do needlepoint and make some of my daughter's and own clothes. I am also a notary public and notarize eye donor cards without charge to anyone I can persuade to donate their eyes to the Missouri Lions Eye Tissue Bank. If people die without donating their eyes, they are literally throwing away the most precious and priceless gift they can bestow."

Other success stories abound. Take for example the work of the Lions of District 22-C Eye Bank and Research Foundation, incorporated in 1957 and located in Seabrook, Maryland. Through the years, mobile health vans have been dispatched to communities for eye screenings and the collection of used eyeglasses to be processed and eventually shipped for distribution around the world. Corneal transplants are, of course, a large part of the foundation's services, and they extend beyond the borders of the district.

A youngster named Francisco Valente de Almedia came to the eye bank from Portugal for a transplant. He returned home with his eyesight restored. Mrs. Miriam Haidar-Akbar, who lived in the Middle East, received corneal transplants and returned home able to see. A young girl from Bolivia was given a successful corneal transplant and another little girl from Nicaragua was treated for cataract in one eye and a corneal transplant in the other.

Francisco, Mrs. Haidar-Akbar, Eric, Jerry, the little girls from Bolivia and Nicaragua are the men, women and youngsters who have moved from darkness to light because of the existence of Lions Eye Banks in countries across the earth.

Lions eye screening programs have aided in preserving the sight of millions. Either at clinics or as a result of mobile vans, detection for such conditions as glaucoma, diabetic retinopathy and other sight-saving afflictions have served to give further meaning to Helen Keller's challenge to be "Knights of the Blind."

Glaucoma is among the most prevalent diseases in causing blindness, but not if detected in its early stages and Lions have played a major role in providing detection. In the development of glaucoma, the fluid that nourishes the cornea and lens drains at a reduced rate, causing increased pressure in the eye. If untended, the pressure destroys the optic nerve, hence irreversible blindness. Glaucoma usually progresses slowly and without symptoms, but the damage it creates can be prevented by periodic examinations and treatment when required. The screening process is fast and simple and can be easily performed on children. Should glaucoma be detected, proper treatment will prevent further damage and eliminate what is certain to be eventual blindness.

The condition was previously treated with eye drops and occasionally by pills. Recently, however, lasers have been used for making microscopic holes through the plugged drainage meshwork in the angle of the eye. This is effective in an overwhelmingly percent of the cases.

The laser's first medical use for sight conservation was treating retinal detachment. If the retina tears loose from the eyeball, blindness can result. A laser beam, focusing through the lens of the eye, reattaches the retina by fusing it to the underlying tissue. It takes a thousandth of a second, while conventional surgery may take hours.

A personal example of one whose glaucoma was detected and blindness prevented can be attested to by Mrs. Maria Delgado de Alvarez, a widow with children who lived in Caracas, Venezuela. She said that she felt fine but a friend, as a precautionary measure, urged her to go along to a Lions-supported eye clinic in that city.

"What for?" she asked. "I feel perfectly well and I don't have any problems with my vision."

"It won't hurt to have an examination," replied her friend.

"It's a good thing I listened to her and had my eyes checked," Mrs. Alvarez said later. "They found that I had undetected glaucoma and required emergency treatment. I was rushed to a hospital for further tests that same day and the doctor prescribed medication that reduced the pressure within the eyeball. Without the glaucoma test and prompt treatment I would have had serious problems and perhaps permanent damage to my sight."

One Very Special Knight of the Blind

The success Lions Clubs International has recorded for more than 90 years is do in large part to its capacity to enlist remarkable men and women to carry on its mission. One such individual is Dr. Muragapa Chenavirapa Modi of India who has personally restored sight to countless thousands of his fellow citizens since graduating from medical school in 1943. Although extensive opportunities for a lucrative practice were available to him, he remained unswerving in his devotion to helping the poor. Because cataract blindness was so prevalent in India, Dr. Modi directed his considerable energy to helping restore sight to people who had no other way to turn. While most surgeons at that time would take an hour or more to remove a cataract, Dr. Modi performed the operation in a matter of minutes at camps throughout his homeland.

Penniless when he began his medical career, the recent graduate rented a small building in the village of Patan and opened a tiny clinic. At first only a few patients came to him, then more and very soon scores came streaming in to this amazing practitioner who performed scores of cataract operations every day. As his fame grew, he became known throughout India, and then the world. Soon he organized a touring eye clinic that served the most remote areas of his country.

Indian Lions began working to help him by arranging trips, organizing clinic sites and supervising patient care. Lions clubs provided funds for his activities and as his reputation grew, Lions clubs in the United States, Europe and Asia began providing equipment, vehicles and other necessities.

Dr. Modi was tireless in his commitment, working nonstop to reverse the plight of the visually handicapped. To take one example, during an eye operation camp organized by the Lions Club of Chirala, India, for poor people, he examined 10,000 patients and performed 42 operations. Traveling by Jeep, Lions spread news of the camp to 80 villages on less than one week's notice. Later in Bangalore City, Dr. Modi examined more than 15,000 patients and performed 350 eye operations, all in eight days. Another 1,351 people were treated without surgery for a variety of eye disorders. In addition to medical treatment, all the patients and the more than 8,000 others who accompanied them were provided meals at the camp, which was sponsored and financed by the Bangalore City Lions Club.

Dr. Modi's dedication and skills did not go unnoticed. In 1962, International President Per Stahl of Sweden visited Dr. Modi and presented him with his International President's Award in recognition of his "deep devotion to others in the field of sight conservation." Years later, in 1989, at the international convention in Miami/Miami Beach, Florida, Lions Clubs International presented him with its highest recognition, the Humanitarian Award, which included a $200,000 grant from LCIF to expand his work.

Lions World Sight Day

This annual program focuses attention on a specific locale in the world, not only to attend to sight needs there, but to demonstrate the global commitment of Lions to eliminate preventable blindness and preserve sight. It is estimated that there are approximately 40 million people in the world today who are blind, an overwhelming percentage of whose blindness could have been prevented. Even more terrible to contemplate is that every five seconds someone in the world becomes blind and a child develops blindness every minute.

Lions World Sight Day seeks to make everyone aware of this condition and to help on an annual basis to bring relief to a pre-determined areas of the world. October was selected as the month each event would be conducted, and it all began in 1998 when major events that included cataract and glaucoma screenings, the collection of used eyeglasses for recycling and the distribution of educational material were held in New York City, London, Cape Town, Hong Kong, Sao Paulo and Sydney. The following year, the second Sight Day was observed in Nairobi, Kenya, when a traveling eye clinic of the Lions SightFirst Eye Hospital in Nairobi conducted hundreds of screenings in remote villages. Many people were transported to the Lions Eye Hospital for immediate surgery and Lions Clubs International pledged to restore sight to 20,000 people each week throughout the year 2000, a goal that was achieved with the assistance of Lions clubs around the world.

The third Sight Day in October 2000 was conducted in Beijing, People's Republic of China. By this time, the Association's SightFirst China Action Program, held in partnership with the Chinese government, had already made tremendous strides in combating blindness and restoring sight through such means as cataract surgery.

The year 2001 witnessed the event in Sao Paulo and Sao Jose dos Campos, Brazil, with nearly 4,000 children receiving vision screenings and the announcement of an LCIF grant in the amount of US$3.75 million to combat the causes of childhood blindness. This would be achieved through the establishment of "centers of excellence" on five continents to train personnel and coordinate blindness prevention efforts. Los Angeles marked Lions World Sight Day 2002 where Lions conducted major screenings and education program targeting Latinos, who comprises nearly half of the area's diabetes patients. In Washington, D.C., the association joined with the National Eye Institute, Lighthouse International and the International Association to Prevent Blindess/North America in conducting a press conference and vision screenings at the Martin Luther King Jr. Library.

In 2003 Lions Clubs International and Lions clubs in Seoul, Republic of Korea, held vision screenings for more than 800 people and disabled children and adults who could not otherwise afford examinations, with the result that 90 individuals were scheduled for eye surgery and treatment to reverse glaucoma, cataract and disorders of the eye muscles. Free eyeglasses were also provided and the Lions of Korea collected more than 30,000 pairs of used eyeglasses to be recycled and distributed in developing countries.

During October 2004, Lions worldwide conducted activities. As its official World Sight Day action, Lions Clubs International screened children in four cities and nearby villages in war-ravaged Bosnia and Herzegovina where a major outreach program aimed at preventing childhood blindness in that nation was announced. Volunteer eye doctors and Lions from the United States, France and the host nation screened screened 548 children in schools, an orphanage and centers for children with special needs, providing eyeglasses where needed and arranging follow-up care for those requiring it.

As in other years, Lions around the world conducted a variety of activities in 2004. In the Czech Republic, for example, a press conference was held at the Lions International Education Centre of Ophthalmology at Prague's Charles University to remind journalists and the public of the importance of blindness prevention. More than 100 volunteers from the Italian and Spanish eyeglass recycling centers met in Salomo, Spain, for a symposium on conducting vision and diabetes screening programs, and, in New Zealand, Lions collected used eyeglasses that will be cleaned and graded at a Lions recycling center for eventual distribution locally and throughout the South Pacific. In Namibia, the Swakopund Lions Club tested the eyesight of more than 600 first grade children at local schools and, in the state of Washington, the Quilcene Lions Club delivered eyeglasses they had collected to the Northwest Lions Eyeglass Recycling Center.

Hyderabad, India, was the location for World Sight Day—2005, an event that also saw the launching of the Sight for Kids project in India. Also, because the number of people with diabetes in this nation is expected to double in the next 25 years, Lions launched a US$398,000 diabetic retinopathy project at the L.V. Prasad Eye Institute in Hyderabad. An LCIF grant will allow the institute to partner with 14 other Lions eye hospitals on a comprehensive diabetic retinopathy education, screening and treatment program that has the potential to provide assistance to nearly 450,000 people with diabetes.

The year 2006, marked the first time a Lions World Sight Day project was held in Africa. In Bamako, Republic of Mali, the association, in cooperation with the Lions of Mali and the Give the Gift of Sight Foundation, screened more than 29,000 children and adults over a nine-day period. It was noted that in excess of two million people in sub-Saharan Africa are blind, 10 times the rate as those of developed nations. A large percentage do not have access to vision care, including eyeglasses. With the help of LCIF, the Lions of Mali arranged for additional care for those who were judged in need of additional attention, including cataract surgery, at the African Institute for Tropical Ophthalmology, the premier eye hospital and training institute in West Africa, funded by LCIF and the Lions of Mali.

More than 50,000 people were given vision screening and 1,500 received cataract surgeries at the 2007 10th annual World Sight Day in Colombo, Sri Lanka, and across that nation. This humanitarian effort actually began months before the official October 7 event with Lions throughout Sri Lanka conducting vision screenings, distributing eyeglasses and arranging free cataract surgeries at the Lions Gift of Sight Hospital in Panadura and the Lions SightFirst Hospital in Hendala. All surgeries were supported by a SightFirst grant from LCIF. Lions also conducted a seminar on childhood blindness and held a press conference to announce the launching of the childhood blindness project in Sri Lanka. In addition, Sri Lankan Lions inaugurated a new ophthalmic ward at Homagama hospital, which was equipped through a grant from LCIF.

Lions in other countries were also active in conducting World Sight Day activities. In Perry County, Pennsylvania, the county commission proclaimed October "World Blindness Month" and Lions raised funds for eye research and treatment for senior citizens in need and those at risk for eye disease. In Jakarta, Indonesia, Lions made it possible for 2,224 primary school children to receive vision screening and in Malaysia the Seberang Jaya Lions Club held a four-day screening for local children and provided eyeglasses when necessary. Elsewhere in Malaysia, Lions clubs in the area of capital city of Kuala Lumpur participated with other groups in a three-week long project to raise public awareness of blindness. In yet another initiative of good public relations, Lions in Bangalore, India, arranged with the postal authority for a special postage cancellation stamp to promote World Sight Day.

Just how extensive is the crucial importance of World Sight Days? To cite one example, hundreds of children in Bosnia and Herzegovina lacked access to even basic eye services. Speaking at the October 2004 press conference in Bosnia's capital city of Sarajevo, International President Clement Kusiak said, "For this reason, we decided to mark the seventh Lions World Sight Day with a series of eye care screenings in Sarajevo and other communities. Every day," he continued, "Lions clubs are making a difference in their communities and around the world, and we are certainly doing so for the children of Bosnia and Herzegovina."

At the conclusion of the screenings, Lions Clubs International announced an important US$130,000 initiative to dramatically improve the country's capacity to prevent vision impairment in children and to treat the most difficult cases of childhood blindness that often require sophisticated surgery. Dr. Jasna Kundurovic, the ophthalmologist who organized the Sight Day screenings and the past president of the Sarajevo First Ladies Lions Club, observed, "the Project for the Prevention of Avoidable Blindness in Bosnia and Herzegovina will establish our country's first pediatric ophthalmology clinic in Sarajevo as well as strengthen eye care services in the cities of Mostar, Tuzla and Banja Luka. The project will also train an eye care team that will be based at the Sarajevo clinic in addition to increasing the number of trained ophthalmologists in the country."

This project is, in fact, part of a US$3.7 million global effort by LCIF and the World Health Organization to establish 30 pediatric eye centers in 30 countries. In reflecting on the 2004 World Sight Day accomplishments, President Kusiak emphasized that "While the people of this nation are making great progress in rebuilding their country after the war, there are still great needs, especially for children. Lions here and around the world are going to assure that these children receive the help they need."

Still another thief of sight is diabetes, with diabetic retinopathy being the number one cause of new blindness in people between the ages of 20 and 74. The World Health Organization in Geneva, Switzerland, estimates that there are more than 30 million in the world today who have diabetes and, tragically, more than half are unaware they have the disease. It is estimated that up to 60 percent of diabetes-related blindness could be prevented with proper diagnosis and treatment Not only is diabetes a major cause of blindness, it is an immobilizer and a killer, which is why the early detection of this disease is so vital. Consequently, examinations and diagnosis will not only help to prevent blindness, but save countless thousands of lives.

Two following examples testify to such commitments and more of the association's attack on diabetic retinopathy and other diseases of the eye will be studied in this book's chapters on the Lions Clubs International Foundation and the overwhelming success of the SightFirst program.

Diabetics who suffer from retinopathy often experience subtle changes in vision long before ophthalmologists can detect the problem. Using sensitive measures, however, retinal diseases can be detected early, explained Gary L. Trick, Ph.D., who served as a professor of ophthalmology at the Washington University School of Medicine in St. Louis, Missouri. He employed a variety of tests to measures vision in patients with diabetes, and reported that at least 30 to 40 percent of them may have subtle changes an ophthalmologist would not detect during a general eye examination.

"There are changes in the visual system that are occurring, and in many cases do so very early in the course of the disease," said Dr. Trick. "Typical examinations of the retina will not show changes until the microvascular disease is there," he continued. "With more sensitive measures, we were able to see functionally different things occurring in patients such as color vision beginning to deteriorate or a lessening of their ability to detect fine detail. Electro-physiologically, we're able to show that the responses of neurons both in the retina and in the brain are disturbed prior to any changes that are typically called retinopathy."

His research was partially funded by an LCIF grant. "One of the nice things about a grant of this nature," he observed, "is that it allows you to proceed with pilot studies in various areas where you might not be able to receive funding from major national sources. The pilot study grants allow you to formulate new ideas, initiate testing relatively quickly and accumulate enough data to support applications to federal sources for further studies."

Dr. Trick said his findings may provide ophthalmologists with a different way to evaluate diabetic patients. "Knowing whether there are visual complications would help them determine if these people need to be followed more carefully. They may need to have examinations more frequently and be studied for other complications, or even have their insulin or blood sugar monitored more closely."

The Joslin Diabetes Center in Boston, Massachusetts, has been still another leader in studying and treating diabetes and its visual complications. The Lions of Massachusetts have supported Joslin's programs for many years and its research has also been assisted by an LCIF grant.

In the mid-1960s, Joslin researchers developed a technique using laser beams to treat diabetic retinopathy. Its eye unit eventually began using lasers and surgery to remove blood and abnormal tissue from the retina, a procedure that helped many people with diabetes regain some vision after being considered permanently blind. Joslin physicians also conducted studies using new drugs they believed could slow or halt the progression of diabetes related eye diseases.

Recycling Eyeglasses

Recycling used eyeglasses has, for years, been a staple of the work of Lions to bring the gift of sight to men, women and children primarily in nations where access to eyeglasses is unavailable or cost prohibitive. Lions collect in excess of 30 million used eyeglasses each year at selected collection points: local businesses, libraries, schools, banks, street receptacles, optometrists' offices and other locations. They are then shipped to the nearest Lions Eyeglass Recycling center where specially trained volunteers sort, clean and determine the prescription strengths of the glasses. The eyeglasses are then packaged and stored until they are requested for eyeglass-dispensing missions to developing nations. At these sites, trained Lions and eye care professionals perform vision screenings and dispense the appropriate glasses, free of charge, to the often thousands of children and adults who arrive at the mission location.

As a result of Lions-sponsored missions, used eyeglasses have found their way to Mexico, Bolivia, Guatemala, Thailand, Peru, Ecuador and other countries where the need is greatest. These eyeglasses have changed lives of the poor who had for years been prohibited from enjoying a full family and social life and, in many cases, even having a source of income. It is estimated, in fact, that

44 percent of people living in developing nations need, but do not have, eyeglasses.

The missions are a joint effort between the Lions conducting the project and local club members who assist with customs requirements, provide advance promotion of the mission, arrange meals and accommodations for the visiting mission team, provide crowd control and translation services when needed during distribution of the glasses and arrange medical treatment for persons needing additional eye care. The Lenscrafters Foundation has been especially generous in supporting and helping to fund a number of these missions.

In all, Lions have, since 1995, distributed more than 13 million pairs of used eyeglasses and in some nations Lions have established permanent used eyeglass distribution clinics. How has the response of the recipients touched the Lions who participated in these missions? Let Past International Director Jim Cameron who led one mission of Indiana Lions to Romania bear witness.

"I remember one little girl, she was about seven years old," he related. "She was so grateful for her new glasses that she sang us the song, *Jesus Loves Me* as payment."

In still another endorsement of this sight-enhancing program, "The gift of eyeglasses gives children a chance for an education, enables adults to find employment and helps senior gain independence," said the late Lion Marilyn Green, who served as executive director of the Lions In Sight Foundation of California. "What you and I take for granted and discard, people in developing countries treat as a miracle."

Past International Director Marshall Cooper shares this feeling when he observed, "The one that stands out was in Catacamas, Olancho, Honduras. Thousands of needy people came to the Lions complex for screening, including a 94-year-old man. He was processed through the screening and a pair of recycled glasses placed on him. When we handed him the chart to read, he began to sob. Thinking we had done something wrong, we asked what the problem was. He said, 'Nothing. I am just so happy that now I can see again,' and added, 'There is one more test I need.' He produced a well-worn Bible from his hat, carefully wrapped in protective paper. Again, he sobbed, 'thank you. I can now read my Bible, the first time in over 15 years.'

He stood outside in the hot sun just to tell all who were waiting what a wonderful thing Lions had made possible for him"

Lions Eyeglass Recycling Centers are located in Redcliffe, Queensland, Australia; Calgary, Alberta, Canada; Le Havre, France; Chivasso, Italy; Johannesburg, Republic of South Africa; San Vicente, Del Respeig, Spain; and in the United States—Tucson, Arizona; Phoenix, Arizona; Vallejo, California; Upland, Indiana; West Trenton, New Jersey; Portland, Oregon; Midland, Texas; Roanoke, Virginia; Olympia, Washington and Rosholt, Wisconsin.

Lions who have led these missions insist it is crucial for everyone to donate their used eyeglasses. In most developing countries, an eye exam can cost as much as one month's wage and a single eye doctor may serve a community of hundreds of thousands. This has grown to be yet another challenge in answering Helen Keller's call to be "Knights of the Blind."

After still another successful mission, Past Indiana District Governor Tom Slattery said, "I wish every Lion could have seen the joy in the eyes of the people of San Martin because we were there to serve."

Guides for the Blind

How often have you observed a beautiful dog leading a blind man or woman along the street or into a building? The chances are excellent that team has been trained at a Lions-sponsored dog guide school.

Intense training and the generosity of Lions are required to help provide these dogs and finance the schools. All dogs are provided to blind individuals free of charge. Among the oldest school is Leader Dogs for the Blind, located in Rochester, Michigan. Founded in 1939 by members of the Detroit Uptown Lions Club, its first class graduated four teams. Today, with a staff of more than 100, it has recorded in excess of 13,000 graduates from around the world and is located on 14 acres with a residence center, kennel and well manicured grounds.

Other dog guide schools in the United States and elsewhere have touched thousands of lives.

Pilot Dogs, for example, was established in 1950 in Columbus, Ohio, and became a state project of Ohio Lions in 1960. Currently, 20 percent of the school's support is funded by Ohio Lions and other states with donations amounting to more than $5 million. The success of Pilot Dogs and all the other Lions-supported dog guide facilities can be summed up in the comments of a woman from Ohio who lost her sight in an automobile accident. "I was angry at first when I realized I lost my sight and didn't think I needed anything or anyone. My Pilot Dog has opened so many doors for me. It's a brand new independence and we've really bonded. Having him by my side has built my confidence and I know I can do anything now. I never thought I'd be this close to a dog, ever. I'm truly amazed at what he can do."

In addition to guides for the blind, Pilot Dogs trains dogs for the deaf and hearing impaired. Chopper, a golden retriever, was teamed with Austin Taylor, a fireman and paramedic, and also Deputy Chief of Homeland Security for DuPage County in Illinois. Austin had progressively lost his hearing over five years due to a genetic disease when he first learned about assistance dogs. A colleague in his fire department happened to breed and raise golden retrievers and when a litter was born at Christmas, he donated a pup to him. Energetic and eager to please, Chopper began training at Pilot Dogs when he was six months old and once his training was complete Austin traveled to Columbus to learn how to work with him. Although Chopper does not go on fire or paramedic runs, he works with Austin in the Homeland Security's underground facility and at the fire station. The team also educates children on fire safety with Chopper even demonstrating "stop, drop and roll." With Chopper at home, Austin no longer misses a knock at the door or a phone call. Of great importance, he knows that at night, Chopper will wake him if the smoke detector goes off. "He's given me my ears back," says Austin.

The Chiens Guides D'Aveugles D'Ile De France, is located in Coubert, 77 miles east of Paris, and heavily supported by the Lions. It has had 32 years of experience and has offered 400 dog guides to blind people. As with all such training facilities, a puppy is first assigned to a family who teaches it sociability and good behavior. When the dog is about a year old, it returns to the school for intensive training such as learning to avoid high and low obstacles, looking for crossovers, stopping at the edge of pavements and waiting for the order to cross, maneuvering stairs and escalators, boarding trains, buses and subways and, to be precise, to become familiar with everything a blind person needs in daily activities. After six to nine months, the dog is ready to be offered to a blind person on the waiting list. The team then begins its own training.

A new school will soon be built here that will be larger and have space for up to 49 dogs, increasing its quantitative and qualitative capacities. A training ground called "miniature city" will include many obstacles necessary for training, such as electric escalator, red light, road crossovers, manhole cover, gate and other elements.

"Our objective is to increase our annual dog guides from 25 to 30. That is nearly three times what we offer today and eight times more than six years ago," said Past District Governor Georges Jolliton, chairman of the association.

Florence, who has been given two dogs by the Coubert school, assured that being guided by a dog is a real security and comfort. "Thanks to first Diva and now Safran, both sponsored by the Vincennes Lions Club, I have more leisure time and relationships with other people. They admire my dogs' appearance, good education and kindness."

In Italy, Maurizio Galimberti, a pilot in the Italian Air Force during World War II, was a commercial pilot after the war and was blinded in plane crash in 1948. Today, he travels with the help of a dog provided by the Lions Guide Dog Service in Limbiate, near Milan. "With the aid of guide dogs," he said, "I've covered more than 200,000 miles as a passenger in planes. I've been able to attend Lions international and multiple district conventions, in addition to traveling all over Italy. My family is me and my dog, Liz. She works 24 hours a day, in good weather and bad. Thanks to her, I'm free."

Another recipient from the Milan service, Olga Baldassi, observed, "Guide dogs can go anywhere and suddenly a new life opened up for me. I can travel around Milan or just about anywhere else in the world with a highly trained companion who never deserts me. I've learned to communicate in a number of languages, but my dog and I communicate in a language that has no words, but is the language of love and companionship. Every day, I am grateful for him."

In Edmonton, Alberta, Canada, Joanne Babineau can also testify to the life-changing gift of these dogs. In an article by Past International Director Bill Webber in THE LION, he wrote that Joanne was 19 when she experienced losing her balance and often falling down. She was soon was diagnosed with Friedreich's ataxia, closely related to muscular dystrophy, which causes progressive damage to the nervous system, eventually resulting in muscle weakness, speech problems and heart disease. "The doctors said I would be dead by my 25th birthday," she said. But Joanne was stubborn and refused to give up. Today, she is almost 40 and much of her determination and support has come lately from a four-footed special skills companion named Anton. A golden retriever, one of more than 1,000 dog guides trained at the Lions Foundation of Canada in Oakville, Ontario, Anton "is like a part of me," enthused Joanne. "It's funny. I was a cat person. I never owned a dog." It's clear that Anton now owns her heart. "I'm okay with my disease," she says. "I have my friends and husband, Andre, and I consider myself truly blessed."

Later she met Cliff Carter, a member of the St. Albert Host, Alberta, Lions Club, who invited her and Anton to a meeting. Not long after, Joanne said she wanted to repay the Lions for their kindness and offered to organize the first Mall Walk for Dog Guides in Canada to be held at the huge West Edmonton Mall and asked if the Lions would help. Of course they agreed and word was spread throughout the Edmonton area. They assisted in coordinating the event and with transportation. The result was that more than 200 walkers participated raising in excess of $27,000 for the Lions Foundation of Canada in support of Dog Guides of Canada.

Joanne says that Anton can do just about everything. If she falls, he will position himself so that she can use him to climb back up. He can get her the phone and hit 911 on the speed dial. He can bring her a drink from the refrigerator, push elevator buttons and open doors. But can he vacuum? "Not yet," she says with a laugh, "but we're working on it." There is genuine love and commitment. "He is everything to me," she says.

These are comments that can be repeated thousands of times by people who have been teamed with these special dogs. Whether their companions be golden retrievers, labradors, German shepherds, boxers, or other breeds, the response is always the same. "My companion has changed my life."

Chapter Five
SightFirst: Enhancing The Legacy

The legacy of Helen Keller is no more vividly and successfully displayed than in the accomplishments and growing potential of the SightFirst program, the association's global objective to conquer preventable and reversible blindness. In 1990, it was noted that blindness affected more than 40 million people around the world and if present trends continued, the number would double in the next 25 years. It was further determined that 90 percent of those suffering vision loss lived in developing nations, those areas least likely to be in a position, economically or technologically, to answer these needs.

It was clear that immediate action was necessary and because of Lions Clubs International's historic involvement in sight conservation, the International Board of Directors, after considerable investigation, declared this to be the direction the association's next major service initiative would take. As a result, the 73rd International Convention in St. Louis, Missouri, in 1990 witnessed the launching of "SightFirst: Lions Conquering Blindness," the most ambitious and far-reaching program Lions had ever undertaken.

Lions would be charged with playing a major role in effectively reversing the course of blindness by the end of the century. It was an objective believed to be attainable because eye care specialists estimated that over 80 percent of all cases of blindness were preventable or curable. Planning for the involvement of Lions actually began years earlier when the board's Long Range Planning Committee initiated a study of a new international program objective. The final decision was made as the result of information provided by world sight conservation leaders at a special symposium held prior to the April 1989 board meeting in Singapore. Early the following year, many of these specialists met with officers and key staff members at International Headquarters in Oak Brook to discuss specific elements of the program.

The program would involve the entire membership through the Lions Clubs International Foundation and quite obviously meant that Lions around the world would need to be increasingly generous both in regular donations and from enrollment of more individuals in the Melvin Jones Fellow Program. Central to this fundraising endeavor was the inauguration of Campaign SightFirst in 1991. The following chapter of this book will illuminate the generosity of Lions both in the original campaign and in Campaign SightFirst II, both of which challenged Lions to respond to a humanitarian need that was considered attainable within the "We Serve" perspective of Lions Clubs International.

First, let us study the impact SightFirst has had on the lives of men, women and children the world over and how Lions have nourished their image of Knights of the Blind. The results have been nothing short of phenomenal.

It was clear that Lions Clubs International would need to work closely with other groups with similar sight-saving goals, such as the International Agency for the Prevention of Blindness, the World Health Organization (WHO), The Carter Center and government and non-government agencies to determine precisely what action would need to be taken. Undoubtedly, it was concluded that diverse approaches would be required to meet needs on a global basis with individual projects tailored for various parts of the world. Each SightFirst project was directed to tie into or become part of a national program, as defined by the local government or national ministry of health.

Specifically, there are six primary causes of blindness throughout the world. The most prevalent is cataract blindness, caused by the clouding of the lens of the eye. It is eminently curable, but necessitates teams of eye care specialists often having to travel to remote areas and providing means of transportation of those afflicted to attend the camps or hospitals. The other common blinding conditions are:

- Glaucoma—pressure within the eye
- Diabetic Retinopathy—a complication of diabetes which often results in blindness
- Trachoma—a contagious infection that causes scar formation and granulation within the eye. It is one of the most common

cause of blindness around the world accounting for six million blind today. Furthermore, an estimated 150 million people are infected with it. It is most prevalent in developing countries marred by poverty, poor hygiene and overcrowding. It is caused by a bacteria which can develop on dirty, unwashed faces and is spread by flies. After repeated infection, the eyelashes turn inward and rub against the cornea, causing severe pain, scarring and, eventually, blindness. Lions are fighting trachoma in Africa in a number of ways. They coordinate the distribution of the drug Zithromax, donated by the Pfizer Company, which will ward off the disease. They also support surgery and antibiotics, teach face washing and promote environmental change. The advanced stages of trachoma can be corrected by a 15-minute surgery and antibiotics to treat an active infection. The Conrad N. Hilton Foundation joined the partnership against trachoma by contributing US$150,000 to LCIF to help battle the disease.

- Onchocerciasis—river blindness—an infection carried by the bite of the black fly that breeds rapidly in flowing rivers and introduces a parasite into the body. The small worms multiply and cause intense itching, skin discoloration and, ultimately, blindness. According to WHO, 17.7 million people are infected, primarily in northern African nations, with 500,000 being visually impaired and 270,000 totally blind. To reverse these grim statistics, Lions work with The Carter Center in distributing Mectizan, a drug donated by Merck and Co. One treatment will last a year. The Lions also offer education and assure the people that this treatment against river blindness is safe, and above all, necessary. In addition, Lions and The Carter Center are seeking to provide training for eye care professionals to treat the disease and to mobilize people in local communities to be able to sustain long-term campaigns against trachoma.
- Xerophthalmia—vitamin A deficiency, usually found in children.

However, venues providing surgery and treatment were lacking in many areas, necessitating Lions to develop or strengthen a viable infrastructure in these locations to ensure that delivery systems could be put in place. They also needed to develop the technology and professional skills of those who would be responsible for conducting sight restoration projects. Lions understood fully that for SightFirst projects to succeed, the local community must be organized and this included medical and health personnel, teachers and all those in leadership positions.

The program required district and multiple district sight chairpersons to be cognizant of the sight needs within their areas of responsibility and aware of the goals and potential of SightFirst. Along with their district governors, they should also be in a position to determine the cost of any projects. It was crucial that they work in conjunction with the program's technical advisor assigned to their area to plan and carry out individual projects. The technical advisor is in close contact with the ministry of health and any other groups with which Lions need to work in order to launch and conduct their project. The advisor was to be instrumental in determining that the project being considered by the Lions conformed to policies on the national level and that it would be part of an overall, long-range national program to fight blindness.

As the Lions meticulously planned the direction SightFirst would take, it became increasingly obvious that many barriers to blindness prevention treatment would stand in the way and needed to be identified and, whenever possible, eliminated.

For example, there was a widespread lack of education and information on the part of the general public and perhaps even among professionals in health care concerning the extent of sight-related needs. Very often, transportation and communications difficulties and the lack of accessible medical services to remote areas impede treatment. There was even the need to overcome the fear many people had of being diagnosed as having a potentially blinding disease. Lions often discovered shortage of trained professionals in eye care and the consequent under-treatment of people in need. Surprisingly, there was a widespread lack of motivation on the part of the public to take action in blindness prevention.

Of great concern, perhaps the most critical, was the seemingly overwhelming backlog of eye disease cases and the continually growing numbers of new cases. It was unfortunately clear that the existing technology, equipment and medical personnel were not available to the extent needed to treat those already suffering reversible blindness, much less to answer all new cases. The first objective of SightFirst would be to eliminate this backlog, a task that demanded the elimination of the aforementioned barriers. By achieving this, treating new cases as they occur could be handled more efficiently by the existing health care systems.

How would SightFirst grants to fund these projects be handled? It was determined that the sponsoring Lions would submit a grant application to the SightFirst program department at International Headquarters. This application needed to be endorsed by the district governor or multiple district chairperson, the technical advisor and the ministry of health or other appropriate government agency. Among the criteria needed for approval is that the program would be self-sustaining once initial Lions involvement and funding ceased. Therefore, the government and local health care professionals along with other private organizations must be committed to its continuing support. Also, the need for the program must be documented and how it fits into an overall national health plan. It was also specified that each project of a permanent nature—clinic, teaching facility, operating room....must carry the Lions emblem and be identified as having been made possible by the association.

"For nearly 75 years, Lions have given clear evidence of their will to success in whatever course they embarked upon," observed then International President William L. "Bill" Biggs. "Our SightFirst program will, I am confident, prove to be a decisive step toward our ultimate goal of conquering blindness."

James T. Coffey, who went on to serve as international president in 1993-1994, agreed. "SightFirst will prove to be our most intensive involvement in our battle against blindness, bringing the world of vision to millions of men, women and children throughout the world."

Since its inception, SightFirst has, indeed, met and, in fact, exceeded the hopes and vision of its organizers. During its first two years, the signs were unmistakable that the new program was on the road to unqualified success. To cite only four examples: Hundreds of people in Brazil who suffered from cataracts had their sight restored through surgery. A community eye care training center was established at the Aravind Eye Hospital in India. Eye camps to provide cataract surgery and eye care were established in Kenya, Tanzania and Uganda. Among the largest projects were SightFirst Zones to provide cataract surgery and eye care for those in need in Mexico, Venezuela, Colombia, Ecuador, Peru, Uruguay, Argentina and Chile. In all, during this relatively short period of time, SightFirst grants totaled US$11,240,140.

The following year, grants were approved for an ophthalmic training center in Mali in order to provide the vital need for trained personnel in west African countries and to Bangladesh to enable Lions to conduct 250 camps where an estimated 20,000 cataract surgeries were slated. Four SightFirst projects were approved for Sri Lanka to construct and equip eye wards in three hospitals and purchase and distribute cataract surgery instruments to hospitals throughout the nation.

"Since 1991, the Lions of the world have given new direction to blindness prevention by contributing more than US$140 million to make possible new initiatives in helping the blind," said Past International President Rohit C. Mehta. "The work in developing countries has been phenomenal. During 1991 in India, approximately 80,000 cataract surgeries were performed primarily in remote camp locations. After 15 years, Lions now make it possible to perform 250,000 cataract surgeries every year in properly equipped facilities. In 1991, there were only six or seven Lion-supported eye clinics or hospitals in India. Today, there are 81 modern hospitals entirely managed by Lions and the number of cataract blindness among blind people in the country was reduced from 80 percent in 1991 to 63 percent now."

The ensuing years witnessed the expansion of SightFirst-funded projects the world over. During 1993, a grant established four permanent eye care and surgical centers in southern Africa, located in hospitals in Kwazulu, Bophuthatswana, Lebowa and Transkei. An acute shortage of eye care in these regions resulted in high rates of unoperated cataract and other diseases. The Lions of Multiple

District 410 worked with the Bureau for the Prevention of Blindness to establish these centers.

To implement the SightFirst cataract project in Indonesia, the Lions of District 307 worked with the Ministry of Health, the Indonesian Ophthalmic Association and Helen Keller International to ensure that the project was able to reach densely populated areas that had no previous eye care services. The first SightFirst project in the Philippines supported a national priority to eliminate the backlog of cataract, which is among the highest in the world. A grant of $269,000 was targeted to perform a minimum of 3,000 cataract surgeries during the first year of what was planned to be an ongoing program. The surgeries were concentrated in the capital city of Manila and the neighboring provinces of Batangas and Bulacan where many urban poor have no access to medical care.

A Giant LEHP for SightFirst

The prevalence of eye disease in developed countries also did not go unnoticed and SightFirst organized an ambitious initiative to inform, test and, if necessary, treat people who were victims of conditions that often went undetected until it was too late. Primary among these were glaucoma and diabetic retinopathy. Lions had supported the National Eye Health Education Program (NEHEP) for many years and were familiar with its objective that people need to understand the warning signs of sight-robbing diseases and that this can be accomplished only through examinations. "I think people sometimes take their eyesight for granted," remarked Rosemary Janiszewski, the National Eye Institute's deputy director of NEHEP. "If nothing is wrong, they think, why should I do anything about it?"

If, however, there were greater awareness and education of sight-threatening diseases, and if those at greatest risk received regular eye examinations, much of the blindness in the United States and other developed countries could be prevented. Lions joined in an intensive education program that, in partnership with NEHEP, included development and distribution of two nationwide radio public service campaigns promoting the message for people at risk for glaucoma and diabetic eye disease and by mailing three NEHEP education kits to 360 SightFirst chairpersons. Lions in their own communities delivered materials outlining the risks of these diseases.

"There are so many Lions clubs throughout the country actively involved in their communities," noted Janiszewski. "We're hoping that Lions will take the lead in bringing people together and mobilizing resources."

One such program was initiated by the Lions of Multiple District 22 (Maryland, Delaware and Washington, D.C.) to inform Americans, especially the elderly, African-Americans over 40, people with diabetes and others at high risk, about proper eye health care. The Lions implemented the program in their communities using educational materials developed by the National Eye Institute. They then evaluated its success in preparation for national participation in *Lions Support NEHEP* by May 1995.

These steps brought about yet another direction for SightFirst, the Lions Eye Health Program, commonly referred to as LEHP. It was launched with a SightFirst grant in 1994 and based on the NEHEP program developed by the National Eye Institute. It was designed to address existing and potential sight-related needs in developed countries where glaucoma and diabetic eye disease pose the greatest dangers to preventable and curable blindness. LEHP is a public awareness program designed to help people avoid the disability, loss of independence and diminished quality of life that accompany vision loss.

Lions were requested to distribute materials to at-risk groups and conduct eye health presentations such as showing eye health videos to diabetics or speaking at senior citizens centers. Lions were urged to partner with eye care professionals to conduct vision screenings because many sight problems go undetected until some vision has already been lost. Periodic screenings have proven to be an effective way to detect such conditions and prevent vision loss. "A public screening is just a really good idea," said Dr. Roger Ede, an optometrist and member of the Honolulu Hawaii-Kai Lions Club. "You can talk one-on-one about the importance of an eye exam." Evidence of such an approach was demonstrated when the Hawaiian Lions joined with Allergan to set up screening equipment at the convention hall where trade union conventioneers were meeting.

They were checked for visual acuity, early signs of glaucoma and told the importance of regular dilated eye exams.

The long-term effects of partnering with eye specialists, community groups and corporate organizations was demonstrated when Allergan, which also sponsors other screenings as the one in Hawaii, donated $100,000 to LCIF to help develop the LEHP CD-ROM and print materials on glaucoma. Another important LEHP partner is the Eli Lilly Co. which, in 2002, provided $50,000 for a diabetic patient survey. It showed that, unfortunately, diabetics are not worried about long-term complications of their disease such as blindness and loss of limbs, even though 75 percent will eventually develop microvascular complications. Lilly also provided $236,000 to publicize the survey results and the work of Lions with diabetic retinopathy, $80,000 to develop diabetes education materials and $55,000 for a highly successful LEHP-related public awareness program.

Although its initial projects were conducted in the United States, by 2007, LEHP projects had been implemented in Japan, the United Kingdom, Canada, Australia and Turkey. LEHP offers specific strategies for raising awareness of eye health. Its new CD-ROM includes detailed instructions for setting up eye health seminars, arranging community eye screenings and otherwise increasing awareness of eye health. It also provides videos on eye disease, public service announcements, PowerPoint presentations and media tips to spread the word about eye health.

All individuals and organizations interested in eye health are invited to participate in LEHP, not just Lions clubs. This leads to the development of new and valuable partnerships and creates a more powerful network for the dissemination of eye health information.

SightFirst Activities Continue to Widen Their Influence

The commitment of Lions to reverse the devastation of vision loss through SightFirst has been enhanced on an annual basis. In his 1995 International President's Report, Dr. Giuseppe Grimaldi stated that LCIF funds were awarded to 57 new SightFirst projects, bringing the total number of endeavors to 201 and that in excess of US$37.3 million had been approved for grants in 43 nations. In fact, seven new countries—Nigeria, Ethiopia, Zambia, Lebanon, Romania, Estonia and Turkey—received SightFirst assistance to provide the resources and build infrastructures to combat blindness. Since the program was launched, sight had been restored to 627,000 people who suffered from cataract and more than five million had received vision screenings. Moreover, new capital construction projects were approved for Nepal, Kenya, Zambia, Bangladesh and Lebanon. Clearly, SightFirst was having an impact worldwide.

In his report, President Grimaldi's observation on the future of SightFirst proved to be prescient: "The foundation has been laid for the most ambitious and far-reaching blindness prevention program ever envisioned. Building on that foundation, we now set our sights on the future. Armed with the necessary resources and a renewed commitment, Lions continue to move forward in their attack on global blindness in a solidarity of purpose I am supremely confident will ensure success."

The following year, grants were awarded for 61 SightFirst projects, including first-time sight-saving action in Cameroon, Italy, Bulgaria, Zaire, Ghana, Papua New Guinea, Nicaragua and the Dominican Republic. In Zaire, for example, a Lions Ophthalmic Center was established at Katana Hospital and in Ghana, a Lions Eye Institute would be financed at the Korle Bu Teaching Hospital.

"A particularly crucial characteristic of each of these projects," said 1995-96 International President Dr. William H. Wunder, "is that they include sophisticated training programs that will have far-reaching effects on blindness prevention."

The pace increased significantly in the next fiscal year when a number of new SightFirst projects were approved, among them, a grant of US$70,466 to provide equipment for the Lions Ophthalmic Center at the Regional Hospital of San Pedro in the Ivory Coast, US$32,400 to fund a cataract zone in Costa Rica, US$138,125 to open a 24-bed eye ward and operating theater at a hospital in rural Sri Lanka and four grants, totaling US$370,000, to help reduce the backlog for cataract surgeries in areas of India not covered by government or World Bank programs.

A milestone was reached early in 1997 when the number of people receiving SightFirst-funded cataract surgeries had exceeded one million. They, and millions to follow, have witnessed the SightFirst mission turn into action. These men, women and children are the beneficiaries of Lions and eye care professionals using all available resources to fight preventable and reversible blindness around the world. The success of SightFirst in just a few years stood as a testament to the commitment of Lions to answer a humanitarian need that was growing and an unbounded determination to address these grievous conditions where blindness was rampant, especially in Africa, Latin America and South and Southeast Asia.

SightFirst continued to expand. In January 1999, the SightFirst Advisory Committee approved 24 grants totaling US$2,035,351 with first-time projects funded in three countries. The Lions of Burkina Faso would develop a multi-faceted eye care delivery program with the goal of providing 300 cataract surgeries and 100 trichiasis surgeries during the first year alone. In Mongolia, a grant would help the Lions in their efforts to reduce the prevalence of avoidable blindness such as cataract, glaucoma and corneal disease in the provinces of South and Middle Gobi. A grant was issued to the Lions of Trinidad and Tobago in the West Indies to establish a cataract zone project with it primary objective to provide free surgery to cataract-blind patients over 50 years of age who were living in extreme poverty.

Also in 1999, 14 grants in the amount of US$690,000 were provided to Lions in Latin America, five grants in the amount of US$105,439 for project in South Asia and US$763,710 to expand the LEHP program in Multiple District 105 (British Isles and Ireland).

In his report to the 2002 International Convention in Osaka, Japan, International President J. Frank Moore III remarked, "SightFirst is maintaining its course to one day conquer preventable and reversible blindness." In tracing the program's success to that point, he stated, "The results of the SightFirst grant projects are measurable and, most certainly, substantial. More than 3.5 million cataract surgeries have been performed and 36 million people have been treated for river blindness. Moreover, the nature of these grants empower the local residents to continue toward their sight-saving objectives once the grant money had been disbursed. Consequently, SightFirst initiatives have built or expanded 136 eye hospitals, upgraded equipment at 273 eye centers, expanded six training facilities and trained nearly 13,000 ophthalmic professionals and 54,000 village health workers, all of which promise to have a positive impact on the future."

The growing victories of the program over reversible blindness was given heartwarming confirmation by a woman in Bangladesh who, after her eyesight was restored as a result of a SightFirst-funded cataract project, exclaimed, "Now I can see my grandchildren for the first time."

Still another example of the effectiveness of SightFirst is found in Madagascar, the fourth largest island in the world. The project is considered a model of SightFirst efficiency in confronting a local condition and cooperating with local health authorities. An initial US$250,800 grant in 1998 enabled the Lions in that nation to expand their routine activity of distributing eyeglasses to developing a sustainable eye care delivery system, primarily to reduce cataract. More than 1,600 surgeries were performed and six hospitals received modern equipment. Two years later a second grant of US$946,876 equipped three additional eye care centers, trained more ophthalmic personnel and provided 8,000 cataract operations. In the course of only four years, Lions and their partnering agencies have altered health care sight services in a manner once thought unthinkable.

"Our first SightFirst project was a complete eyeopener," said Project Chairperson Fidy Rakotozafy. "Before Lions were involved, there was no recognition of the prevalence of cataract. We not only helped to build capacity for services, but also gained the respect and trust of the Ministry of Health."

As one cataract surgery recipient remarked, "I am so thankful to the Lions. Before they came here, I didn't even know my sight could come back."

The People's Republic of China Opens its Door to SightFirst

Among the program's most ambitious ventures was bringing sight-saving services to the People's Republic of China. Launched in April 1997 in cooperation with the Chinese government's State Council Coordination Committee on Disability and two of its subsidiaries, the Ministry of Health and the China Disabled Persons' Federation, it was named SightFirst China Action and began with a US$15.3 million grant to the Lions of District 303 (Hong Kong and Macau) who would coordinate the program. This was the largest grant for a project since the inception of SightFirst and the first time the Chinese government had chosen to participate directly with an international service organization in a national program. The government agreed to provide 15-to-one matching funds to the SightFirst grant.

The reasons for this endeavor were obvious. Of the estimated 37 million blind people in the world, 20 percent who were blind from cataract lived in China and 400,000 new cases were recorded each year. The goal of SightFirst China Action was to mobilize 100 surgical teams to travel to remote rural areas of the western provinces where the need was greatest. The program's span had five years during which it was to sponsor 1.75 million cataract surgeries. The SightFirst grant would also establish an efficient database system to collect and manage data on blindness from rural and remote areas; train 3,500 ophthalmologists, technicians and nurses to provide cataract surgeries and other eye care services; develop ophthalmology departments in local hospitals in more than 400 rural counties; publicize eye health prevention nationwide and create an organization that would include Lions, the government and eye health professionals to administer, control and manage the project.

In commenting on the historic initiative, Dr. William H. Wunder, chairperson of the LCIF Board of Trustees, said, "The Lions are proud to play a role in accelerating the elimination of blindness in the world's most populous country."

The program went on to exceed expectations. At the end of the five-year period, 2.5 million cataract surgeries had, in fact, been performed in China and 104 surgical eye units established in rural counties that previously had none. More than 12,000 ophthalmologists and paramedics were trained and 260 medical teams dispatched to areas most in need. So successful was this program that, in 2002, the Chinese government and LCIF extended SightFirst China Action for another five years. Applying a second grant of US$15.8 million, the objectives of Phase II of this program were to expand the accomplishments of Phase I by completing at least another 2.5 million cataract surgeries, creating more medical teams and training additional medical personnel. In order to assure the sustainability of the program, more clinics in rural areas would be built and equipped and training courses offered to prepare medics to continue to deliver quality treatment for reversible blindness.

Phase II was approved at the SightFirst Advisory Committee meeting in May 2002 and officially launched in Beijing in August 2002 when association leaders met with Jiang Zemin, president of the People's Republic of China, along with other national and provincial leaders, including Deng Pufeng, chairman of the China Disabled Persons' Federation. "President Zemin expressed his deep appreciation for all the Lions achieved during Phase I," said International President Kay K. Fukushima. "He also remarked that he looked forward to more Lions clubs being established in his nation, clubs he was certain would sponsor still more sustainable sight programs."

Phase II of SightFirst China Action built on the success of the initial phase and presently more than 705,000 cataract surgeries have been performed.

The overall accomplishments of the program's two phases witnessed the number of poor people receiving surgeries annually increase from 200,000 in 1996 to in excess of 600,000 and extended the coverage of surgical services, increased the capacities of training centers by constructing 31 new centers and strengthened infrastructures to provide comprehensive eye care, particularly in poorer provinces and counties. Initial SightFirst activities were also conducted in Tibet by equipping hospitals in four prefectures, performing 11,000 sight-restoring operations and providing training for local doctors. As a result of SightFirst funding and the support of local Lions, which provided the cost for sight-saving surgeries, medical team training and equipment, the Chinese government declared Tibet a "cataract free zone" in 2007. These zones are declared when an existing cataract surgery backlog has been addressed and existing eye care systems can manage all new cases. Because of the success of the Lions in Tibet, the China Disabled Persons' Federation in May 2007 announced its intent to achieve cataract free zone status in 500 counties throughout China by 2010. Training workshops and public education campaigns for medical teams in the counties are now underway. The announcement also included a memorandum thanking the Lions and LCIF for their support.

Beyond the medical achievements, SightFirst China Action also increased the association's visibility and interest in Lions.

SightFirst and The Carter Center: A Winning Alliance

The SightFirst program's success has in large part been due to partnerships with local government and United Nations Agencies and private groups. Among the most enduring has been the association's alliance with The Carter Center, forged in 1999, to fight trachoma and river blindness in Africa. Former United States President Jimmy Carter is a past district governor of Georgia's District 18-C and has given unstintingly of his time and resources to enable Lions to implement the goals of SightFirst. A recipient of the 1996 Humanitarian Award from Lions Clubs International, he pledged in 1997 to help Lions gain access to high-level government officials in African countries where SightFirst projects were being conducted or under consideration, remarking, "I would be honored to be called upon."

The Carter Center and SightFirst were already partners in onchocerciasis projects in Nigeria and Cameroon and would soon expand to other African nations, including the Sudan. In 1995, The Carter Center established a presence in Sudan and was positioned to provide both technical and data management assistance to Lions in developing river blindness control activities. A SightFirst grant of US$1,567,796 was targeted to treat people afflicted with blindness and to expand training of Sudanese eye-care specialists. The funds were channeled through Global 2000 offices of The Carter Center and then to project offices. It was expected that 380,000 individuals would be treated annually.

Another giant step was taken in the Lions-Carter Center SightFirst Initiative in the year 2000 when an LCIF-SightFirst grant in the amount of US$16,020,915 was approved for a five-year program that would focus on preventing and controlling onchocerciasis (river blindness) in Nigeria, Uganda and Ethiopia, eliminating it in Latin America and controlling trachoma in Sudan and Ethiopia. Millions of people have been treated through the distribution of the drug Ivermectin donated by Merck & Co. and, in cooperation with

The Carter Center, millions more will be prevented from incurring blindness by receiving Ivermectin on an annual basis.

To cite one example of these cooperative efforts, The Carter Center, with the support of Lions, is the only non-governmental organization in Ethiopia fighting onchocerciasis. In 2005, more than 2.5 million people were treated in that war-torn nation and because of this partnership, in five years, 32,000 community-based distributors of the drug were trained, providing a cumulative total of nearly 9.3 million treatments in remote villages.

Commenting on a story on river blindness that appeared in the *Houston Chronicle,* Dr. Clement Kusiak, who was serving as 2005-2006 LCIF Chairperson, wrote, in part, "You will be pleased to know that since 1995 SightFirst has targeted river blindness in Africa and Latin America through our partnership with The Carter Center. Working primarily with national health ministries, LCIF and The Carter Center have delivered more than 70 million treatments of Mectizan, donated by the pharmaceutical company Merck. We've delivered these treatments at an average cost of only 50 cents per person.

"Lions in the endemic countries are a critical part of the 'volunteer' army that distributes the drug. Local Lions also help lead workshops for policy makers and community leaders and lobby for local spending and programs to control the disease. So you can see that Lions are at the very heart of the battle.

"One of the primary aims of SightFirst is to eliminate river blindness as a public health concern. Because of the campaign, Lions will be able to effectively eliminate the disease in Latin America by 2010, as health experts agree is possible, and control its blinding effects in Africa by 2020.

"Think for a moment about those school children in the (*Chronicle*) story. They are taking Mectizan. They plan to grow up. They say they are determined to become a doctor, a professor, the president. We need to keep them and others safe. We can protect them and their future. The reporter says it's unbelievable that a fly and a worm can be so tough a battle. Well, that's partly correct. This disease has been a tough foe but, its days are numbered."

In the Amhara region of Ethiopia, trachoma threatens 90 percent of its 19 million persons and the Lions-Carter Center SightFirst initiative is poised to expand its activities. The Pfizer Company is supplying all necessary amounts of the drug Azithromycin needed for the required surgeries. The transmission of trachoma in Ethiopia and southern Sudan is severe and increasing and Lions along with The Carter Center have pledged to meet this challenge.

The New York Times featured a story on trachoma control as part of a series on neglected diseases. President Carter sent a letter to the editor which read in part: "For more than 20 years, The Carter Center has worked to control, eliminate and eradicate neglected diseases, including river blindness and trachoma, that affect the poorest of the poor. Your coverage of these diseases will mean the alleviation of suffering for thousands more people like those you profiled. The Carter Center is honored to be mentioned in some of these articles and is appreciative of the many partners who support our work. In fact, none of our efforts in Ethiopia, as illustrated in your trachoma article, would be possible without the active partnership and financial support of Lions Clubs International, an organization of more than one million members who address blindness diseases."

The SightFirst program continues to expand around the world in its determination to eliminate preventable and reversible blindness. By 1999, the total number of countries that benefited from SightFirst projects stood at 71, and three years later, in 2002, the numbers stood at 572 projects with grants totaling US$136 million approved in 78 countries. Also in 2002, it became apparent that specialized eye care was a growing problem in the Czech Republic. A SightFirst grant helped to build and equip the Lions International Educational Center of Ophthalmology, now part of Charles University in Prague. In addition to reversing the backlog of cataract surgeries, the center will train ophthalmologists in surgery who, in turn, will meet needs in eastern and central Europe.

In yet another large-scale project, since 1993, the Tropical Ophthalmology Institute of Africa (IOTA) has been awarded nearly US$3 million in SightFirst grants for the development of human resources. Located in Bamako, Mali, IOTA is the primary force for blindness prevention activities in west and central Africa. Its training capacity now includes a fully-equipped teaching laboratory, library, classrooms and pharmacy and has trained of hundreds of ophthalmologists, cataract surgeons, ophthalmic nurses and eyeglass technicians from nations across the continent.

Childhood blindness was also a growing concern, especially in poor areas of the world. It was estimated that a half million children go blind every year, mostly from preventable conditions such as Vitamin A deficiency, measles, cataract and untreated infections. To reverse this trend, Lions Clubs International teamed with the World Health Organization in 2002 to launch the Project for the Elimination of Avoidable Childhood Blindness. A SightFirst grant of US$3.75 million was announced during a conference at WHO that brought together 45 global experts on blindness. A three-pronged approach was adopted. First, primary eye care services would be brought to 30 countries to treat preventable causes of blindness through the training of health workers. Second, a network of 25 regional centers in developing areas would be developed to provide advanced treatment and surgical care. Thirdly, low vision services would be created in 25-30 countries to ensure that children with diminished eyesight would have access to the proper devices to improve their vision and, when necessary, receive mobility training.

By the year 2004, SightFirst's record of giving the gift of sight was far-reaching. Through the application for 642 grants totaling US$152 million in 79 countries, it had made possible 50 million treatments for river blindness, 3.5 million cataract surgeries, the construction or expansion of 154 eye hospitals, equipment upgrades for 296 eye centers, the expansion of six training facilities and the training of 68,000 health workers.

LCIF began preparing for the future of SightFirst at the International Sight Symposium held in Seoul, Korea, in April of 2004. It brought together Lion leaders and 24 experts on the subjects of blindness, vision rehabilitation and vision research. All examined the role of Lions in preventing blindness, assessed old and new threats to vision and discussed current and emerging initiatives, strategies and technologies to combat blindness.

Insofar as specific regions are concerned, as 2005 approached, SightFirst had awarded US$77.7 million for 258 grants in South and

Southeast Asia, supported 875,000 cataract surgeries in India, and in cooperation with The Carter Center in attacking river blindness, had transformed lives in 12 nations in Africa and Latin America.

It was abundantly clear that that SightFirst was enabling Lions to be the world's primary champions of sight. At the conclusion of 2005-2006, it had awarded US$187 million for 771 projects in 89 countries. Since its inception, five million people had their sight restored through cataract surgery; five million men, women and children had avoided vision loss as a result of timely treatment and eye care services were improved for hundreds of millions. SightFirst grants provided 70 million treatments for river blindness, constructed or expanded 207 eye hospitals, clinics and wards; upgraded 314 eye centers with modern equipment, provided management training at 109 facilities and trained 300,000 ophthalmologists, ophthalmic nurses and professional care workers and village health workers.

The expanding scope and reach of SightFirst is demonstrated through the expansion of the Sight for Kids program in Latin America. As a result of SightFirst joining in partnership with Johnson & Johnson, Sight for Kids is now addressing the critical problem of uncorrected refractive error among 100,000 children in Argentina and Brazil. Supported by US$100,000 in funding, Lions are helping to provide a solution to a situation that is entirely reversible. Sight for Kids also expanded into India and the Philippines because of US$320,000 in renewed funding. In Bangkok, Thailand, alone, Sight for Kids has screened more than 345,000 children in 431 schools. Eyeglasses were prescribed for 6,245 and an additional 231 youngsters required hospital treatment for eye disease. The program is expanding to other schools in Thailand's capital city and beyond, with vision training skills given to school teachers to make it possible for them to continue caring for the vision health of their students.

To further demonstrate the commitment of Lions worldwide to eradicating preventable and reversible blindness, in January 2006 the SightFirst Advisory Committee issued 13 grants totaling US$4.7 million. Nations receiving these grants included Mexico, Argentina, Sri Lanka and Ethiopia. The largest was US$3,100,984 to District 403-B in Cameroon. It will extend the river blindness control program in seven provinces and will begin in the one province which was not covered at the time. In a splendid example of cooperative effort, the work would be done in partnership with The Carter Center, Helen Keller International, the International Eye Foundation and PersPective.

The following year, the SightFirst Advisory Committee awarded US$14,538,959 for 71 projects.

Reflecting on the program and looking to the future, 1997-1998 International President Howard L. "Pat" Patterson said, "More than 40 million people are blind today—most of them needlessly blind. This is appalling. SightFirst can make this figure a thing of the past...and it will. But it needs the commitment of every Lion and every club in the association. Look to the future and imagine one where blindness has been conquered. Can you envision a brighter future?"

In commenting on the tremendous success of SightFirst, 2007-2008 International President Mahendra Amarasuriya observed, "It has met the needs of millions of poor and deserving people all over the world by establishing new sight centers and hospitals in various parts of the world, completing around eight million cataract surgeries, delivering millions of doses of antibiotic to combat river blindness in Africa and Latin America and providing eyeglasses to the poorest of the poor. Our efforts have touched the lives of countless people who would otherwise continue to be blind with cataract, affected by blinding diseases and who would never have the opportunity of seeing their loved ones and enjoying the beauty of nature."

Past International President Austin Jennings also expressed his thoughts on the success of SightFirst: "It is amazing what can happen when we focus the energy and resources of Lions around the world toward a common goal—eliminating reversible and preventable blindness. A sleeping giant has been aroused. The future is bright for Lions Clubs International. We have found a sense of direction, a common objective, a place in the major leagues of humanitarian service providers. We have earned worldwide recognition for having changed the lives of more than 85 millions people. And we have only begun."

SightFirst continues its humanitarian mission wherever the need is greatest, thanks to the generosity of the Lions membership and its forging of successful partnerships with other organizations and agencies. However, an undertaking of this magnitude requires funding—generous funding. This had been the challenge of Campaigns SightFirst I and II and Lions predictably responded as expected as members of the world's largest service club organization.

Chapter Six
The Campaigns that Financed the Path Toward the Objectives of SightFirst

The first steps in the monumental Campaign SightFirst (CSF) fundraising program were taken by the LCIF Board of Trustees during its June meeting at the 1991 International Convention in Brisbane, Queensland, Australia. The goal was to raise US$130 million over a three-year span with the year 1991-1992 designated as the Year of Planning and Preparation. Past International President Judge Brian Stevenson was appointed the campaign's International Executive Fundraising Coordinator and its chief spokesperson. Past International Directors were named members of the International SightFirst Fundraising Committee and charged with establishing campaign policy and overseeing the progress of the drive. They represented each of the association's seven constitutional areas:

United States & Affiliates: Robert J. Drabek and
    Norman M. Dean
Canada: W.W. "Bill" Webber
Mexico, South & Central America and the Caribbean:
    Rodolfo Alfredo Marinelli
Europe: Heinz J. Ondrejka
Orient, Philippines and Southeast Asia:
    Hiromasa Shinoda
Africa & Southwest Asia: Ashok Mehta
Australia, New Zealand, Isles of the South China Sea &
    South Pacific: Dr. R.J. "Bob" Coulthard

To ensure still further coordination and eventual success, 45 National/Multi-National Coordinators were named to provide leadership worldwide and 133 Sector Coordinators were appointed and responsible for working with an average of six districts each.

In addition to the recruitment of top campaign leaders, the first year witnessed requests for large gifts from foundations, corporations, government agencies and a select few individuals. As a matter of fact, during the year CSF received its first Lead Gift from an anonymous Lion in the OSEAL area. These are gifts initially of at least US$100,000 that, as the name suggests "lead" the way by inspiring others to donate at their greatest potential.

During 1991-1992, extensive information, marketing and public relations plans were developed to foster support of the foundation and SightFirst.

"In this, our 75th Anniversary year, we are celebrating the association's decades of commitment to sight conservation," said International President Donald E. Banker in his report to the 1992 Hong Kong Convention. "During 1991-1992, Campaign SightFirst has become a symbol of this long-standing involvement. Indeed, it is much more than that. It reflects a fulfillment of our commitment to sight conservation, an opportunity for Lions to have a lasting effect on sight needs around the world. Campaign SightFirst is vital to the success of SightFirst. CSF-funded projects make the goal of conquering blindness a real and practical possibility."

The International Fundraising Committee further outlined the objectives of the three-year drive. Year two, 1992-1993, was designated the Year of Organization and Motivation when leaders would join the SightFirst fundraising campaign at the district, zone and club levels and orientation would be provided to the campaign leaders. During this fiscal year, there would be a continuing effort to receive large gifts and clubs would maintain their commitment to raising funds for LCIF and SightFirst.

The final year, 1993-1994, would be the Year of Campaign SightFirst, to be launched at the 76th International Convention in Minneapolis, Minnesota. Comprehensive campaign manuals, audio-visuals and other operation materials would be made available and there would be widespread fundraising efforts by clubs throughout the world. It was fully anticipated that the campaign's success would be celebrated at the following year's 77th International Convention in Phoenix, Arizona.

During the first year of the campaign, many examples could be provided to demonstrate how funds were able to help those in need. In commenting on the effect Lions can have, Campaign Chairperson Stevenson observed, "The leading causes of blindness are all preventable or reversible; tragically 80 percent of those who are blind lose their sight needlessly. All that is lacking is enough money for treatment, medicine, facilities and trained professionals. To seize this opportunity, Lions must step beyond all that has gone before and unite behind CSF to help raise the US$130 million needed to conquer blindness. Campaign SightFirst is not another program in Lions' traditional commitment to sight. It is an opportunity to fulfill that commitment. I ask Lions the world over to look beyond local projects and reach across international borders to become a part of this historic worldwide effort. The sight of millions depends on it."

Among the most important and visible examples of this commitment were the *Model Clubs*, those which set an example for all Lions clubs by conducting intensive fundraising campaigns in advance of The Year of Campaign SightFirst. The campaign's first Model Club was the Albany Evening, Georgia, Lions Club and was so designated by raising more than US$76,000. "This money," said Past President Stevenson, "will help blind people by supporting special CSF-funded projects. But its value will also be multiplied many times because of the outstanding example that has been set."

Model clubs were seen as leading the way in the campaign to conquer blindness. They demonstrated that CSF's plan for seeking important financial support from individuals and businesses in the community. Employing tested and effective ways to raise US$130 million showed that, when fully informed about the seriousness of the worldwide problem of blindness, Lions are extremely generous.

Another important large-scale element in the campaign singled the Lead Gift donors. 1992-1993 International President Rohit C. Mehta stated that more than 30 had been received, all in excess of US$25,000 and most at or above US$100,000. "These figures, " he said, "when combined with the growing success of our Model Clubs program, demonstrate conclusively that, when offered the opportunity, "Lions will give generously to help their fellow Lions fight the scourge of preventable and reversible blindness."

The international president continued, "Not only has 1992-1993 been one of preparation, in excess of US$30 million was raised. Furthermore, I am extremely pleased to report that 3,500 clubs earned the *Lions Conquering Blindness* banner patch by raising at least US$1,500 for the campaign."

The stage was now set for the third and final year of the campaign and the international convention in Minneapolis was up to the task.

The Year of Campaign SightFirst

"Lions, our year together has begun...Let us each assume our responsibilities," exclaimed James T. Coffey, the newly elected 1993-1994 president of Lions Clubs International at the closing session of the 76th International Convention in Minneapolis. "As international president, it is my honor and privilege to officially launch The Year of Campaign SightFirst." The words reverberated through the Target Center and to members around the world. Thus did President Coffey begin his year with this challenge for the Lions membership to join in the greatest fundraising program in the history of the association.

The SightFirst program and the campaign's goals were central to the theme of the entire convention. During the opening session, a re-enactment was staged of Helen Keller's speech at the 1925 International Convention when she challenged Lions to become "Knights of the Blind." Three local actors portrayed Ms. Keller, then International President Harry Newman and Anne Sullivan, the "Miracle Worker," to a hushed audience that provided a standing ovation upon their conclusion.

Also at the opening session, Past International President Judge Brian Stevenson introduced committee members representing the association's seven constitutional areas who announced the funding goals of Lions in their areas toward the campaign's minimum target of US$130 million by June 30, 1994. These announcements were followed by the introduction of Campaign SightFirst Honorary Chairperson, future Olympic figure skating medalist Nancy Kerrigan, who encouraged all Lions to support the program and for registrants to the convention to attend the SightFirst/Campaign SightFirst

Seminar the following day. During pre-game ceremonies at Lions Night with the Twins she was on hand to help present a check in the amount of US$12,000 to association officers that the Twins baseball club donated to the campaign.

During the convention's second session, the 1992-1993 Lead Gift donors of at least US$100,000 to the campaign were introduced. Each received the prestigious "Global Vision" statue in recognition of their generosity. The 76th Convention closed with President Coffey stating with confidence that the next year's convention in Phoenix, Arizona, would be the scene of celebration for the successful conclusion of the Year of Campaign SightFirst. But what exactly did this year, one of the most important in the history of Lions Clubs International, entail?

It was a time for each member to reflect on what it meant to be a Lion, to evaluate his or her commitment to conquering blindness and to bring all Lions together in unity as never before. Lions were being asked to consider a meaningful personal gift to CSF and to understand that fundraising was not an end in itself, but a means to an end, that being to eliminate needless blindness. It was a year to appreciate that a united global fundraising effort would enhance the association's image and to realize that the success of CSF would build membership and have a positive effect on the future of Lions Clubs International. It was a year when every Lions club was asked to make the campaign its top priority and for club leaders to join in comparing progress and to encourage one another. Moreover, it was a year when all Lions were to ask themselves, "Do I have a special responsibility to help assure the success of my association's greatest sight initiative in history?"

World leaders were generous in complimenting Lions for their commitment to Campaign SightFirst.

"Throughout my public life," said Margaret Thatcher, Britain's longest serving prime minister, "I have been guided by the principle that private citizens, acting together, can do much that governments cannot. Campaign SightFirst is an excellent example of such action. Only an international organization with members in 178 countries can bring to bear the worldwide resources needed to combat the global problem of preventable and reversible blindness. I congratulate the Lions of the British Isles for their role in Campaign SightFirst and I thank Lions for undertaking this most ambitious humanitarian effort."

Former United States President Jimmy Carter, who served as a district governor in Georgia, remarked "Rosalynn and I are pleased to join in supporting Lions Clubs International's Campaign SightFirst. The world's largest humanitarian service club is to be commended for this most ambitious fundraising project. We send our best wishes for success in your efforts to eliminate preventable blindness."

"I have been an honorary member of the Grand Rapids, Michigan, Lions Club for many years," said former U.S. President Gerald Ford, "and have always been proud of what my good friends there have done for people in need. Now I am asking them all and all the Lions in the world to get behind Campaign SightFirst and to work hard to meet and exceed its goal. I congratulate you for setting your sights so high and am confident that you will reach them."

Former President Ronald Reagan remarked "Your efforts are helping to make this a better world for everybody," and former President George H.W. Bush remarked, "During the past three quarters of a century, Lions clubs have been a shining example of the importance of community service and the spirit of volunteerism. Members of Lions Clubs International can be proud of their organization's 75 years of service. On this occasion I especially applaud Campaign SightFirst, your greatest effort to prevent blindness around the globe."

Another very special testimonial was offered to Lion Ashok Mehta in 1993, a past international director at the time who years later would become international president. He was in Calcutta, India, with a delegation of Lions to visit the convent of the Missionary Sisters of Charity. "We were escorted into a small room," he recalled, "and were joined by Mother Teresa, Nobel Prize winner and recipient of the 1986 Humanitarian Award of Lions Clubs International. Upon hearing that Campaign SightFirst was to provide eye care to the poor throughout India and the world, Mother Teresa commended Lions, quoting from the Bible, 'As Jesus said, whatever you do for the least of my brethren, you do for me.'

"I returned to my home in Bombay eager to share news of my visit with Lions of all faiths working for the success of Campaign

94

SightFirst," said Lion Mehta " For, as Mother Teresa observed, 'The fruit of love is service.' And the fruit of service through Campaign SightFirst is a world free from preventable blindness."

Leaders of Lions Clubs International were equally enthusiastic as the Year of Campaign SightFirst approached.

"This campaign is most assuredly a colossal undertaking, an extraordinary financial endeavor that will determine our capacity to conquer preventable and reversible blindness" observed Rohit C. Mehta, then serving as international president. "But for this goal to be attained, every individual Lions club needs to participate and participate generously."

Past international presidents also lent their support and encouragement.

"Through our involvement in Campaign SightFirst Lions can change the entire world—the entire world, not just a small corner of it," said Donald E. Banker. "We're going to involve ourselves as we have never been involved before in the lives of people."

"Show your pride in Lions Clubs International by learning as much as possible about CSF and spreading the word among fellow Lions and members of the community," encouraged Judge Brian Stevenson.

Past International President Joseph Wroblewski stated, "New extraordinary CSF-funded projects must stand on the shoulders of our traditional sight preservation programs in order to close the gap between what is being done and what must be done to conquer blindness."

"Lions are once again being asked to do more," observed Edward M. Lindsey. "No other organization, can match our record in sight preservation and help for the blind. Yet, it is not enough. Despite all we have done, the number of blind people in the world continues to grow at an alarming rate. Campaign SightFirst," he assured, "will make the difference between victory and defeat in our historic battle against blindness."

Anticipating success of the campaign in his vision for the future, Austin P. Jennings, the CSF International Lead Gifts Coordinator, predicted, "By participating in Campaign SightFirst, we were able to play an integral role in the greatest humanitarian effort ever. We were involved in what no other organization could do. We could selflessly help those in parts of the world where needs are far greater than ours. We changed the world because we had the interest, experience and commitment of our members to do it. Lions conquered blindness!" In addition to his responsibilities as the coordinator for International Lead Gifts, Past President Jennings was involved in many other aspects of the campaign that concluded in its extraordinary success over its three-year period.

First, however, it would be necessary for Lions the world over to join in the spirit of 1993-1994 and the Year of Campaign SightFirst. The road to Phoenix and the 77th International Convention was open, a road that would test Lions Clubs International in the greatest fundraising effort in its history.

At the time of the launching, Lead Gifts of US$25,000 to US$250,000 had already been contributed and 31 Model Clubs were demonstrating what could be achieved when Lions were determined to reach out to blind people wherever the need is paramount. In addition, a select group of Lions were being invited to become Advance Gift donors by considering gifts of US$5,000 to $10,000 and above to set the pace of giving in advance of intensive fundraising in the clubs. The donors were eligible to receive the Melvin Jones Fellowship or a Global Vision statue specially designed for the campaign, symbolizing the vigilance with which Lions stand guard over the world's eyesight.

As The Year of Campaign SightFirst dawned, more world leaders were prompted to show their support and to compliment Lions for their actions.

"It is a terrible tragedy that blindness afflicts so many millions of people around the world," said U.S. President Bill Clinton. "Even more tragic is that the great majority of these cases could be prevented or reversed, yet go untreated every day. I am very pleased that Lions Clubs International has created the SightFirst program to address this great world need. Your program is making significant advances toward stopping blindness."

Remarked Henrik, Prince of Denmark, "During the last couple of years, I have been following the impressive Campaign SightFirst. I feel strongly entitled to encourage the Lions of the world to make an extraordinary effort in this last stage of the campaign in order to save and restore the sight of millions of needy people."

"I am delighted to give my endorsement to the Lions Clubs International program, Campaign SightFirst, and to congratulate your members on their efforts to rid the world of preventable and treatable blindness," said John Major, Prime Minister, the United Kingdom.

"It is my wish that all men and women of goodwill join in this humanitarian effort to bring victory in the battle against blindness," declared Edward Cooke, Governor General of Jamaica.

"I call upon all Lions clubs members to participate in the fight for the end of needless blindness so that children and all peoples, especially those in developing countries, may see without fear of what the future may bring," said Cesar Gaviria Trujillo, President, Republic of Colombia. "I salute the Lions of Colombia and the world and urge that you make this great initiative a reality for the benefit of all humanity."

"On behalf of the government of the Republic of El Salvador, we express our congratulations to worldwide Lionism and particularly the Salvadorian Lions clubs, to whom we offer our support to the best of our abilities for the success of Campaign SightFirst," stated Alfredo F. Cristiani, President, Republic of El Salvador.

With endorsements from these and other world leaders and the commitment of leaders in the association, Lions worldwide embarked on meeting the object of the most important fundraising program in its history.

Lions were assured that a gift of US$1,000 would help fund cataract surgery for some 133 older adults in parts of Asia, or rescue 1,000 people from river blindness, or save 2,500 children from blindness or death due to Vitamin A deficiency, or train people in four African villages to prevent the spread of trachoma. Donors of this amount were told they would take their rightful place in history when their names are entered in a computerized display at International Headquarters commemorating Lions as "knights of the blind."

These and other incentives were in place. Now was the time for Lions to put their sense of responsibility to the test. Projects were initiated and Lions dug a bit deeper into their pockets, especially as February 28 loomed. This was designated as Worldwide Report Day when campaign leaders would report the total funds raised in cash and pledges. It was designed to provide a clear picture of the status of the campaign in all areas of the world. "On that day, we will know whether we must continue to focus our efforts on reaching our minimum goal of US$130 million, or can begin our sprint toward our challenge goal of an additional US$70 million by the end of this year," said the campaign's executive coordinator Judge Brian Stevenson. "In either case, Lions will be running hard down the home stretch toward our victory celebration this July."

International President James T. Coffey further emphasized the crucial importance of Lions joining together in this common cause.

"Today, Lions are confronting perhaps the greatest challenge any group has ever faced: that of conquering preventable and curable blindness," he observed "Upon our shoulders rests not only the success of Campaign SightFirst, but the fate of millions of people who are needlessly blind, the future of millions more at risk of losing their sight, and the very prestige of our association.

"This is a job which no man or woman, no district or multiple district, no one country or continent can tackle alone. For the first time in history, Lions have been called to stand together, shoulder to shoulder, 1.4 million members strong. Together, we are committed to raising a minimum of US$130 million by June 30, 1994."

Indeed, Lions worldwide accepted the challenge. In the first few months, the following are but a few examples of how serious Lions were to raise those funds.

Italian Lions sold postcards which declared, "Those who cannot see are not alone," and in India CSF T-shirts were designed to help raise funds. Leos in that country also sold special postal covers bearing the CSF logo. The Ganlose, Denmark, Lions Club sponsored a journey for sight that included blind runners and a poster advertised a similar journey in Finland.

Raffles were popular around the world. For example, a miniature car was the prize of the River Valley Lions Club in Gore, New Zealand; another car was provided by the San Lorenzo, Argentina, Lions Club and a colorful quilt was sewn by the Mayodan, North Carolina, Lions Club.

Lions in Sweden held a nationwide collection and, in Canada, a "lumberjack day," that raised $5,000, was sponsored by the Lachute, Quebec, Lions Club.

Testimonials to what campaign-generated funds accomplished were many. In Bangladesh, Alam Khan and his brother lived in a small farming village and he and his brother regularly walked through the rice paddies to reach the shallow river where they could cast nets to catch fish and feed their families. Both, however, suffered from cataract. "I could not see to mend my net," said Alam, and his brother had trouble negotiating the trail. When a group of Lions came to the village and explained how they could have their sight restored at a SightFirst eye camp being set up in a neighboring town, Alam decided to go, but his brother refused, fearful of the procedure.

Alam had his sight restored and is now able to again farm and fish. He also convinced his brother that the Lions spoke the truth and soon led his brother to another SightFirst camp so that he, too, could once more see.

Rosa Gargurevich attended to children at an orphanage in Lima, Peru. She developed cataracts, but could not afford the cost of an operation, so decided to live with the impairment. Then they got worse. "It was difficult to work; I could barely see anything," she said. She was faced with the prospect of losing her job when she heard about local Lions offering free cataract surgery. It was, in fact, part of a pilot project for SightFirst in Latin America.

She traveled to the location, the surgery was performed and when the bandages were removed, "I cried for joy to be able to see again." When asked if she had any message for the Lions of the world who were working to make SightFirst possible, tears welled in her eye once clouded with cataract. Her words echoed the sentiment of hundreds of thousands of others who had been and would be given the gift of sight because of campaign funding, "Thank you for all the work you are doing to help the blind in our country," she added.

Special events increased worldwide to generate funds for Campaign SightFirst. Among the most successful was staged by the campaign's honorary spokesperson herself, future Olympic Silver Medalist Nancy Kerrigan. In addition to making several appearances to Lions on behalf of the campaign, she presented International President Coffey with a check for US$50,000 to Campaign SightFirst before a special skating exhibition on February 4. The gift represented proceeds raised at this nationally televised skating benefit, "Nancy Kerrigan & Friends," performed in front of 3,400 well-wishers at Northeastern University in Boston, Massachusetts. She was scheduled to leave for Lillehammer, Norway, in less than two weeks to participate in the Winter Olympics and her coaches and trainers were pleased to afford her the opportunity to perform in front of a live crowd before she departed. The exhibition took place little more than month after she was clubbed in her right leg by an attacker, causing injury to her knee and forcing her to withdraw from the U.S. Figure Skating Championships.

Thrilling to her performance that evening was her legally blind mother, Brenda, who peered at the performance through a television monitor. She was the main reason Nancy agreed to support the campaign. Nancy was a one-year old when her mother became visually impaired from complications of a virus that damaged nerves in her eyes. So she knew the realities of day-to-day blindness. "My mother's blindness could not be prevented and cannot be reversed," said the champion figure skater in a public service announcement for the campaign. "Yet 80 percent of all blindness is preventable or curable. As honorary spokesperson for Campaign SightFirst, I support Lions clubs in their efforts to conquer needless blindness."

The types of fundraising events varied. A fortuitous project occurred in Oregon where the Gresham Breakfast Club took advantage of a truly singular opportunity. Although the campaign's objective was to raise a minimum of $146 per member, the Gresham Breakfast Club pledged to raise $200 per member, or a total of $12,000 from the 60-member club. Serving as the club's Campaign SightFirst Committee Chairman, charter member Carl Berry's firm provided moving and storage services for Benjamin Franklin Savings and Loan Co. The institution had recently been purchased by Bank of America, located in San Francisco, and began moving into most of their branch offices in the Portland, Oregon, area. The Franklin furniture was moved to Berry's storage area to make room for the Bank of America's furniture. What to do with the Franklin chairs, tables, etc.? Berry received permission from Bank of America to donate the furniture to a charitable group and, knowing his club's pledge to SightFirst, received permission to auction everything of Franklin's in the warehouse. Lions loaded the 13,500 cubic feet of furniture onto trailers and stored them in a vacant office building until the auction was held. It was conducted by a professional auctioneer, Len Zakula, who knew of the Lions' humanitarian work and cut his sales fee in half. The result—Lions netted more than US$17,000 from the auction, with US$12,000 going to Campaign SightFirst to meet their pledge and the remainder to the Oregon Lions Sight and Hearing Foundation.

Lions around the world continued their fundraising efforts, motivated by the ambitious goals promoted by the campaign. All this activity led to one of the most significant days in the history of Lions Clubs International. On April 14, 1994, club reports catapulted the campaign's fundraising total above the US$130 million minimum goal...US$130,335,734 to be precise. A Worldwide Victory Report was compiled and a directory of the final reports of all clubs was compiled for distribution at the forthcoming international convention. Phoenix was set to celebrate the most successful chapter in the history of the association. But the financial results were witnessed in still more tangible ways. More than 2.5 million people had been screened for vision problems at CSF-funded projects and the campaign made it possible for more than 350,000 cataract surgeries to be performed. Through CSF donations, Lions were able to construct and equip 30 new eye hospitals and hospital wings, enabling eye care professionals to treat tens of thousands additional patients per year. Moreover, because of CSF, over 1,000 additional eye care professionals were soon trained to bring the gift of sight to those most in need.

Phoenix, Arizona, did, indeed, prove to be a celebration of triumph. Final results showed that the campaign had raised in excess of US$146 million and, in his farewell address at the Arizona Veterans Memorial Coliseum International President Coffey thanked Lions for their generous support. "There are so many people we need to recognize for their leadership in this accomplishment," he said. "Past International President Judge Brian Stevenson, who served with such dedication on the SightFirst International Committee, the 7,500 CSF coordinators, 41,000 club presidents and their CSF chairmen and committee members, our district governors and international directors, past and present, and of course, you—the Lions of the world—for your generosity and commitment."

The grand celebration continued with campaign leaders from around the world announcing their final fundraising totals. Balloons were even dropped from the ceiling to add to the excitement of the celebration. Past President Stevenson then introduced songstress Tina Fusco, daughter off Past International Director Ted Fusco, who sang "A World of Thanks," especially for Lions who helped reach and exceed the campaign goal. Spokesperson Nancy Kerrigan was also on hand, then officially a Silver Medal winner, and spoke at the SightFirst seminar, congratulating Lions for their success. She was presented with a Melvin Jones Fellowship in recognition of her enthusiastic work on behalf of the campaign.

SightFirst was now in a position to expand its grants to Lions the world over in their fight to conquer preventable and reversible blindness. From projects to confront river blindness and trachoma in Africa and Latin America, to cataract surgeries in India and throughout Asia, LEHP programs in developed nations and other sight-saving programs, CSF funds proved decisive. The campaign's impact was nothing short of phenomenal.

Campaign SightFirst II

Money, however, has a habit of running out and if SightFirst was to continue its course of humanitarian endeavors, additional funds were required shortly after the turn of the century. Hence, the association's second great fundraising initiative: the launching of Campaign SightFirst II.

"During the next three years," announced incoming International President Dr. Ashok Mehta in his 2005-2006 program, "our foundation will have the goal of raising US$150 million to carry on the traditional services of SightFirst and pursue new opportunities for eliminating causes of blindness. I am very confident that our passion to help people in need will motivate us to exceed our past performance as humanitarians."

CSFII, in fact, began with a bang, or to be exact the sound of a gong that Immediate Past International President and CSFII

Chairperson Dr. Tae-Sup Lee struck at the second plenary session of the 2005 International Convention in Hong Kong to officially launch the campaign. "Lions have done great things, and we can do much more," he said. "Our job is not finished, but the successes of SightFirst show that we are on the right road and that our goals are attainable. Of course, numbers only tell part of the story," he continued. "The hard work and generosity of Lions around the world stand behind these numbers. Each tells a personal success story of one individual's victory over blindness—multiplied millions of times." And the SightFirst accomplishments and numbers at the start of the Hong Kong Convention in July 2005 were, indeed, impressive:

- 24,000,000: the number of people who have been saved from blindness with SightFirst
- 37,000,000: the number of people who will be saved from blindness with CFSII
- US$150,000,000: the minimum amount required by CSFII to fund future initiatives of SightFirst
- 4,600,000: the number of cataract surgeries provided to date by SightFirst
- US$6: the average amount cost to save one person from blindness through CSFII
- 2010: the year river blindness can be eliminated in Latin America through funds provided by SightFirst, the Bill and Melinda Gates Foundation and The Carter Center
- 15: CSFII will enable SightFirst to expand trachoma-control activities from the current five countries to 15 countries by 2010. This will increase the population served by Lions SightFirst trachoma-control projects from two million annually to 30-40 million annually.
- 65,000,000: the number of treatments for river blindness provided to date by SightFirst

Before the gong was sounded, however, International President Dr. Clement Kusiak called Dr. Lee forward to address the convention. He began commenting on the success of the first Campaign SightFirst and was especially complimentary of Past International President Austin P. Jennings, who organized the initial meeting that led to the development of the SightFirst program, and Past International

President Brian Stevenson, who served as the campaign's chairperson. He also credited the support and leadership of the past presidents who served during that time. Chairperson Dr. Lee then called forth Past International President J. Frank Moore III, the campaign's vice chairperson and international coordinator.

"I wish to introduce some of the people who will make it possible for SightFirst to continue and expand its crucial work in the future, said Past President Moore. "Campaign SightFirst II designates gifts of US$100,000 or more as Lead Gifts, and these Lions are truly leaders," said Moore. "Their gifts speak eloquently of their dedication to Lions Clubs International and demonstrate a keen understanding of the need for urgent action." He then went on to call to the stage the 24 donors of Lead Gifts pledged at that time.

He explained many of the advances that will be possible because of the funding through CSFII and emphasized, "Through the extraordinary success of SightFirst, we have made ourselves indispensable in the international battle against avoidable blindness. The world looks to us for leadership as never before."

Following these introductions, a recording was played of an actress portraying Helen Keller challenging Lions to be "Knights of the Blind in the Crusade Against Darkness," and Lions were asked to rededicate themselves to the mission ahead. The answer was a resounding "yes," and Dr. Lee then announced that with this expression to act, CSFII could officially commence.

The gong was then about to be struck "This is an ancient tradition of Asia," explained the chairperson. "Each strike of the gong is said to lessen the suffering of one soul somewhere in the universe, just as we seek to relieve the suffering of those who are blind. When I strike this gong, Campaign SightFirst II will be officially underway." The gong was then struck, reverberating throughout the arena, and the Lions of the world began their monumental efforts to attain the ambitious goal of US$150 million and an extended goal of US$50 million during the coming three years.

In addition to SightFirst's stated objective of eliminating river blindness in Latin America in five years and controlling its spread in Africa in 10 years, it was fully anticipated that CSFII funds would expand successful programs that screen and provide eyeglasses for children, create new eyeglass distribution clinics, train hundreds of low-vision specialists, create vision clinics to serve populations of 10 million to 20 million people, establish centers of excellence in pediatric eye care and fund quality research initiatives at Lions eye centers.

Funding received a gigantic boost months after the convention when Past District Governor Sung Gyun Choi of Korea pledged a Lead gift of US$500,000. At that time, Choi's gift was the largest single gift from an individual in the history of the Lions Clubs International Foundation. "We are most grateful for this milestone gift," said Past President Lee. "A gift of this magnitude opens new horizons for the campaign and shows what is possible when Lions work together in worldwide unity."

By that time, 30 Lead Gifts had already been received from Lions in Bangladesh, Ethiopia, Hong Kong, India, Japan, Korea, Singapore, Sri Lanka, Multiple District 300 Taiwan, Thailand and the United States.

Model Clubs Also Lead the Way

More than 400 Lions clubs worldwide had, by that time, also volunteered to serve as Model Clubs, 240 in Japan alone, setting their fundraising goals of at least US$400 per member or US$500 per member. In the first six months of the campaign, these clubs alone had raised US$1.5 million. Per-member averages were looked upon as a key measuring tool for the campaign. "They make it possible to compare small and large clubs in a proportionate way," explained Past President Moore. A brief sampling of a few Lions clubs demonstrates the success the campaign had already achieved at that time.

The 124-member Bonita Springs Club in Florida expected enough income from its resale shop to raise US$100,000 for the campaign and in Spartanburg, South Carolina, Lions kicked-off the campaign by announcing 12 gifts of US$1,000 each from club members at a banquet observing the club's 75th anniversary. In Bozeman, Montana, the 46-member club planned to raise US$100,000 with the Lions already acknowledging plans for personal gifts of more than US$50,000. The Marbella Francofono, Spain, Lions Club had already raised US$5,000 through personal gifts from its members and the

Istanbul Fatih, Turkey, Club planned a benefit concert featuring some of that nation's most famous entertainers. In Italy's District 108-TA1, six clubs joined forces to fanout across the region in a joint orchid sale they called "Orchid for Sight," and went on to raise more than US$50,000.

All Model Clubs that reach their goals would receive appropriate recognition at international, multiple district and district conventions. Lions providing a personal gift of US$100 or more would be recognized with CSFII "Knights of Sight" pins and the clubs would receive a special banner patch upon reaching their goals.

The campaign continued to gain fundraising momentum—and in support from world leaders and the individual often called *the most trusted man in America.* "In these opening years of the 21st Century, international cooperation is more important than ever if we are to overcome the worldwide problems that confront us," said Walter Cronkite, in February 2006. "Preventable blindness is such a problem, threatening millions of people on all continents.

"For more than 85 years, Lions Clubs International has been a model of international cooperation and, in the past 15 years, has established an unsurpassed record of achievement with coordinated projects that have saved millions of people around the world from blindness or severe vision loss. I encourage all Lions to continue this extraordinary work by giving their full support to Campaign SightFirst II."

This declaration is from Maj. Gen. Michael Jeffrey, governor-general and the Queen's representative in Australia. "Lions clubs around the world have long been associated with the prevention and reduction of blindness. For over 80 years, Lions clubs have worked in this field with great success with millions of people from around the globe benefiting from surgery, medicines, vision care and training.

"I commend the International Association of Lions Clubs for developing Campaign SightFirst II which, following the successful and very effective SightFirst I programme, will target preventable and reversible blindness internationally, and particularly in the developing world. I would like to thank all those who work tirelessly in support of this programme and wish you all every success in your important work."

International President Mehta was especially successful in obtaining campaign funds during a visit to Model Clubs in northeast India. More than US$100,000 to be exact. The Lions Club of Howrah and the Lions Club of Siliguri Greater reached their minimum goals of US$70,000 and US$35,000 respectively. The Howrah Club also announced that it was commencing to work toward its challenge goal of US$100,000.

The Bangalore East, India, Lions Club had already reached its target of US$34,000 and was enroute to its challenge objective of US$100,000. In Michigan, the Muskegon North Lions Club had pledged a minimum of US$37,000 and was looking forward to the club's challenge goal of US$50,000. Many of the Lions in the area are eye-care professionals and the club recognized the great potential in requesting gifts from members of that profession. "We just jumped in with both feet," said Past International Director Dennis Cobler, a club member and a campaign sector coordinator.

As the end of the year 2005-2006 approached, the gong that was heard around the world inspired 8,000 volunteer coordinators to work on behalf of CSFII. They inspired fellow Lions to raise more than US$45 million toward the US$150 million minimum goal. "We have made an excellent beginning," said Chairperson Lee, "but now it is time for Lions in all parts of the world to do their best for those who are blind or may become blind." To do "their best" meant getting down to business to institute intensive fundraising. Dr. Lee cautioned that, "The ultimate success of Campaign SightFirst II depends on what is done by individual Lions at the club level."

The association now looked forward to its 2006 International Convention in Boston, Massachusetts, "the 11th hour" replacement site for Hurricane Katrina-devastated New Orleans. Here, Campaign SightFirst II was to take center stage at the second plenary session, accompanied by unprecedented fanfare and celebration, with a focus on reaching the goals of the greatest fundraising initiative in the history of Lions Clubs International. The year 2006-2007 would be the year of "Inspiration and Motivation" when clubs the world over formed CSFII committees and continued local fundraising.

The presentation began with a special video message from former United States President, Nobel Laureate and Past District Governor

Jimmy Carter who spoke of how proud he was of the work Lions were doing in sight conservation and encouraged their participation in CSFII. The nation's 39th president and a Lion for over 53 years, President Carter taped several public service announcements to raise awareness of the world's growing blind population and the need to support the SightFirst program through CSFII.

"To date, SightFirst remains one of the world's most effective blindness prevention and eye-health programs," said Carter in a special message in the November 2006 issue of THE LION Magazine. "Since 1990, the program has improved, saved or protected the vision of more than 100 million people around the world, in both industrialized and developing nations. By raising a minimum of US$150 million through Campaign SightFirst II, Lions will prevent vision loss in 37 million people by continuing the services provided by SightFirst-funded projects.

"The world is full of difficult problems," he continued. "Preventable blindness should not be one of them. As Lions, we have the knowledge, the means and the dedication to save the vision of millions. All that is needed is the will to act. As a fellow Lion, I urge you to act in order to achieve the goals of Campaign SightFirst II."

Model Clubs and Lead Gifts donors were then honored at an awards ceremony at the second session when it was announced that, as of that date, Lions worldwide had raised in excess of US$45 million for the campaign. This was followed by a moving address by Jaimi Lard, who is deaf and blind and a graduate of Helen Keller's alma mater, The Perkins School. She reminded Lions of their role as "Knights of the Blind." Following her address, those in attendance were asked to demonstrate their appreciation in the only way she could recognized, by stomping their feet in applause so she could feel the vibration on the floor. The first year of intensive fundraising had gotten off to a rousing start.

At the time of the Boston convention, Model Clubs had raised more than US$25 million, nearly half of all funds raised. Each of these clubs was inspired in its own way. "When the Model Club program came along," said Jeff Cottrell, a member of the Bozeman, Montana, Lions Club, "it breathed new life in our club, and allowed us to approach a fundraiser both with individual goals and a club goal. As a Model Club, you know what you can do for CSFII, and no one can take that away from you. Our members are challenging themselves," he continued. "They see what they are capable of doing, many are giving generous personal gifts, and they feel a self-worth they've never felt before." The 50-member plus Bozeman Club had a once unimaginable goal of raising US$100,000. It grew to US$125,000, a $2,500 per member average.

Other Model Clubs have also been generous in their commitment. The Braemar Hill Lions Club in Hong Kong, with 21 members, adopted a US$100,000 goal and the Lebanon Host Lions Club in Beirut pledged to raise US$500 per member by selling jams and local fruits and packaging them in CSFII-labeled jars. The story was much the same throughout the world, with increasingly more Model Clubs committing themselves to the success of the campaign. As a result of this overwhelming participation, the Model Club program was extended throughout the remainder of the campaign, ending June 30, 2008. To further encourage the generosity of Lions, a progressive Model Club program was established to recognize clubs that greatly exceed their original goals, honoring clubs, for example, that achieve two, three, four or even five-times their original per-member Model Club objective.

By the beginning of the 2006 year, Lions around the world had raised more than US$60 million toward the campaign's minimum goal of US$150 million. The number of Model Clubs had risen to 1,600 and a goal of 2,007 Model Clubs was established for the 2007 International Convention in Chicago. Also, as the new year dawned, 44 Lions had become Lead Gift donors. Eighteen months remained and Lions were urged to reinvigorate their efforts on behalf of the campaign. They were reminded that although members have given so very much through the SightFirst program, they had the power to achieve even more. Since 1990, Lions had saved 27 million people from blindness, US$6 at the time, the average cost per patient. They had also improved eye care for more than 100 million people. These were figures Lions needed to keep in focus as CSFII kicked into high gear.

"Thanks to Lions, there are less blind people today despite a rapid rise in the world's population," said 2006-2007 International

President Jimmy M. Ross. "That should instill a whole lot of pride in each and every Lion. It also ought to instill a rock-solid commitment to support Campaign SightFirst II."

Lions Clubs International's other executive officers reinforced the president's feelings. "I am proud to be associated with all the Lions of the world who have personally committed their time and resources to ensuring our success in Campaign SightFirst II," said then Second Vice President Albert F. Brandel, and First Vice President Mahendra Amarasuriya stated, "Reaching our goal of US$150 million will be a joyful day, not only for Lions, but for those millions of individuals to whom we give sight."

"Every dollar donated to CSFII goes toward a SightFirst grant and to the people who need it," Immediate Past President Dr. Ashok Mehta observed. "SightFirst is Lions' premiere vehicle of service. It is the epitome of LCIF and 'Lions helping Lions'."

By the time the 90th International Convention convened in Chicago, Lions had raised more than US$101 million, two-thirds of the campaign's minimum goal. There were 2,070 Model Clubs that had raised in excess of US$45 million and 48 percent of all Lions clubs worldwide had raised funds for CSFII. Lead and Major Gift donations from individuals had reached US$16 million, including a gift of US$600,000 from Lion Karosandas Babla of Kenya, the largest personal gift in the history of Lion Clubs International and CSFII at that time.

****

As this book goes to press, in excess of US$200.3 million has been raised for Campaign SightFirst II. There are presently 3,465 Model Clubs and 87 Lead Gift donors, including a landmark personal donation from Past District Governor Aruna Oswal of India. Her family's donation of US$3 million is the first seven-figure donation from an individual in LCIF's 40-year history The result of this generosity and commitment of members of Lions Clubs International during the span of Campaign SightFirst II is that millions more men, woman and children throughout the world will be saved from the devastating loss of sight, thanks to the commitment and generosity of the members of Lions Clubs International.

Chapter Seven
Lions Clubs International Foundation
Lions Helping Lions Serve the World

The programs, the initiative, the selfless objectives of Lions had spread worldwide. Individual Lions clubs and districts had for decades strived to bring critical services and hope to people in desperate need in their own communities and to other shores. This they had strived to do since the association's founding in 1917 and the results were remarkable. As the years passed, however, these human and community needs had expanded beyond their own means and, if they were to carry out the "We Serve" imperative with greatest efficiency, funding assistance from yet another source was demanded. It arrived in 1968 with the incorporation of the Lions International Foundation...the name was changed to the Lions Clubs International Foundation in 1980. Contributions from Lions throughout the world would be transformed into grants to Lions districts where the needs were greatest and most compelling.

To be precise, the Lions Clubs International Foundation, or simply LCIF as it became known, is a public, non-profit, tax-exempt corporation and the charitable arm of Lions Clubs International. It was established to receive donations from the membership and others interested in supporting humanitarian causes. Through careful disbursements, the foundation uses donated funds to help meet needs in communities around the world. It operates from a strong financial reserve which guarantees that it has a sufficient base to undertake large projects. A hallmark of the foundation is that all administrative and promotional expenses are paid from interest income and not from donations.

The foundation is governed by a board of trustees, the chairperson of which is the immediate past international president, and must approve all grants. Standard grants are made for Humanitarian

Services, Vocational Training and Disaster Relief. Emergency, and Catastrophe and Core 4 grants are also important elements in the foundation's total grant program.

The grant applicant is a Lions district. The district is required to develop a blueprint explaining precisely how it will administer the money to improve living conditions with the districts themselves expected to match the grant amount in standard grant cases. Throughout each particular project, the local Lions provide a meticulous accounting for all funds received from LCIF.

The foundation eventually grew into one of the most generous and far-reaching agencies of its kind, encompassing projects that enabled Lions to confront hunger, disease, inadequate housing and the needs of those with physical disabilities; support research into diabetes, build schools, hospitals, clinics and eye research facilities; construct wells to provide potable water, provide disaster relief in the wake of hurricanes, earthquakes, floods and other tragedies, recently to administer the Lions Quest Program and, of course, fund its most singularly successful venture, the SightFirst program.

Thanks to the dedication of the membership, millions of dollars have passed through the foundation over the years to Lions districts requesting grants. Its overall success, however, cannot be counted in mere dollars alone, but most significantly in what it has meant to those people who had nowhere else to turn.

"Through LCIF, Lions ease pain and suffering and bring hope and healing to people worldwide," said Past International President Dr. Clement Kusiak, 2005-2006 LCIF chairperson, in his LCIF Annual Report of that year.

Past International President Kay K. Fukushima observed, "Because of the many projects made possible by LCIF grants throughout the world, and the high visibility of programs that have helped bring life to the true meaning of *We Serve*, Lions can be proud of the many footprints they have left behind. The result has been countless dedication ceremonies marked with the unveiling of LCIF plaques on the walls of new hospitals, schools, clinics, community service buildings and emergency vehicles of all kinds that attest to the effectiveness of LCIF grants, accomplishments that have brought about the sincere gratitude of the thousands of recipients. Also, the foundation's immediate and long-term response after natural disasters are remembered and talked about for years by people whose lives have been impacted by Lions who helped with their gift of love."

The Lions Clubs International Foundation has, indeed, been a tremendous force for concern and service around the world. Tracing its success is a study in the ideals of a service club organization that, in essence, has twin roots---in the local community and in the global community.

The very first grant consisted of US$5,000 to District 5-SW in South Dakota in 1973 for aid in flood relief. Not long after, thousands of dollars were provided to Lions in New York, Pennsylvania, Virginia and Maryland for relief in the wake of Hurricane Agnes. A sight conservation program in Bangladesh received US$10,000 and US$20,000 was disbursed to Nicaragua to assist earthquake victims. That year's largest grant, US$26,809, was provided to a district in India, to help bring relief to people caught in the grip of a severe drought.

It was the beginning, and new horizons for active humanitarian service unfolded over the decades.

As an example, the foundation, in the year 2000, provided a US$75,000 Standard (matching) grant to District 11-A1 (Michigan) to help expand the Penrickton Center for Blind Children, a facility which for years had been supported by Lions clubs in the state. The grant's primary goal was not only for the center's physical expansion, but to expand the horizons of children with special challenges. One of its many heartwarming success stories is found in Nicholas Randall, who was born in 1985 with only one eye which was just one-third the size of a normal eye. Surgery was performed at age six weeks and neurologists told his parents he would not live to his first birthday and should be institutionalized. If, they said, he did manage to survive that long, he would never be able to walk or talk and would, in short, be a vegetable. His parents didn't give up and continued to care for him as best they could. But by the time he reached his second birthday, he had been diagnosed with cerebral palsy and chronic asthma. "He was not even able to sit. All he could do was roll," said his mother, Mary.

It wasn't until a local teacher recommended Nick be taken to the Penrickton Center that my husband, Fred, and I visited the center," said Mary, "and we were surprised how bright and cheerful everything was. The children were playing happily and the staff was attentive to their needs. It was easy to make our decision to place Nick in their daycare program."

It was a wise decision. Under the guidance of the staff, he soon learned to sit, walk, feed and dress himself, and he was happy there. The Randalls placed Nick in the center's residential program and he joined his fellow students in field trips, movies and amusement parks. He even came to enjoy horseback riding and swimming and take part in typical childhood experiences. Penrickton, it must be noted, does this without any state or government funding, operating completely on private contributions from individuals and organizations such as LCIF.

Nick graduated from Penrickton in 1998 when he was 13, but returns for parties, picnics and other events. His only complaint is that the center didn't expand when he was there. It now serves 33 children in its residential program, instead of 21, and its multipurpose room, made possible through the LCIF grant, enables the youngsters to enjoy a variety of activities, including equipment that teaches "active learning." Blind children are encouraged to explore their environment and programs are in place to promote walking skills for children with disabilities. Thanks to the staff here, Nick did develop his skills and has been playing percussion instruments since fourth grade and was the first chair snare drummer in his high school band. In 2004, he was one of 27 children in the United States and Canada to receive the "Yes I Can Award" for outstanding achievements in the arts.

"We are eternally grateful to Penrickton for all their help and guidance, as well as to LCIF and the many Lions clubs who so strongly support it," said Mary Randall. She admits that they didn't know much about the Lions until Nick was enrolled, but soon attended fundraisers sponsored by many clubs. "In fact," she continued, "Fred was so impressed that he became an active Lion himself and served as president of the Taylor Lions Club and is a past zone chairperson."

The foundation's roots do grow deeply and one of its earliest successes was in the wake of a devastating earthquake. It lasted only 33 seconds when it struck at three o'clock in the morning, February 4, 1976, completely destroying the San Juan Zacatepeque Children's Hospital in Guatemala. Originally designed to restore health to tubercular youngsters in that Central American nation, it was founded by the Guatemala Central Lions Club of Guatemala City in 1943. After TB was wiped out in 1970, the hospital's purpose was then furnished on malnourished youngsters.

The hospital is located 18 miles from the capital city and, although the hospital was completely destroyed, none of the 98 children was seriously injured, although the director suffered a fatal heart attack. The hero was its janitor, Roman Cano, who forced his way through the wreckage to rescue the terrified boys and girls who ranged in age from six months to seven years. "Because of the design of their beds," said Cano, "the frames held off the falling debris. The children couldn't get out by themselves so I found a pair of wire cutters to cut through the bedsprings and get them out from the bottom. My wife ran to the village nearby for help and three men came at once to help me."

Cano continued, "We fed the youngsters during the day and at night. They spent two nights in makeshift tents until real tents arrived, donated by the U.S. Air Force and the U.S. Embassy. They lived outside for five months until we could get enough of the hospital rebuilt so they could be inside again."

The Lions Clubs International Foundation acted quickly, providing a US$10,000 Emergency grant to the nation's Lions immediately following the quake. They used it to build shelters for the thousands of homeless in the devastated area because the rainy season was about to begin. That left the fate of the children's hospital. Two weeks after the disaster, Lions began collecting money and in a few days raised $15,000. "We then contacted the Lions Clubs International Foundation for assistance with the project," explained Past District Governor Eduardo Escobar, "because we wanted to rebuild the hospital quickly and could not have raised enough money ourselves to do it."

In June 1976, LCIF approved a grant in the amount of US$125,000 for the rebuilding and work began. An added bonus was that many of the local Lions were engineers and architects; others were in the construction business, all of which dramatically reduced building costs. The total cost to rebuild and equip the hospital was US$164,000. Dr. Milton Zapeda Nuila, a past president of the Guatemala Central Lions Club at the time, advised "the building is far better than the one destroyed. That's important because last year alone we had about a thousand tremors in the country."

Help also arrived from Lions in the United States, Germany, Spain, Mexico, Costa Rica and other nations. Today, the new hospital is equipped with 200 beds and complete diagnostic and treatment facilities. "Funds from LCIF enabled us to rebuild the hospital quickly and get on with our work of helping malnourished children in our country," said Past District Governor Lorenzo Hasbun. The facility was finished on July 18, 1977, and was back in service just 18 months after the earthquake."

In addition to rebuilding the children's hospital, LCIF also provided another US$81,600 to help in the construction of 34 schools, amounting to 60 percent of the total cost. Guatemalan Lions contributed the remaining 40 percent.

Accounts of foundation funding grants could fill volumes.

Allow Sivamani, who was a resident of the Goodwill Children's Village in India, to explain another of the foundation's successful early ventures. The Goodwill Village had been a recipient of an LCIF grant in the 1980s. "It is a sad day for me," he wrote in a letter to LCIF, "for the time has come to the end of my school days. It also means my happy days at Goodwill must come to an end. When I was a poor boy four years ago, Goodwill Village came to my aid. I shall be grateful all my life through.

"I cannot leave this place without writing to some of the wonderful friends who have helped Goodwill and children like me. That is why I say with love in my heart, thank you to everyone at Lions Clubs International Foundation."

This village in India is a powerful example of the good that LCIF dollars can do. It combines a loving home atmosphere with a superior educational system. While the orphanage was progressive educationally, in other ways it remained very primitive. Youngsters had to carry water a mile and a half each way because the village had no well. A US$5,000 grant from LCIF was enough to build a well and a pumphouse. With cool fresh water only a few steps away, the youngsters had even more time to learn and play. Through LCIF, Lions everywhere shared in the expanded lives of these young residents.

The deaf and blind in Finland are also testimonials to the foundation's early capacity to answer crucial needs. In the 1980s, there were only about 450 people in that nation who suffered the twin disabilities, with the result that facilities aimed at their special needs were few. Communication, travel, work and routine living are all especially difficult for the deaf and blind and at the time, Finland had no organized program targeted for them.

The Lions of District 107-E recognized the problem and began cooperating with the Finnish Deaf-Blind Association to build a center in order to expand opportunities for these people. The Lions received land from the city for the building, worked with an architect on plans, negotiated funding and took bids for its construction. The Lions of Finland then proceeded to spearhead an appeal for funds. LCIF soon gave the Lions a major boost with a grant of US$30,000. The money bought indoor and outdoor equipment to provide stimulation, enjoyment, education and opportunities for the Finnish deaf-blind. For the first time they were able to live in a center equipped for individuals with neither sight nor hearing.

In December 1984, Past District Governor Martti O. Hirvonen wrote the following to LCIF: "We want to thank you again for your grant for the multiple-use-building for the deaf and blind."

The deaf-blind of Finland and Sivamani in India, along with tens of thousands of other people and Lions worldwide, were certain to agree with the observation of 1986-87 International President Sten A. Akestam when he stressed the need for quality in living and pointed to the foundation as the ideal vehicle to accomplish this. "I must stress how important it is for all members to recognize themselves as *International Lions*," he said. "International in thought and in action. Support for LCIF is one of the most significant ways possible for Lions to demonstrate their commitment to the international concepts of Lionism. Your generosity will enhance the image of our international association by making it possible for foundation funds to *Bring Quality To Life* in communities spanning the globe.

The compliments of the earliest beneficiaries of LCIF funds were certainly to have been echoed later when, for example, in 1992 funds were granted to answer needs local Lions would have been unable to do. A US$49,000 grant helped the Lions of Portugal's District 115-CS begin construction of the Cercilei School for the Disabled. When completed, the facility consisted of three floors for workshops, offices, a kitchen, dining room and gymnasium. The school provides teaching and rehabilitation for children in Leiria, a village near the west coast of Portugal. Here they are taught basic skills and preparation for further training. The new building enabled 80 mentally disabled children to receive a quality education at any one time.

A clinic for disadvantaged people in need living in the Central American nation of Belize was soon to benefit from a cooperative venture of the Lions in their country, Lions in Texas and LCIF. The Belize City Lions Club, along with other Lions clubs in District 59, had long supported local sight-related projects. When they received donated land from the city the Lions determined to build a clinic that would provide eye, ear, nose and throat treatment, and received a grant of US$20,000 to assist with construction. To further establish a first rate clinic, LCIF forwarded a US$29,000 grant to the Texas Lions of District 2-E2, the funds designated to complete the exterior of the clinic and purchase needed equipment. This equipment made it possible for the clinic to be 100 percent operational, in addition to enhancing the services of nurses, ophthalmologists and doctors from the United States who each provide their time and skills to help the patients.

Once again LCIF funding was making it possible for Lions to be "international" in thought and action.

As the association entered a new decade, the 1991-1992 LCIF Annual Report announced that the foundation's board of trustees approved grants in the amount of US$15,134,132, an increase of US$5 million over the previous fiscal year. Of that amount, US$100,000 was given to AIDS research related to blindness, US$150,000 for the international expansion of the Lions Quest program and US$250,000 for diabetes research. More than US$9.7 million was invested in SightFirst and US$5 million was provided in Standard grants. Among these Standard grants were US$11,495 to District 111-MN in Germany to purchase playground equipment for a school for disabled children, US$39,000 to District 300-A1 in Multiple District 300 Taiwan to establish an eye bank at a hospital in Taipei for vision screening, and funding to District 106-D in Denmark to develop a forest management program in Nepal. The district is part of the Nordic Quadrille comprising Lions clubs in Denmark, Norway, Sweden and Finland. Their cooperative efforts with Nepalese Lions educate the community in managing forest areas, improving living conditions through the development of water systems, reducing the rate of environmental degradation and creating employment.

That year's report also showed that US$24,367,846 was contributed to the foundation by Lions worldwide, an increase of US$7 million from the previous year. Through such growing generosity, LCIF was demonstrating it had the momentum to continually enhance its leadership in funding programs that bring hope, health, opportunity and relief to people in greatest need. Lions had accepted the challenge to support their foundation and were proud of their efforts to be able to do so. One single program, however, has proved year after year to be decisive in this success story, one that came to represent to most potent individual fundraiser in the history of Lions Clubs International. Its name: the Melvin Jones Fellowship.

A Fellowship for the Ages

The Melvin Jones Fellowship was created in 1973 to honor individuals who have made outstanding contributions to humanitarian endeavors. It is presented to anyone who makes a donation—or in whose name a donation is made—of US$1,000 or more. Melvin Jones Fellows receive an inscribed plaque and a special lapel pin.

In discussing the impact of this program, 1980-81 International President William C. Chandler said, "The most effective ways to support this program are the Melvin Jones Fellowships and Contributing Memberships (an annual gift of at least US$20). I challenge you to recognize outstanding Lions in your club or district by making them Melvin Jones Fellows. They are honored and the foundation can better meet critical human needs whenever they may occur in the world."

Each grant does, in fact, translate into hope. A few examples: early grants in the amount of US$10,000 helped construct a blood bank in India, expanded a vocational center in Uruguay, purchased a microscope for an eye bank in Brazil, erected a primary school in Kenya and bought a wide-angle camera for eye research in Washington.

The first Lions honored with the Melvin Jones Fellowship were William G. Clayton, a member of the Fort Lauderdale Downtown, Florida, Lions Club in November 1973 and Dr. Luciano Nunziante of the Barletta, Italy, Lions Club in June 1974. Since then the list has expanded to include Lions and non-Lions throughout the world. As of December 31, 2007, there were 269,097 Melvin Jones Fellows and 48,299 Progressive Fellows, those who have contributed an additional US$1,000 or more to the foundation.

The 1994 International Convention in Phoenix, Arizona, was an auspicious occasion for the fellowship and particularly for Lion Lloyd Larson of the Randall Cushing, Minnesota, Lions Club when he was recognized as the 100,000[th] Melvin Jones Fellow. He received the plaque and pin from International President James T. Coffey and Immediate Past President Rohit C. Mehta when it was also announced that the number of fellows at that time stood well in excess of 110,000, with 62 Lions clubs having achieved 100 percent membership. Only eight years later, in 2002, the 200,000[th] Melvin Jones Fellow, Lion Kiyokazu Kaneda, of the Nagoya Minato, Japan, Lions Club, was enrolled, and by the end of 2002-2003 the number of fellowships stood in excess of 203,000. The 250,000[th] fellow, Kazuhiro Seno of Japan, was recognized at the 2007 International Convention in Chicago.

The fellowships, contributing memberships and other club and private donations were making it possible for LCIF to provide necessary programs and relief when circumstances dictated. In 1996, for example, a US$50,000 LCIF grant to Multiple District 118 (Turkey) made it possible for the Lions Eye Bank to open at the Istanbul Medical Facility. The Turkish Lions and the university hospital were then able to develop an eye bank to provide quality eye tissue, research and medical support. The LCIF seed money has been of crucial importance to individuals needing treatment and corneal transplants. Osman, who lived in a rural area of the nation, can vouch for that. When he was five years old, he fell on a broken tree branch and injured his right eye. He was taken to a local hospital about 1,500 kilometers from Istanbul where the doctor diagnosed the cornea as being badly damaged and recommended a transplant. Corneas were not available at that hospital and little Osman was rushed to the Lions facility in Istanbul where he underwent surgery to replace the damaged cornea. Doctors say that without the surgery, the boy would have developed severe vision problems.

Emergency assistance in the wake of natural disasters has always been a priority for the foundation. When the April 1997 flooding of the Red River in the upper Midwestern United States and Canada left thousands of victims displaced, local Lions took action. In addition to teams combining their resources to assist communities in helping to restore homes and damaged buildings, LCIF provided a US$175,000 grant to help Lions in North Dakota, Minnesota and Manitoba in their rebuilding efforts.

The Lions of Iceland were able to purchase equipment for their Lions House for the Disabled, thanks to a US$35,261 grant. It is a home for people who are so disabled they cannot help themselves and prior to the opening of the home had little choice but to live in an institution. Most were confined to wheelchairs and had limited abilities to communicate. This modern facility suited their personal needs that were essential to independent living.

Foundation grants often enable Lions to cross boundaries to assist people in need. This was true when the Lions in District 334-A in Japan received an International Assistance grant for use in Zimbabwe's District 412. In the African nation's town of Kadoma it was estimated that 20 percent of the families were headed by mothers who possessed no marketable skills; hence no employment opportunities. Children in these families were required to work instead of attending school. The Nagoya Kinjo Lions Club established a training center where sewing and knitting were taught to women who would then manufacture clothing made from locally-grown cotton. General education classes were also taught at the new facility. The grant funds were used to construct the building and to purchase sewing machines and other equipment. A truck was then purchased for use in delivering raw materials to the center and the finished product to dealers. Dedicated in 1995 and attended by members of the Nagoya Kinjo Lions Club, the center is managed by the town council of Kadoma and the Kadoma Lions Club, with guidance from the Lions of District 334-A.

In still another across-the-borders project, District 101-VG in Sweden received an LCIF grant to initiate an enterprise establishing a complete dairy program in the community of Oravita, Romania. Fifteen large tanks were purchased to place in farms around the town for use in helping farmers store surplus milk. The Swedish Lions also purchased a truck for transporting the milk and for equipment that ensured a complete dairy production line. Upon completion of the project, Past District 101-VG Governor Bjorn Wahlenius observed that the Lions were very inspired by the support of LCIF and believed that it will benefit people in need of help.

Two recent natural disasters demonstrated the foundation's capacity to take immediate steps to provide long-term assistance to help Lions answer human needs in areas of severe devastation.

The Agony in South Asia

It roared across the coastal areas of the Indonesian island of Sumatra in the morning hours of December 26, 2004. It is safe to say that most people in the world hadn't any idea what a tsunami was. They soon found out. The result of an intense 9.0 earthquake a few miles off the Sumatran coast, it produced, with no warning, a wall of water estimated at 30 to 60 feet high, completely wiping out villages in its path. It was impossible for the men, women and children living there to escape. But the tsunami wasn't finished. Within hours, it devastated coastal areas of Thailand, Bangladesh, Sri Lanka and India, as well as locations in Malaysia, Myanmar, Maldives and even Somalia, thousands of miles away in East Africa. The death toll in all these nations exceeded 165,000, with the vast majority of the fatalities occurring in Sumatra. Thousands of bodies were never recovered in this, described as the greatest natural disaster in human history. Immediate relief was necessary throughout South Asia. But where to begin and how was it to be carried out? For decades, Lions have exercised leadership in efforts to provide assistance to victims of tragedies. This, however, was a new test, the scope of which neither they nor anyone else had ever encountered.

Early reports estimated that more than 75,000 Lions were at the scenes of devastation almost immediately to provide whatever assistance they could, either directly or in coordination with local governmental agencies. LCIF at once issued 22 Emergency grants totaling US$220,000 for districts in India, Indonesia, Sri Lanka and Thailand to help enable Lions to provide food, blankets, water and other items. A Major Catastrophe grant of US$250,000 was also approved to attend to needs of both short-term and long-term natures.

The total commitment of local Lions and LCIF exceeded anything heretofore recorded. It was determined that assistance in recovery would be made possible through LCIF reserve funds and by designated donations to the foundation. Less than a month following the disaster, LCIF approved an initial US$5 million to enable the Lions of South Asia to rebuild homes, schools and child welfare centers for orphans. "The tsunami disaster has prompted a tremendous outpouring of support from Lions around the world, and Lions in the affected countries worked day and night to bring essential supplies to victims," said then LCIF Chairperson and Immediate Past International President Dr. Tae-Sup Lee. "Thanks to Lions, victims are receiving necessary food and water, and communities will be rebuilt."

The foundation also established what it called the South Asia Tsunami Disaster 2004 fund for Lions worldwide wishing to lend their support. The Lions of Sweden immediately responded with a donation of US$120,000 and the Lions of the Republic of Korea with US$200,000. By the time the second anniversary of the tsunami was reached this disaster fund had allocated US$15 million. Every dollar was applied to relief efforts.

In Sri Lanka, for example, 500 of the 1,452 planned homes had been completed at this time. International President Jimmy Ross visited the nation in December 2006 and remarked, "The Lions of

South Asia have helped put lives back together and have given hope to thousands of people. It's very emotional when a child comes up to you and thanks you for their new home."

Lions constructed 195 homes in two villages in Thailand, encouraging Multiple District 310 Secretary Dr. Wallapa Wisawasukchol to state, "I am so proud of the Lions village project. We've never accomplished a project of this magnitude before, but we were able to because of LCIF." Lions in India used grant money to build 851 homes along with community rehabilitation centers, potable water facilities, health centers, schools and orphanages.

In Indonesia, Lions established three villages with 545 homes and plans were underway to construct a school and medical clinic in each of the villages. This was achieved through the foundation's partnership with the Lions of Indonesia's District 307-A, Malaysia, Australia, the Netherlands and Sweden. LCIF funding also replaced fishing boats and nets to help villagers once again earn a livelihood. Lions were rewarded in special ways for their efforts. When Wahjudin Wahab, who headed the committee in District 307-A that oversaw relief efforts, asked one little girl if she liked her new home, she nodded and answered, "For me, this is my palace." Lion Wahab said he felt tears welling in his eyes as he hurried to his car.

Katrina Was No Lady

A few months later, the Lions Clubs International Foundation and members worldwide faced yet another stern test to the ideals of "We Serve." It appeared in the wake of the most destructive hurricane ever to hit the United States, a Category 4 storm that was to be a living nightmare for citizens of the Gulf Coast, from Louisiana to the Florida Panhandle, and especially New Orleans, Louisiana, virtually destroying that historic city. Designations for hurricanes had already reached the letter "K" and on Monday, August 29, 2005, Katrina made landfall with an impact of colossal proportions.

Winds reach 145 miles-per-hour and a 20-foot storm surge along the coastline caused enormous loss of life along with catastrophic damage to homes and businesses. New Orleans itself was 80 percent under water and huge areas of Louisiana, Alabama, Mississippi and Florida were devastated. New Orleans was to host the following year's international convention. Quite obviously it wasn't to be and Boston, Massachusetts, was selected as the convention's site. Funds and hand-on relief efforts were immediately needed and Lions and LCIF once again answered the call.

The foundation immediately awarded a US$200,000 Major Catastrophe grant to help victims. Soon, 15 US$10,000 Emergency grants were made available to districts directly affected. LCIF also established a designated fund for Lions and others wishing to assist in the tremendous relief efforts. A steering committee of Lions from the four states most affected was appointed to facilitate the efforts of Lions.

One significant form of assistance resulted from an online Help Link set up by LCIF to partner Lions clubs on the Gulf Coast with clubs in other areas of the United States and the world wishing to assist in relief efforts. It took only two days for 21 clubs to make arrangements to send money, provide toys for Christmas, send supplies, repair houses and do other work. In addition, because thousands of people lost their eyeglasses, Lions in the affected regions arrived with mobile vision vans, providing free vision screenings and new eyeglasses. The direct assistance provided by Lions could fill volumes. Members of the Mount Prospect, Illinois, Club, for example, drove a truck full of supplies to the Biloxi, Mississippi, Lions distribution center and Connecticut Lions arrived on the coast with a truck full of saws, hammers and nails donated by Stanley Tools. Wisconsin Lions sent a truck full of school desks, paper and other classroom supplies while the Lions of Liberty, Indiana, delivered yet another truckload of supplies to Bayou La Batre, Alabama. A few months later they also sent a fire truck they purchased at public auction.

"Government is good at fixing roads and infrastructure," observed Connecticut Lion Glenn Boglisch who drove a tractor-trailer to Mississippi with his wife and daughter to deliver supplies donated by Lions in his district, "but it takes a civic group or non-profit to help feed people or help them one-on-one."

While immediate relief is necessary when natural disasters strike, "we realize that our strength lies in providing long-term assistance even after the news cameras and the media leave and the major relief organizations move on to the next disaster," said Past International

President Dr. Clement Kusiak. "In the case of Hurricane Katrina," he continued, "LCIF is providing funds for Lions of Mississippi and Louisiana to continue important service projects such as sight screening, an eye bank and eye care services for the poor. Along with many other volunteer groups, we each contribute what we know best. And that adds up to quite a bit."

In all, the foundation mobilized more than US$5 million for disaster relief and long-term reconstruction efforts in the Gulf states. Not only this, but LCIF and local Lions distributed UNICEF "School-in-a Box" kits to children whose schools were destroyed. Each kit served 80 children and contains books, pencils, scissors, chalkboards, plastic cubes for counting and a set of three laminated posters (alphabet, multiplication and number tables). The kits enable teachers to establish makeshift classrooms until permanent facilities can be built. To further help to support the program, a check in the amount of US$36,183 was presented to UNICEF at the 2006 Lions Day with the United Nations. This equates to uninterrupted schooling for 13,784 children who have been displaced by war and natural disasters.

LCIF funding has also been made available to Lions to help people rebuild their homes, communities and lives following numerous tragedies the world over. Earthquakes, volcanic eruptions, typhoons and other disasters have brought about cooperative efforts between LCIF and local Lions in the highest order imaginable. In the aftermath of the killer 2001 earthquake in Gujarat, India, foundation funding allowed local Lions to build hundreds of homes and scores of schools, and other earthquakes in Pakistan and Turkey spurred the awarding of additional grants for rebuilding. Response to the attacks on the World Trade Center and the Pentagon proved to be special challenges for LCIF and for Lions in the United States and throughout the world.

LCIF immediately set up a special World Trade Center/Pentagon Disaster Victims Fund to receive donations from Lions and other concerned citizens. The foundation committed an initial US$100,000 grant to support relief efforts and a coordinating committee was established to determine how best to use donations to help those in need, especially the families of the victims. Lions responded with their usual generosity and the association's 2003 annual report stated that US$1.59 million of the more than US$3 million in the September 11 fund had already been disbursed or committed to various relief activities. Of special note, nearly US$600,000 went toward victim bereavement camps that primarily served the emotional needs of children who were orphaned by the attacks.

Ultimately, in excess of US$3.2 million was donated by Lions worldwide to the foundation. Every dollar was designated for a specific need such as immediate aid, ground zero assistance that included seven 20-foot long shipping containers used for a number of purposes—sleeping and warming centers for workers at the site, staff offices and even as a temporary kennel and respite center for rescue dogs and their handlers. Sadly, another was used for victim identification purposes. Eventually, the single largest share of the donation to the LCIF fund, US$1,600,000, was provided to the family camping retreats. Among these was Camp Sunshine in Casco, Maine. The week-long camps, with their theme, "Ray of Hope," were conducted from June 2002 to July 2005. Each session was open to 40 individuals and funded at a cost of US$72,000 per session.

In a special report summarizing the response to the tragedy Past International Director Robert Klein, chairperson of the 9/11 Central Steering Committee, said, "After the horrific event of September 11, Lions in the affected areas, across the country and even around the world, moved quickly yet deliberately to map out a plan of action. Those decisions and the resulting plan can serve as a blueprint for Lions to use in times of disaster.

"Flexibility, autonomy, careful oversight and unselfishness were the lynchpins of the Lions' approach to its 9/11 relief efforts. In addition to local hand-on activities, Lions leveraged their capabilities through networking with other organizations and agencies to achieve the maximum benefits possible for victims.

"The effort to assist victims was funded through the contributions of Lions worldwide who raised US$3.2 million. The money was sent to LCIF and made available through grants requested by the 9/11 Central Steering Committee."

Past Director Klein concluded, "This report cannot include the names of all the people who provided time, talent, skill, and unselfish devotion. We still don't know who they all were, but without them doing what had to be done, the help and assistance provided by Lions everywhere would not have been possible. We can only say 'thank you' to whomever you are...you are the real heroes of 9/11."

J. Frank Moore III was president of Lions Clubs International on September 11 and observed, "The aftermath of the tragedy once again demonstrated what Lions can do when put to the test. Lions in the affected areas joined to bring assistance and comfort to those whose lives were forever changed. Many were on the scene immediately to bring food and equipment to rescue workers at Ground Zero and at the Pentagon to help in any way their services were needed. Club members throughout the world not only expressed their most profound sympathy, but generously donated to the special LCIF fund that was established to support the relief efforts. It was an unspeakable assault not only on the United States, but on the world community, and its aftermath nonetheless demonstrates the compassion, the decency and the faith of people of good will who recognize the common bond that joins us all."

LCIF and Habitat for Humanity

Lions have now been involved in a very special way to offer a helping hand to people in need. In 1999, LCIF inaugurated a partnership with Habitat for Humanity and committed $12 million to build homes for people having a family member with a disability. Thus far, 990 homes have been built or approved for construction, many in partnership with The Carter Center. Nations in which Lions-Habitat homes have been constructed include the United States, Canada, the Republic of Korea, Poland, Australia, South Africa, Kenya, the Philippines, Hungary and Romania. The effect of the new homes on the residents has been heartwarming. To cite one example:

"One of my life's dreams was to give Frankie a house," said Alice Penny on the front porch of her new residence in Belleview, Nebraska. "Now it's our house," declared the mother of three in September 2000. Frankie, the family's oldest son, has muscular dystrophy and is confined to a wheelchair. He is also a student at Metropolitan Community College in Omaha.

"The Greater Belleview Habitat for Humanity chapter approached the Papillion Area Lions Club with a proposal," said Papillion Lion Martin Malley, who eventually served as the project manager. "They had heard about the international partnership and had a family in mind that met the requirements. The project was born and to further ensure success we also brought in other local Lions clubs to assist." The Habitat for Humanity chapter along with the Papillion Area, Millard, Bellevue, Ralston and Hanson-Shris-Betty Lakes Lions clubs then applied for and received a $30,000 grant from LCIF. The grant covered 75 percent of the construction cost, with the Lions and Habitat contributing the remaining 25 percent. The 1,000-square-foot wood home includes several special features to accommodate Frankie, including wheelchair ramps, wide doors and a special emergency exit from his bedroom. The Lions and Habitat also learned after beginning construction that Frankie must always lie on his left side and to accommodate this, special door arrangements and electrical and cable TV outlets were configured for his room.

"It was a real pleasure to contribute in such a tangible way to this family's quality of life," observed Lion Malley. Alice Penny said that they could not have afforded the house without the help of the Lions and Habitat, emphasizing that "it was like one huge family that worked on the house."

Lions Quest: Enabling Young People to Develop and Maintain Skills for Living

Lions around the world had long been involved in promoting drug awareness among young people and working with them in helping to avoid drug and alcohol abuse. In 1984, Lions Clubs International joined with Quest International to elaborate upon this goal and to eventually add newer dimensions. It began with Skills for Adolescence, geared for students in grades 6-8 and soon grew to two additional categories: Skills for Growing for students in kindergarten through fifth grade and then to Skills for Action for young people in grades 9 through 12. While resisting pressure to use drugs and alcohol is a high priority in each of these programs, emphasis is also placed on teaching skills they need for everyday living:

- Learning to accept responsibility

- Communicating effectively
- Setting goals
- Making healthy decisions

In addition, these three life-skills curricula emphasize community service, with sponsoring Lions clubs often helping the young people plan and implement projects. In effect, the local Lions partner with the schools to provide financial support for Lions Quest training and relevant materials. In focusing on teaching life-skills, Lions Quest fully understands how their implementation will have the positive effects on young people as outlined by the World Health Organization. These effects fall into the areas of decision-making, creative thinking, communication, self-awareness, coping with emotions, problem-solving, critical thinking, relationship skills, empathy and coping with stress.

In 2002, Lions Clubs International purchased the Lions Quest curricula and it is now fully absorbed into LCIF. This complete support has allowed it to expand its base of operation still further. By purchasing the program, LCIF has been able to increase its reach and to offer greater support and visibility for the Lions who work with their local schools and communities to implement it. Under the Core 4 program, LCIF offers grants for up to US$100,000 for multiple districts or two or more single districts applying jointly and US$25,000 for individual districts. These grants are used for establishing new programs or expanding the scope of existing Lions Quest activities.

As this book goes to press, Lions Quest is operating in schools in 24 countries and, since its inception in 1984, has been offered to more than 11 million young people. "Lions Quest has been established as the foremost youth development program in the world," says 2007-2008 International President Mahendra Amarasuriya. "By providing the necessary inputs to make youth gain confidence in themselves and to be able to refuse to participate in activities which are detrimental to their futures, Quest has been a boon to many young people in all parts of the world."

Past International President Rohit Mehta added, "Though Lions Quest was developed to keep children away from the abuse of drugs and alcohol, it actually also promotes value-based education by helping them in developing positive thinking and a disciplined life. Lions have this opportunity to help the community and, in coming years, are looking forward to many more millions of children around the world to learn those skills that will enable them to have a better and healthier life."

Educators the world over have been certified to teach the Lions Quest curricula. Consequently, Lions Quest is the most widely used life-skills/drug abuse prevention program in the world. The numbers tell the story: more than 130,000 educators are certified to teach Skills for Growing; in excess of 200,000 have been trained to teach Skills for Adolescence and over 7,000 are now certified to teach Skills for Action. It is required that all these teachers complete a special training session before they can teach the curricula and this must occur before schools can obtain Lions Quest materials. Local Lions help to organize, support and finance training in their respective areas.

All three curricula have been named "SELECT" programs, the highest rating, by the Collaborative for Academic, Social and Emotional Learning (CASEL). Lions Quest has also been endorsed by the U.S. Department of Education, the Ministries of Education in Australia, Iceland, Italy, New Zealand, the Republic of South Africa, Thailand and all provinces in Canada; the Canadian Association of Principals, the U.S. National Association of Elementary Schools, the U.S. National Association of Secondary School Principals, and the U.S. National Council of Juvenile and Family Court Judges.

Special Olympics and the Opening Eyes Program

The numbers were ominous—and challenging: Sixty-eight percent of Special Olympics athletes hadn't received an eye examination in three years, 37 percent were in need of eyeglasses and 18 percent wore clinically incorrect eyeglasses. This was the situation when Lions Clubs International joined in partnership with Special Olympics and founded its Opening Eyes Program in September 2000 with a Core 4 grant of US$3.3 million. In the ensuing years it has grown into one of LCIF's most successful and personally rewarding links with another organization. Cindy Bentley, a Special Olympian who benefited from the initial LCIF grant through cataract surgery and new eyeglasses, put it quite clearly when she said her motto is, "Don't look at the disability, but look at the talent." The involvement of Lions is now making it possible for those athletes to build on their talents.

The foundation issued another grant of US$2 million in 2003 and a third grant of US$3.85 million in 2004. Special Olympics is a year-round international program of competition for children and adults with mental disabilities and the partnership set into motion a cooperative program to help a segment of the world population that is often underserved. Opening Eyes is conducted at Special Olympic events and, beginning at the 2001 Winter Games in Alaska, Lions now provide hands-on services in areas such as registration, color vision testing, visual acuity tests and the distribution of eyeglasses and protective sports goggles for the athletes needing them. Eye-care specialists also test the athletes for glaucoma and other diseases of the eye, thus preventing blindness through early detection.

Special Olympics was founded in 1968 by Eunice Kennedy Shriver. The Opening Eyes program, however, began 10 years before the Lions came onboard. Dr. Paul Berman, a board member of the Sports Vision section of the American Optometric Association and a Lion, and now Global Clinical Director of Opening Eyes, offered vision screening for athletes at the Special Olympics World Summer Games in Minnesota. Examinations were given by Dr. Berman and other optometric volunteers, but they discovered that diagnosing the problems and providing prescriptions were not enough. The Special Olympians needed corrective lenses, and the sooner the better. At the 1995 Games in Connecticut, Dr. Berman and his colleagues turned the corner by providing direct clinical care and recycled eyeglasses on site. More than 900 athletes were evaluated that year, with 400 pairs of prescription eyeglasses distributed free-of-charge.

With the launching of LCIF's partnership, the number of athletes who have been screened exceeded 100,000 by 2007 with eyeglasses provided to more than 44,000. Significantly, in excess of 8,000 Lions clubs members have offered their services at sites the world over where Special Olympics games have been held. During the 2002 Lions World Sight Day, only one year after LCIF joined the program, Special Olympics was cited for the success of Opening Eyes, drawing further attention to preventable blindness in the world and raising awareness concerning the importance of sight preservation and identifying effective programs and partnerships to address the challenge of preventable blindness.

During an Opening Eyes program at the 2005 International Convention in Hong Kong, nearly 100 Special Olympics athletes were given sight screening and about two dozen received eyeglasses at no charge. This screening was additionally significant because it represented the first time a service project was conducted on the floor of the convention, and it was replicated at the following conventions in Boston and Chicago.

"We are proud of the work that the Lions-Special Olympics partnership has achieved," said Dr. Clement Kusiak, international president at that time. "We look forward to sharing more successes with Special Olympic athletes worldwide."

Dicken Yung, Special Olympics East Asian president, added, "Looking at all the people who have benefited from the work of Lions clubs worldwide gives you countless reasons to be proud of your work as Lions clubs members. What a way to say We Serve."

The latest grant of US$3.85 million extended the partnership through the August 2007 Special Olympics World Summer Games in Shanghai, China. The new funding also assured further expansion of Opening Eyes in East Asia, Eastern and Central Europe and other regions. The grant also made it possible to implement a training curriculum in optometric schools and eye care training institutes around the world. Upon receiving the Optometrist of the Year Award in 2005, Dr. Paul Berman, the founder of Opening Eyes, stated, "The work that Lions Clubs International has done to advance sight and sight preservation is simply incredible, and I am honored to do my small part to ensure that all are afforded this opportunity."

As further testament to this partnership, Dr. Timothy Shriver, CEO of Special Olympics received the association's Humanitarian Award at the 2007 International Convention in Chicago, along with a check for US$200,000 from LCIF to help in continuing the work of the program.

"LCIF has grown to be one of the leading foundations of its kind precisely because Lions have been passionate in their support since it was established in 1968," remarked 2005-2006 International President

Dr. Ashok Mehta. "It has come to exemplify the *international* in our name and has made it possible for our proud emblem to appear on clinics and hospitals, homes for the elderly, camps, community centers and other facilities. Through SightFirst, it is successfully helping Lions fight trachoma, onchocerciasis and cataract blindness. The Lions Clubs International Foundation enables us to exercise our passion to serve freely and generously in helping others and provides the means to turn dreams into realities. It gives us confidence in knowing that we gain so much for ourselves by making life better for someone else. It is a vehicle for Lions helping fellow Lions reach their service objectives and be able to look forward to still greater achievements."

He concluded by asking Lions to "continue along this well-traveled path and remain confident of the fact that the Lions Clubs International Foundation stands as our most potent global instrument for responding to the needs of humanity."

Chapter Eight
Membership Growth: The Road to Global Success and Respect

Growth in members and in clubs has been a central objective of Lions Clubs International since its organization in 1917. This emphasis has resulted in it becoming, in 2008, the largest service club organization in the world. Its beginnings were cautious and heavily scrutinized to be certain that those who volunteered their services were, indeed, serious and committed to improving their communities and assisting people in need of their undivided attention.

"The local Lions club represents a truly broad spectrum of community life," observed 1991-1992 International President Donald E. Banker. "Its membership includes leaders in various professions: successful, energetic, forward-looking people who are in the habit of getting the job done. We all wish to be associated with individuals such as these, to join with them in fellowship and community service. This is how we need to present Lions club membership when seeking to interest prospective members. We must emphasize that being a Lion is a proven way to become involved in one's community, to develop an awareness of all aspects of the community's structure and to be a positive force in serving community needs. Stress that ours is a *service* club, not a fraternal or social organization, and that through membership one will most assuredly be a full participant in the life of that community."

It is a formula that Lions have been following for more than nine decades, all the time improvising new strategies and approaches to bring in more members and charter both traditional Lions clubs and, beginning in the 1990s, clubs targeted to specific groups of prospective Lions.

At the end of 1917, three months after the association was officially established, there were a modest 25 clubs with a membership of about

800. One year later, membership had nearly doubled to 1,526 in 28 clubs and by 1919, there were 2,364 Lions in 42 clubs. As the year 1920 came to a close, membership stood at 6,451 members in 113 clubs. Clearly, the association was gaining momentum. A defining deliberation concerning the association's name was voted upon, however, at the 1919 International Convention in Chicago. During a luncheon on the convention's first day in the Red Room on the LaSalle Hotel, the same location that witnessed the initial steps in organizing Lions Clubs International, a young attorney recommended that the word "Lions" should stand for *Li*berty, *I*ntelligence, *O*ur *N*ation's *S*afety. The board's education committee recommended its adoption and it has served as the association's acronym ever since.

The association became international on March 12, 1920, with the chartering of the Border Cities Lions Club in Ontario, Canada. It included the communities of Ford, Walkerville, Windsor, Sandwich and Ojibway. Shortly thereafter, Lions clubs were formed in Toronto and Hamilton, Ontario. The Border Cities club was later renamed Windsor and stands as the forerunner to the establishment of clubs worldwide. At the beginning of 2008, clubs were active in 202 nations and geographic areas.

The association's explosive growth and mounting prestige has been an ongoing saga since its early days.

Denver, Colorado, was the site of the 1920 convention and witnessed 284 delegates representing 32 clubs in nine states. They elected Jesse Robinson of Oakland, California, as international president. Melvin Jones was elected secretary-treasurer and was soon thereafter named editor of THE LION Magazine. It proved to be a busy convention. Delegates established a home office in Chicago and increased the number of directors from three to nine. The powers of the board were enlarged and an executive committee of five members was given the authority to act on behalf of the board between its scheduled sessions. Happily, financial problems had disappeared and the association was solvent and growing.

In regard to THE LION Magazine, it became more professional in appearance and content and played an increasingly important role in the organization. The early issues of 28 pages contained a blend of articles of national interest, news of individual clubs and essays describing the host cities of new clubs. Readers profited from specific tips on ways to hold better meetings, attract new members and retain present ones. As it evolved, the magazine gradually expanded coverage of service projects conducted by clubs worldwide.

Several stories concerned clubs that had adopted lion cubs as mascots. Some brought them to the table during club luncheons and fed them bowls of milk. Understandably, as the lions grew larger and stronger the club members quickly lost interest in having them at lunch.

In March 1920, the very first wives' club was established. It was called the Lioness Club of Quincy, Illinois, and was organized "for the express purpose of being a helpmate organization to the Lions and Quincy." Mrs. Lois Dudley of Benton Wells was its first president.

The April issue of THE LION devoted its cover to displaying the new Lions emblem as it appears today. The design was submitted by the Oklahoma City Lions Club and had been adopted at the Board of Directors meeting in January 1920.

The Lions spirit was flying high in 1921 when famed World War I aviator and ace Eddie Rickenbacker was the special guest of the Stockton, California, Lions Club. He spoke to the group and entertained them with an array of photos demonstrating exciting aerial maneuvers.

For the record, the Lions song, "Don't You Hear Those Lions Roar?" was introduced at the 1924 International Convention in Omaha, Nebraska. Written by Robert Kellogg of the Hartford, Connecticut, Lions Club, it was performed by the Lions who comprised the Pittsburgh Quartet. It has since been sung countless times in restaurants, meeting halls, convention arenas and anywhere else that Lions gather.

Proving that a Lion is likely to turn up anywhere, Admiral Richard E. Byrd, Jr., flew over the North Pole on May 9, 1926, with fellow aviator Floyd Bennett. A member of the Washington, D.C., Lions Club, Admiral Byrd sent a letter that was read during that year's international convention in San Francisco that said in part, "We carried the Lions club flag with us to the top of the world and felt it the greatest possible honor to do so."

Not to let his accomplishment rest with that, on November 28 and 29, Admiral Byrd and his chief pilot Bernt Balchen, flew to the South Pole. In doing so, Lions had been to both the top and bottom of the earth.

The news was all good at the 1926 convention, especially when Melvin Jones announced that the previous year had seen the greatest growth in the history of the association with 186 new clubs organized. He also advised that the name of the association's magazine was now THE LION and that membership stood at 49,239.

China became the third nation to host a Lions club when the Tientsin club began meeting on October 1, 1926. Truly international, the Tientsin club's 55 members included Chinese, British, German, Italian, French, Japanese, Austrian, Hungarian and United States members. A second Chinese club was established in Tsing-tao in 1927. Chinese Lions were active in those early years, founding an eye clinic in Tsing-tao, sponsoring a Boy Scout troop and establishing a soup kitchen in Tientsin.

Mexico was next with the chartering of a club in Nuevo Laredo on March 15, 1927. In part, it was the result of efforts by the Waco, Texas, and Tulsa, Oklahoma, Lions who had entertained high ranking Mexican officials traveling in the United States during 1922.

Cuban Lions held their first meeting in Havana on June 23, 1927. Lions clubs in that nation were, in fact, strong and vigorous for more than three decades, but became inactive after the 1959 revolution.

The number of Lions clubs had actually passed the 1,000 mark in 1926.

World War I hero Sergeant Alvin York spoke to the international convention in Miami, Florida, in 1927. Decorated by 12 governments, York remained unassuming in the midst of his fame. He had been named by French Marshal Ferdinand Foch as the greatest soldier of the war. His decorations included the Medal of Honor from the United States.

Calling for an "aggressive campaign in foreign extension so that Lions may have the stimulation of world contact," International President Ray Riley set the tone for the 14th International Convention in Denver, Colorado, in July 1930. Those in attendance cheered when it was announced that 8,935 new Lions had been inducted during the year and 398 clubs had been established. In 1930, club totals stood at 2,202 and membership was now 79,414.

In 1931, Lions in Toronto, Ontario, Canada, hosted the first international convention held outside the United States. Membership had hit a high of 80,456 with 2,491 clubs, but began to dip the following year, and triggered by the bleak economic picture, the slide continued.

International President Julian Hyer challenged members during the 1932 International Convention in Los Angeles to reach deep within themselves to keep the association growing. In his address titled, "Real Lionism Means Actual Sacrifice," Hyer urged Lions not to be quitters but to be a steadying influence. "There are members in every club," he said, "who are facing a real problem in business. They need your help. Along with the blind and underprivileged let us give close attention to our own membership. Some of our best leaders of other days are wavering financially. The Lion looks after the inmates of his own den." Judge Hyer urged members to "sacrifice everything but our membership."

Despite these kinds of efforts, dwindling bank accounts caused by the Great Depression made club dues impossible for many. The figures bore witness to this grave situation. There were 79,203 Lions in 1932, 75,022 the next year, 77,218 twelve months later, and 78,871 members in 2,707 clubs in 1935.

The association received a major international publicity boost with the Chicago World's Fair in 1933 and 1934. When the "Century of Progress" opened on May 27, 1933, Lions Clubs International was represented. Visitors from around the world learned about the work of Lions from members manning a booth in the fair's Social Science Division. Moreover, some 5,000 Lions representing in excess of 1,300 clubs attended the event.

A special achievement was cheered at the 1935 International Convention in Mexico City when Amelia Earhart, an honorary member of the New York City Lions Club, completed a record-breaking, nonstop flight from Los Angeles to the convention site. Appearing on a Mexico City radio broadcast, she congratulated the association for "doing its full share toward the furtherance of Lionism and international relationships."

Also during the convention, Melvin Jones told the assembly that 171 new clubs had been formed along with a membership gain of 7,500. Finances were solid and the organization's net worth was nearly $4,000. Membership had reached a new high of 85,539 and three more nations welcomed Lions clubs: Panama, Costa Rica and Colombia and clubs now totaled 2,725. With the exception of China, all international growth was confined to the Western Hemisphere. In a little more than a decade, that would change.

International President Richard Osenbaugh told Lions gathered at the 1936 Convention in Providence, Rhode Island, "Today, we face a wider citizenship, a citizenship not only of the city, not only of the state, not only of the nation. As Lions, we face the responsibility of the citizen of the world. It is our work to hold and maintain the proper environment and to build a proper type of future for men to carry on."

The following year's international convention in Chicago was special for the association's founder. Fifteen members of his Chicago Central Lions Club assisted in giving him a medallion in his own image. Clubs were urged by President Roderick Beddow to observe the January 13 birthday of Melvin Jones by bringing in new members during that week. The month of January was given the title of Founders and Rededication Month.

In 1938 International President Frank Birch's New Year's message was optimistic. "Lionism was never in a more flourishing condition than it is today," he stated. "Almost without exception, clubs are more active. Attendance is improving, finances are better, membership is on the upgrade and activities are more varied."

His optimism was founded on solid achievement. Membership soon passed the 100,000 mark and statistics showed that Lions Clubs International was leading the way as the largest service club organization in the world. However, the world picture was growing gloomier. With the Hitler-Stalin Pact, August 23, 1939, it became clear that the world was rushing toward war. On September 1, Germany invaded Poland from the west and a few days later, Stalin sent his armed forces smashing into that ravaged nation from the east. Six years would pass before the end of what became a worldwide struggle.

As the war in Europe spread, International President Alexander Wells said, "In the present period of strife, turmoil and unrest throughout the world...one cannot but feel a deep concern for the need for a stabilizing influence. In Lionism, I feel we have such a stabilizer and inasmuch as we represent a true cross-section of the best in citizenship, much of our feeling of concern may be to a very large extent at least be allayed."

Wells' statement came in the spring of 1940 when France, Norway, Denmark, Belgium, the Netherlands and Luxembourg had surrendered to Germany. One month later, Italy declared war on Great Britain. Then on December 7, 1941, the Japanese attack on Pearl Harbor made the conflagration worldwide in scope.

Despite the war, the association continued to grow. The Guatemala City Lions Club began operation in 1941 and the following year saw Lions clubs founded in El Salvador, Honduras and Nicaragua in Central America and in 1943 and 1944 clubs were chartered in Venezuela and Peru.

When World War II finally ended in August 1945 there were 4,856 Lions clubs with 218,184 members in 14 nations. Following the war, much of the world needed rebuilding and Lions Clubs International moved into the post-war period poised for vigorous expansion.

Full Speed Ahead Around the World

The association's postwar extension began with a flourish as three new countries—Netherlands Antilles, Bermuda and Ecuador—joined the international family during 1945-46. When the 30th anniversary was celebrated in October 1947 at the Waldorf Astoria Hotel in New York, it had become the world's largest service club organization with Lions clubs active in 19 nations and a membership of 324,690. Lions Clubs International had grown so large, in fact, that it had outgrown its headquarters in Chicago's McCormick Building on South Michigan Avenue. As the workload grew and more employees added, it had become cramped, prompting Melvin Jones to suggest at the board meeting prior to the anniversary celebration that a Research Committee be formed for a purpose of establishing a new more spacious International Headquarters. This was officially acted upon at the 1951 International Convention in Atlantic City, New Jersey, when the Board of Directors voted to find a permanent home for Lions Clubs International. After careful study, the Research Committee decided to purchase a building and remodel it for International Headquarters.

Led by Third Vice President S.A. Dodge, the committee selected a site on the northeast corner of Michigan Avenue and Lake Street in downtown Chicago. It contained six floors and transportation was deemed excellent for the staff. The total cost of the building was $750,000 and another $150,000 would be required for remodeling. On August 29, 1952, International President Edgar M. Elbert and Association Secretary William R. Bird made the necessary arrangements and 209 North Michigan Avenue became Lions Clubs International Headquarters. As a final act, a large purple and gold Lions' emblem was placed high on the building's south wall and for nearly 20 years it greeted visitors from throughout the world until 1971 when headquarters moved to suburban Oak Brook.

Lions Clubs International took a major jump in 1948 when it began chartering clubs in Europe. The extension was propelled in large part by the efforts of Jones, International President Fred W. Smith, Assistant Secretary General Roy Keaton and future French Lion A.A. DeLage.

DeLage was instructed by Jones in January 1948 to investigate the establishment of the continent's first Lions club and the following May, President Smith traveled to Geneva, Switzerland, to represent the association at a meeting of nongovernmental organizations. Earlier in March, DeLage and Keaton met with 20 key leaders in Geneva about starting Europe's first club. When these men asked for more time to discuss the proposal, Keaton and DeLage flew to Stockholm, Sweden, and met with local leaders in the capital city.

The extension of voluntary service under the banner of the Lions only three years after Europe had been torn apart by World War II was on track and President Smith presented a charter to the Geneva Lions Club on May 19 and to the Stockholm Lions Club on May 23. The Swedish club, however, completed the organizational requirements before the Geneva club and, therefore, was designated as Europe's first Lions club and its eventual multiple district was announced as 101.

While this grand extension was hailed throughout the association, one of the most inspiring Lions clubs was formed April 24, 1948, in Kalaupapa on the Hawaiian island of Molokai. Kalaupapa is a leper colony founded in the 19th Century by the Belgian missionary priest, Father Damien. The charter members all suffered from Hansen's Disease (leprosy) and soon became one of the most active Lions clubs in the world. Now a landmark on Molokai, a cross was built by the Lions on a high point of land near their colony. A bronze plaque at the base reads: "Love Never Faileth."

The United Kingdom welcomed Lions in 1950 with the establishment of the London Club, "a highlight of my year as international president," related Walter C. Fisher of Canada. It was an honor he especially held dear because it was Canadian District A Secretary Bruce Malcolm who traveled to London in 1949 and contacted Colonel Edward Wyndham. It was a contact that resulted from the war when Canadian Lions pooled their money and were able to send nearly $5,000 to England to help house the thousands of children who were orphaned by the war. Colonel Wyndham was connected with the Waifs and Strays Society, which administered the funds. The colonel went on to become the charter president of the new Lions club.

Two years, though, had elapsed since the organization of Europe's first two Lions clubs and the London club. During that time, Lions had been welcomed in Chile, France, Bolivia, Norway, the Philippines, Guam and Denmark. Australia had, in fact, joined the association in 1947 with the chartering of the Lismore, New South Wales, Lions Club. Consequently, at the close of 1950, 402,841 members were active in 8,055 clubs in 28 countries.

The flag ceremony at the 1952 International Convention in Mexico City witnessed six new nations: Iceland, Germany, Japan, Belgium, Brazil and the Netherlands. The establishment of the Manila (Host) Lions Club in the Philippines three years earlier, however, led to a chartering that was especially significant and heartwarming, for it spoke of the global goodwill that had become a hallmark of Lions Clubs International.

Although the Philippines and Japan had been bitter enemies during World War II, the Filipino Lions decided to carry of message of

Lionism to Japan in the year 1952. Speaking to that year's convention, newly installed International President Edgar M. Elbert told of a moving event he had experienced as first vice president. "How it encouraged me to have taken an active part in establishing Lionism in the land of Japan, to have heard Kin-ichi Ishikawa, president of the first Lions club in Tokyo, say, and I quote him, 'Filipinos should detest and hate us, but then, from these same Filipinos came an invitation for us to join Lions Clubs International. International Director Manuel J. Gonzales, on the occasion of charter night, presented to me a Filipino flag and I presented him with a Japanese flag. When I hugged his flag to my bosom, I could not push back the tears. From all over the world of Lionism, letters of congratulations have come to us since our charter night. We Japanese have qualities that are intrinsically good and beautiful. We can contribute these to the rest of the world through Lions Clubs International.' "

Prior to the Mexico City Convention, Lions clubs had been established in Finland, Italy, Uruguay and the Yukon Territory. The recent influx of new clubs and countries caused President Elbert to declare the year 1952-53 as the beginning of the glory years of the association. He had reason for such optimism, for at the end of 1953 there were 46 nations hosting Lions clubs and the association continued to move forward.

Service had been central to Lions clubs since the founding of the association in 1917. Other than a commitment to responding to community and human needs, there had been no official motto to which Lions could point as their standard for resolve. This changed in 1954 when, after a contest among Lions around the world to select a motto, the two words now familiar to Lions everywhere were announced at the international convention in New York. After more than 6,000 suggestions were considered, "We Serve," submitted by Lion D.A. Stevenson of Font Hill, Ontario, Canada, was chosen.

For nearly four decades it was deemed as symbolizing the moving spirit of Lions Clubs International: to help others, to tear down the shrouds of ignorance and distrust that often separate one human being from another. "We Serve" is now translated every day from two words into a living reality in nations spanning the earth.

This global awareness was clearly demonstrated by both the membership and the services at International Headquarters. During the 1950s, an international language department was developed and, today, specially trained employees translate correspondence, newsletters, reports and other types of communication into Spanish, French, German, Italian, Finnish, Japanese, Chinese, Portuguese, Swedish, Korean and Hindi, in addition to English, now considered the official languages of Lions Clubs International. Members of staff research at all levels of the association to ensure that materials are reliable and of use to members around the world.

Through the years, a number of prominent individuals had been and are still being named as Honorary Lions, including heads of state, royalty and others who have made personal contributions to humanitarian service and global good will. Helen Keller and Amelia Earhart have already been mentioned, but in 1957 a figure world renowned was bestowed this recognition. During a visit to French West Africa, then International President John L. Stickley conferred honorary membership in the Ysounde Lions Club of the Cameroons upon Dr. Albert Schweitzer. He was also given the Lions Humanitarian Award, one of the first individuals to receive this, the highest recognition of the association. In a letter to the president, Dr. Schweitzer said, "I hope that the movement of Lions progresses. It has such a good influence on men of our era."

The growth of Lions Clubs International continued unabated. The 14,000[th] club was organized at Bastad, Sweden, during the year 1958-59 and the association entered the 1960s with 606,740 members in 14,723 clubs located in 104 countries and geographic areas. The "We Serve" spirit also arrived in a place one would be surprised to find the Lions emblem.

United States Air Force Major A.G. Thompson spoke at a meeting of the 49ers Lions Club in Las Vegas, Nevada, and told them there was a spot on earth that didn't have a Lions club—the South Pole. The Lions were quick to catch on and agreed to symbolically plant the Lions flag at that frigid location. Major Thompson was with the 12th Air Force headquartered in Waco, Texas, and when the Waco Lions learned of the plan they decided to join in the extension effort. As a result, South Pole Antarctica officially became the 101st area on the Lions' map with the somewhat chilly chartering of the 59ers Lions Club, the southernmost Lions club in the world. There were 16 charter members, all part of a group of U.S. scientists and military personnel based at the Pole's Amundsen-Scott station for Geophysical Year research.

The Passing of a Legend

The 44th International Convention in Atlantic City, New Jersey, in 1961 was a time for both celebration and reflection. Founder Melvin Jones had died at his home in Flossmoor, Illinois, on the afternoon of Thursday, June 1, 1961. He was 82 years old. Although partially incapacitated by a stroke two years before, he appeared regularly at his International Headquarters office to greet visiting Lions and to lend his counsel to the growing association. He never missed an international convention and at the 1960 convention in Chicago, he was helped from his wheelchair to acknowledge a sustained standing ovation from appreciative Lions from around the world.

Jones had stated that "You can't get very far until you start doing something for somebody else" and "the lion stands for something; not so much as a noble animal, but rather as the traditional symbol of great ideas and high accomplishment."

In a tribute to the founder, 1960-61 International President Finis Davis wrote, "Once in every generation or era a man appears and in his fleeting hour upon the stage leaves and indelible imprint upon the lives of his fellow men, and upon generations yet to come.

"Such a man was Melvin Jones. All over the world today he is the symbol of man's concern for his fellow man; the guiding spirit of a great movement for human welfare; the eternal inspiration for men of good will who find unselfish rewards in human service.

"I do not think the world of Lionism mourns the death of Melvin Jones to the degree that it glories in his life. For while there is universal sorrow at his death, surely there is greater universal happiness that he lived. He saw his dream of a world brotherhood of men in the service of others come true; he saw the surge of Lion growth and influence break barriers of creed and nationality to bring the world nearer to mutual understanding and peace; he saw a dedicated army of men marching hand in hand in the fellowship of service, teaching his doctrine that the helping hand will forever be more powerful than the mailed fist.

"Today, in death, countless hosts revere and bless this kindly man whose dream has brought happiness into the hearts and lives of the poor, the stricken and the handicapped of the world.

"The good works of Melvin Jones under the Lions emblem will go on and on in spirit and deed, for in its moment of sorrow the world of Lionism takes new heart and new pride in his memory."

His funeral was held Monday afternoon, June 5, 1961, at the First Methodist Church of Chicago—the Chicago Temple—with last rites conducted by Dr. Preston Bradley, pastor of the Peoples Church of Chicago, who delivered the eulogy, and Dr. Charles Ray Goff, pastor of the Chicago Temple. Melvin Jones was laid to rest at Mount Hope Cemetery in suburban Worth.

Fifty Years and Growing

Lions Clubs International entered its golden anniversary year of 1967 with a membership exceeding 800,000. The year before, the 20,000[th] Lions club was organized—the Walnut Creek (Rossmoor), California, Club. Nations the world over recognized the association's Golden Anniversary, many with the issuance of commemorative postage stamps. The stamp issued by the United States, for example, depicted International President Edward M. Lindsey's theme "Search for Peace." Other countries issuing 50th Anniversary stamps included Brazil, Senegal, Colombia, Morocco, Paraguay, Bolivia, Luxembourg, Australia, Chad, the Philippines, the Central African Republic, Upper Volta, Dahomey, French Somaliland, Nigeria, Peru, Korea, Monaco, Belgium, Japan, Iran, Chile, Cameroon, El Salvador, Vietnam, Ethiopia and Ecuador.

A total of 118 countries hosted 21,479 clubs as the association prepared to enter a new decade. In his farewell address at the 1968 International Convention in Dallas, Texas, President Jorge Bird observed, "I returned from my world travels convinced that Lionism is at its peak of enthusiasm and accomplishments. Its spirits are high, its mood confident and optimistic. Its presence is secure and its future glows with promise."

A New International Headquarters is Dedicated

"This building is a temple built without hands," declared International President Dr. Robert D. McCullough on April 21, 1971, at the dedication of the new International Headquarters in Oak Brook, Illinois. "It was built with the hearts of 950,000 Lions around the world. The Headquarters," he continued, "is a memorial to those who have served Lionism from the beginning."

The 108,000 square foot, tri-level structure doubled the space of the former building at 209 North Michigan Ave. in downtown Chicago. Nonetheless, with the association's continuing worldwide growth, even the new suburban structure became too small by the middle of the next decade. Extensive remodeling to create more space expanded the building by about 30 percent in 1986 and, today, more than 300 staff members serve the needs of the membership.

The year 1971 also witnessed yet another milestone with the formation of the 25,000th Lions club in Fred, Texas, that boasted 32 charter members. As if in anticipation of the association's fast pace forward, the international convention in Las Vegas, Nevada, attracted an attendance of more than 30,000 Lions and their families. Newly installed International President Robert J. Uplinger stated in his inaugural address, announcing his year's theme, *Lionism Is Commitment*, "It would be wonderful if I, by some miracle, could manage to distill into a serum all of the motivation and psychology necessary for this commitment and then inject it into each one of our nearly one million members. Of course, this would be impossible. But if you will assume with me that I have such power, I would mix it into the serum to energize our theme for 1971-72."

Lions Clubs International continued its global commitment for growth with the flag ceremony at the 1972 International Convention in Mexico City, introducing two new island nations in the burgeoning family: Nevis and Macao. The following year's international convention in Miami Beach was of special note with incoming International President Tris Coffin introducing his 1973-74 theme: *One Million Men Serving Mankind*, for it was in his year that the one millionth Lion, Barney Gill of Virginia, did indeed don the lapel pin to become "one in a million." As the year drew to a close, there were, as President Coffin's theme proclaimed more than a million members serving mankind in 149 countries and geographic areas.

"The scope of your many activities is an impressive demonstration of what active and concerned citizens can accomplish by working together," said California's Governor Ronald Reagan in welcoming Lions to San Francisco for the 1974 International Convention. "Your efforts are helping to make this a better world for everybody...And because this help stems from humanitarian concern for people, it represents something very special and very precious, especially in today's world where there is so much cynicism and distrust."

A Flaming Tribute

The year 1975 was special to the Lions of the world in one special regard, and it was a tribute that burned brightly. International Headquarters in Oak Brook was mortgage free. International President Johnny Balbo was happy to intone: "During the March 1975 board meeting, Lions Clubs International reached a new milestone. We had the pleasure of burning the mortgage of the International Headquarters building. In less than four years, we had paid off all our indebtedness on our new building."

President Balbo continued with enumerating the successes of his year in office. "I visited many heads of state," he said. "Two of these visits stand out in my mind. One was to His Holiness, Pope Paul VI, and the other to Dr. Rudolf Kirschlager, the president of Austria. Both spoke of the strong force our association was for peace around the world. It filled me with pride when the Pope referred to the great humanitarian services performed by Lions around the world, and he was well versed in our goals."

The third session of the 1975 international convention in Dallas was special in a number of ways. A special tribute was paid to the memory of Helen Keller who, at the international convention 50 years earlier in Cedar Point, Ohio, offered the challenge to Lions to take up the cause of the visually impaired. Actress Carolyn Jones read Miss Keller's message. This historic address was followed by a speech by Dr. Richard Kinney, at that time director of the Hadley School for the Blind in Winnetka, Illinois, the world's foremost correspondence school for the visually impaired. "Lions," said Dr. Kinney, deaf and blind himself, "you are playing a tremendous role in attacking the most terrible blindness of all--the blindness of ignorance and prejudice that sets one man against another, one race against another, one nation against another...It was once said, 'Live and let live,' but Lionism has raised this principle to that nobler 'Live and help live.' "

The Dallas convention also witnessed an address by United States Senator Jennings Randolph of West Virginia, a past district governor and co-sponsor of the bill that made it possible for the blind to operate concessions stands in public buildings.

The following year's international convention was once again a special occasion. Held in Honolulu, Hawaii, it boasted an attendance of well over 40,000. Also, it was announced that a record total of 1,420 Lions clubs were established that year with the 30,000th club chartered in Callaway, Minnesota. In his inaugural address, International President Ralph Lynam stated of the privilege it is to be a part of the global family of Lions. "We must cherish and protect this tremendous international flavor of our organization," he stressed, "for a better world is within our reach."

THE LION Magazine: Telling the Association's Story

Through nearly all of the association's history, THE LION Magazine has been a highly effective means of informing Lions of the work of their fellow members and to promote the service and fundraising objectives of Lions Clubs International. The Headquarters edition first began publishing in November 1918 and is the oldest. The Spanish language edition was established in 1944. Today there are 21 language editions of the magazine. In addition to English and Spanish, it is also published in Japanese, French, Swedish, Italian, German, Finnish, Korean, Portuguese, Dutch, Danish, Chinese, Norwegian, Icelandic, Turkish, Greek, Hindi, Polish, Indonesian and Thai. Only the English (Headquarters) and Spanish editions are published at International Headquarters; the others are printed in the areas of their distribution.

"The magazine's purpose is two-fold," said Jay Copp, senior editor of the Headquarters edition. "One is to give credit to individual Lions, clubs and districts to services they have performed. The other is to inspire Lions to carry out similar projects and to be proud of what Lions and Leos are accomplishing around the world.

"By informing and inspiring," he continued, "THE LION also makes its contribution to growth. The more pride individual Lions take in what they are doing, the more apt they are to help organize new clubs and to invite friends and business associate to join. The magazine also becomes somewhat of a 'how to' manual—how to get doctors together in a caravan, or set up a relief mission to a disaster-torn village. The inspiration, the practical points, the learning are all there."

The association continued to expand. Between 1979 and 1982 Lions clubs were chartered in Swaziland, Lesotho, Sierra Leone, Bophuthatswana, the Comoro Islands, Benin, Gambia, Ghana and Equatorial Guinea. As growth continued, so did the responsibilities of the international officers to reach out to the membership. Outgoing International President Kaoru "Kay" Murakami reported at the 1982 convention in Atlanta that "during the past 12 months I only spent 14 days at my home in Kyoto, Japan. The rest of the time was devoted in working for Lionism." He told the audience that he had traveled 764,344 miles, or the equivalent of 32.5 trips around the world...equal to more than three trips to the moon.

United States President Ronald Reagan brought delegates to their feet at the 1985 International Convention in Dallas with his ringing support for the spirit of volunteerism Lions bring in answering human needs. It was first time a U.S. President still in office spoke to an international convention. Another guest speaker at that convention was former U.S. Secretary of State Dr. Henry Kissinger.

During 1984-85, a total of 791 new Lions clubs were organized, bringing the worldwide total more than 37,000 in 158 countries and geographical areas. To further underscore that commitment of Lions to service, a highlight of 1986-87 International President Sten Akestam's year was when syndicated columnist Ann Landers printed his letter urging those at high risk to seek diabetes testing. The letter appeared in 1,200 newspapers and resulted in tremendous public interest, with more than 1,000 phone calls being received at International Headquarters. To meet the demand for additional information on diabetes, Lions were offered thousands of diabetes brochures available from headquarters.

During his term of office, club strength reached 38,700 and membership increased to 1,352,177. Two new flags waved at the 1987 flag ceremony: Cape Verde and the Republic of Guinea.

The 1987 International Convention in Taipei, Multiple District 300, also proved to be one of historic importance for Lions Clubs International. It was here that the amendment was passed to the International Constitution and By-Laws, opening the doors after nearly 70 years to women membership. It proved to be of signal importance to the association. Outgoing International President Brian Stevenson told the following year's packed gathering in the convention hall in Denver, Colorado, "The amendment to our International Constitution, eliminating the word 'male' as a condition for membership in a Lions club, has encouraged women the world over to become Lions. At present, approximately 10,000 women are members of clubs in 69 countries, and I am certain women will continue to demonstrate their wish to serve communities and human needs through membership in Lions clubs."

How right he was. By February 29, 2008, women membership exceeded 245,000 in 188 nations.

The new international president, Austin Jennings, indicated still another avenue for membership growth. "A scrutiny of demographics," he advised, "will show large influxes of people in the suburban areas, not to mention sections within our cities which are being populated more and more by young business and professional people. We need to arouse the interest of this 'new breed' of individuals to the benefits of serving through Lionism."

During the coming decade specialized Lions clubs would focus on this 'new breed' and on men and women and young people with new opportunities to become Lions. First, however, an entirely new vista was opening for Lions Clubs International to organize clubs and attract quality members.

After "The Wall" Fell

Who can ever forget the sight of those individuals, young people for the most part, atop the Berlin Wall in November 1989 tearing down that barrier that had so long divided East and West Berlin and, symbolically all of Europe? It marked the end of Soviet domination in eastern Europe and the beginning of a new era for people who for so long had been denied the freedom of association. Among the first organizations to benefit from this new freedom was Lions Clubs International and at the 1989 international convention in Miami/ Miami Beach, Florida, President Jennings could point to two new countries to host Lions clubs, even before the wall came down: Hungary and Poland. He emphasized that the clubs in Budapest and Poznan respectively permitted us to become the first service club organization to be represented in what was generally considered the Eastern Bloc. Soon Lions clubs would be flourishing in Estonia, the Czech Republic and Slovakia, Romania and even the Republic of Russia itself along with other nations in that area of the world. The association had undeniably become still more international in scope and voluntary service.

"I attended the organizational meetings of the first two clubs," said President Jennings, "met with the new Lions and with their sponsoring Lions from Finland, organizers of the Budapest club, and Lions from Sweden, sponsors of the Poznan club. I realized fully what an important step this was for the expansion of Lionism."

Two new Lions clubs that year also pointed to the direction specialized clubs could take in the future. Fifty-four young professionals formed an urban Lions club in Sacramento, California, with future International President Kay K. Fukushima serving as the Guiding Lion. The membership was primarily middle to upper level management, men and women in their late 20s to late 40s. Most lived in the suburbs and none had ever belonged to a service organization. Another specialty Lions club was chartered in Toronto, Ontario, Canada, with its roster composed exclusively of medical personnel. It was, quite obviously, referred to as the "doctors club" and its main objective was to deal with medical needs in the Toronto area, assist underprivileged children and raise funds for research at the University of Toronto.

Another path to strengthen individual Lions clubs and the entire association was a resolution adopted at the June 1989 Board of Directors meeting in Orlando, Florida, providing for the establishment by each club of a three-member membership committee. It put into place an organization structure for membership which ran from local clubs through the zone and multiple districts.

The resolution created the position of membership director, which automatically was bestowed on the chairperson of the membership committee. Each member is elected to a three-year term, consistent with the three-year term served by multiple district membership chairpersons. In the second year, the elected member becomes the committee vice chairperson, and in the third, the post of chairperson. It was deemed that this rotation system better prepares that Lion and assures continuity of the committee's work.

The club membership director is responsible for:

- Developing a growth program for the club and presenting the plan to the board of directors for approval;
- Encouraging Lions during meetings to bring new members into the club;
- Setting up membership orientation sessions; and
- Serving as a member of the zone level membership committee.

As Lions Clubs International moved into the final decade of the 20th Century, new countries were continually being added to its roles, thanks in great part to the fall of the infamous *wall*. Membership at the beginning of 1990-91 stood at 1,369,955 Lions active in 39,734 clubs. The year, however, began with the association taking steps in the succession of international presidents that had never before occurred. First International Vice President Mathew Seishi Ogawa of Tokyo, Japan, had died September 21,1989, following surgery. He would have assumed the office as president in July 1990 in St. Louis, Missouri, and, consequently, it was necessary to name a president for the year 1990-91.

"Mathew Ogawa was a distinguished citizen of Japan and a great and dedicated Lion," said International President William L. Woolard. "He was one of those chiefly responsible for the tremendous success Japanese Lions have recorded in humanitarian service."

The Lion who took the oath of office at that post as 1990-91 International President was Past International Director William L. Biggs, of Omaha, Nebraska.

In his inaugural address to the 73rd International Convention in St. Louis, President Biggs said, "I was extremely honored to have been elected last Saturday by all the past directors, past presidents and our current international board, meeting together in Oak Brook. I want to thank each one of them for their confidence in me and for allowing me to be a part of the leadership team of our association during this very exciting and challenging time in our history."

At the end of his term, membership stood at more than 1,383,000 Lions in 40,100 clubs and with the chartering of clubs in Russia and Lithuania, the association had grown to 171 nations and geographical areas.

"We can all be proud of these achievements this year," stated President Biggs in his report to the 1991 convention in Brisbane, Queensland, Australia, "and proud that we are members of our international family at such a tremendously challenging time in our history."

By June 1992, club strength had surged to 41,152 and with the addition of three new countries—Latvia, Ukraine and Bulgaria and the geographical areas of Saipan, Isle of Man and the Leeward Islands—along with the association's recognition of the independence of Slovenia and Croatia, the association was represented in 177 lands worldwide.

International President Donald E. Banker was extremely proud of one area of growth and observed in his 1992 convention report in Hong Kong, "The admission of women into Lions clubs has proven to be instrumental in our membership growth. Currently, there are more than 46,000 female Lions serving in clubs in 131 nations worldwide. Many are officers of their clubs and a growing number are beginning to serve on the district level, testimony to the eagerness of women to serve their communities through Lionism."

He also commented on the launching of Campaign SightFirst during his year at the helm of the association. "In this, our 75th anniversary year," he stated in his report, "we are celebrating the association's decades of commitment to sight conservation. During 1991-1992, Campaign SightFirst has become a symbol of this long-standing involvement. Indeed, it is much more than that. It reflects a fulfillment of our commitment to sight conservation, an opportunity for Lions to have a lasting effect on sight needs around the world."

Lions Clubs International maintained its pace by witnessing the establishment of clubs in additional countries. During 1992-93 Lions clubs became active in Albania and the Republic of Belarus. Also, the association recognized the newly independent nations of the Czech Republic and Slovakia and re-established Mozambique as a member of the international family, thus bringing the total number of countries and geographical areas to 180. When the year drew to a close, the number of Lions clubs stood at 41,152.

Commenting on the need for growth, International President Rohit C. Mehta proclaimed that "one of our greatest acts as Lions is to give more individuals the opportunity to share membership with other leaders in the community, to develop their personal skills and to serve their communities as members of the largest service club organization in the world. Bringing in new members is our own opportunity to demonstrate how proud we are to be Lions and our confidence in the programs, the objectives and the potential of Lions Clubs International."

Mongolia became a member nation during 1993-94 and by June 30, 1994 there were in excess of 42,100 clubs. "Throughout the year," said International President James T. Coffey, "I stressed the crucial need for growth and asked that clubs make this a priority item on their list of objectives. I know our programs are sound and that Lions everywhere are committed to the tasks which lie before them. The more men and women who proudly wear the pin identifying them as Lions, the more far-reaching will be our achievements." Membership at the conclusion of his year in office stood at 1,417,300.

The following year, the association continued its drive in establishing new clubs. At the end of 1994-95, an increase of more than 1,000 Lions clubs was recorded to bring club strength to 42,710. International President Dr. Giuseppe Grimaldi viewed with great satisfaction the "significant increases occurring in eastern Europe where, only recently, we had the opportunity to establish clubs." He elaborated that, "the organization of new Lions clubs and steady net gains annually will test our ability and potential to accomplish all that we have set out to do in making 'We Serve' a more efficient force in the cause of humanity."

Emphasizing the role of the association's growing strength, Dr. Grimaldi, in his farewell address to the 1995 International Convention in Seoul, Republic of Korea, asked everyone in attendance in the hall "to stand and join your hands in solidarity and compassion, love and thought, and pledge yourselves to be forever the moral conscience of the community and the makers of a splendid future for coming generations.

"That is what we want!

"That is what we will do!

"No one will break the chain of our international humanitarian solidarity."

The 1996 International Convention convened in historic Montreal, Quebec, Canada, where it was reported that 43,373 clubs with 1,425,310 members were active in 181 countries and geographic areas, the addition of the former Soviet republics of Georgia and Kyrghyzstan bringing the association to this new global total. There were, in fact, 1,200 new Lions clubs organized during 1995-96. A key element in this growth was the Lioness Conversion Program. International President Dr. William H. Wunder emphasized in his report to the convention that this initiative "is proving to be a most effective means to build the membership roles of Lions clubs worldwide. Not only does it allow Lions who were once Lionesses to record their past Lioness service years on their current Lions record, it also encourages women who are Lionesses to join Lions clubs because they are now able to receive proper credit for their years of service as Lionesses clubs members. This number now stands at more than 4,900."

Growth continued unabated the following year and by June 30, 1997, club totals were 43,700 with 4,436,000 members. With the addition of Cambodia, Bosnia-Herzegovina and the former Yugoslav Republic of Macedonia Lions clubs were now active in 185 countries around the world. Furthermore, the establishment of Palau and the Republic of Guinea-Bissau as independent nations were part of this expansion.

"I have continually encouraged bringing more women into our clubs because they are, indeed, a largely untapped potential for building our membership," observed International President Augustin Soliva in his convention report in Philadelphia. "Currently, there are in excess of 106,000 women in Lions clubs," he continued. "I find this most noteworthy, since the initiation of the Lioness Conversion Program, nearly 11,000 women have claimed their Lioness service years on their current Lion record. Also, the program has encouraged more than 1,000 Lionesses to become Lions for the first time."

Lions Clubs International moved into the year 1997-98 with a renewed commitment to fortify its strength in answering community and human needs, geared by the words of new International President Howard L. "Pat" Patterson's theme, "Proud Past—Bright Future." It looked to the association's decades of accomplishment to provide the inspiration to expand its programs as Lions moved forward to the 21st Century.

The number of clubs by the end of the year had risen to 44,122 with 1,421,992 members. President Patterson underscored the importance of retention in net growth, saying "It is imperative that we close that back door and close it securely in order that Lions do not leave and forfeit their membership. A club cannot strengthen its membership if, though it brings in new Lions, an equal or even greater number choose to resign."

As Lions Clubs International approached the new millennium, it boasted as of June 30, 1999, 44,551 clubs and with the addition of Cape Verde and the cancellation of Liberia, the number of countries hosting Lions clubs stood at 185. An important membership goal continued to emphasize bringing in Lionesses and spouses of Lions. Central to this was the waiver of the entrance and charter fees for those individuals that was established on January 1, 1999 and extended through December 31 of that year.

"I am pleased to advise," reported International President Kajit "KJ" Habanananda, "that most recent statistics show that more than 2,400 spouses of Lions have joined our Lions family and in excess of 230 Lionesses have chosen to become Lions. In many cases, Lioness clubs voted to become Lions clubs, taking advantage of this one-year waiver offer. Furthermore, in excess of 146,000 women have become

Lions since 1987—over 10 percent of our total membership." All of the association's leadership admitted that considerably more women needed to join Lions clubs and encouraged districts and clubs to make concerted efforts to ensure that this was achieved.

The association now prepared to enter the 21st Century with a growing emphasis being taken to organize clubs that answered special needs of potential members. In recognizing its importance, the International Board of Directors initiated steps for the establishment of three new structures of Lions clubs.

Club Branches

Many men and women found it difficult, if not impossible, to join a Lions clubs because of the time devoted to their professional duties or where they lived relative to the nearest Lions club's meeting place. Furthermore, and this was important, their numbers did not support the formation of traditional clubs which required the enrollment of at least 20 members in order to receive a charter. This barrier was remedied by the action of the International Board at its 1999 meeting in Atlanta, Georgia, with the creation of club branches, allowing an existing Lions club to, in fact, *branch out* and establish clubs in locations such as nearby small towns and rural areas, ethnic neighborhoods, professional groups and business parks, hospitals and medical complexes and such places as shopping malls, markets and retail stores.

In essence, a club branch is a small group (less than 20) of service-minded individuals who, though officially full members of their existing parent club with the attendant privileges and responsibilities, hold meetings and conduct service activities at locations separate from that of its parent club. Each of these club branches has a branch coordinator and liaison from the parent club who are on call to assist in their programs and establish objectives.

The program was an immediate success with six clubs being formed by June 30, 2000. The first branch club was established February 2, 2000, in Iceland, the Reykholar Club, with the Bogarnes Lions serving as the parent club. The new branch went right to work, donating books to a local school and sponsoring a Christmas program for children. The new club branch, in cooperation with its parent club, also conducted fundraising events and became involved with homes for the elderly and for mentally challenged individuals.

By June 30, 2001, club branches numbered 120 and the innovative approach was well on its way to filling a crucial gap in membership growth. "I am confident this number will increase significantly," said International President Dr. Jean Behar in his report to the convention in Indianapolis, "as more Lions clubs see the benefit of bringing in new quality members in localities where they have previously been unable to do so."

To energize the program, Club Branch Bulletin Kits were developed along with other materials outlining the uniqueness of the program and providing guidelines for the formation of club branches. All were submitted for translation into the official languages of the association. After initiating the club branch program, the kit was mailed to all district governors, council chairpersons and multiple district chairpersons in July 2000.

Still another encouraging outgrowth of the program is the option for club branches to become traditional Lions clubs once they reach 20 members. To date, 225 branches have converted to Lions clubs.

As of July 31, 2008, there were 832 club branches in 70 nations. Their activities are clearly diversified.

For example, the Youth Program Branch of the Schaumburg-Hoffman Lions Club in Illinois reaches parents of youth program participants. The members are bound by their common interest in serving young people in their community. Still another example of how club branches reach out is the Educator's Branch of the Sweeny, Texas, Lions Club. The parent club had not traditionally participated in youth activities and the Educator's branch filled that gap by sponsoring Youth Exchange, Lions Quest, essay contests and presenting an Outstanding Youth Award. In keeping with the commitment of Lions to sight conservation, the Eye Bank Branch of the Allentown Alton Park, Pennsylvania, Lions Club serves the hospital that houses the eye bank through corneal donations and other volunteer activities, such as participating in the Adopt-a-Senior program and donating games and materials to the hospital's psychiatric unit.

New Century Lions Clubs

In surveying the need to broaden membership, the board sought to provide an opportunity for younger career-minded men and women (through the age of 35) to serve their communities and to benefit from the personal rewards of membership. These opportunities took the form of what was designated New Century Lions Clubs, specially designed for this peer group. This new door to the future of Lions Clubs International was opened at the April 2000 Board meeting in Acapulco, Mexico, with the introduction of the proposed program's core concept during James M. "Jim" Ervin's year as president. It was subsequently launched at the 2000 International Convention in Honolulu, believing these clubs would be a magnet to attract young adults in the community as well as outgoing members of Leo clubs. During its first year, 35 New Century Clubs and one club branch were chartered with a membership of more than 350 in 15 countries.

The program accelerated and by July 31, 2008, there were 118 New Century Lions Clubs in every constitutional area, with the greatest number of these clubs being in India, Southwest Asia, Africa and the Middle East and in Europe. The young members have demonstrated an energetic capacity to become involved in their communities. Two examples will demonstrate how these young men and women are becoming involved in their communities.

In Jakarta, Indonesia, for example, young Frank Mulyadi and some friends had daily walked through poverty-stricken areas. They were appalled at the deplorable conditions in which families were forced to live and were especially concerned about the children who were often forced to do whatever was necessary to earn money in order to survive, often becoming street children and resorting to begging or turning to illegal means. Mulyadi and his friends decided to answer these needs by first distributing food and clothing to then establishing "open air free style" classrooms where they would teach reading, writing, math or simply listen to the children. Their work came to the attention of Past Council Chairperson Djoko Soeroso and members of his Jakarta Kota Lions Club. He and his fellow members were convinced these young volunteers would make excellent Lions, but the club's membership was mostly over 50 years of age and didn't think the young people would really fit in. The solution: charter a New Century Lions Club with members of Mulyadi's group.

Consequently, on April 17, 2004, the Jakarta Kota Raya New Century Lions Club held its charter night ceremony with the induction of 22 members. The new Lions have now expanded their open school to a daily preschool for more than 350 pupils taught by professional teachers in a permanent building. Lion Mulyadi and his members still worked with the street children they initially encountered. The club conducted an Achievement and Creativity Appreciation Day which attracted nearly 1,000 street children. The club was also chosen by the United Nations Volunteers to join a campaign supported and initiated by the United Nations to help homeless youngsters from becoming street children. Since the chartering of their Lions club, Frank Mulyadi and his friends have dedicated themselves to helping impoverished children and given them hope for a better future.

Still another example of success is the Vancouver Cathay New Century Lions Club in British Columbia, Canada. Originally chartered and sponsored by the Vancouver Cathay Lions Club in 1997 as the Vancouver Cathay Leo Club, the young members, all ambitious high school graduates, were afforded opportunities to explore and develop their personal and team skills and understand fully the goals of Lions Clubs International.

In 2005, the Leos, grateful for the guidance and encouragement they received from their sponsoring Lions, were prepared to meet new challenges. They became established as the Vancouver Cathay New Century Lions Club. Since then, the new 25-member club has become involved in numerous community and humanitarian activities. Among them are the Third World Eye Care Society, Covenant House, the Lions Foundation of Guides, World Vision and the Union Gospel Mission. As further evidence of their enthusiasm, the club was awarded first place in the Web site category of the association's 2006-2007 International Contest, the results announced at the 90th International Convention in Chicago.

As are all Lions clubs, regardless of their structure, the Vancouver Cathay New Century Club members are concerned with making a difference in their community and, whenever possible, to people the world over by providing a wide variety of voluntary services.

Campus Lions Clubs

Establishing Lions clubs on college and university campuses was actually the first of these three new concepts for specialized clubs to be initiated. A club was chartered in 1995 at the Pennsylvania School of Optometry in Philadelphia and went on to be a huge success. After consideration and study were given to expand this vision for growth, a core concept was launched at the 1998 International Convention in Birmingham, England. It was designed to provide an avenue for students and other young adults to develop a Lions club that appealed to their ideals and their desire to become directly involved in community service.

The year 1997-98 was the new program's first test year when the association participated in trade shows for the purpose of conducting research and measuring market potential. One important item was introduced—a Campus Club Kit to assist Lions, especially extension chairpersons, in chartering these clubs. Early results showed that at the end of that year, five clubs had been organized, four in the United States and one in Canada. One year later, it was reported that eight new Campus Lions Clubs had been formed in the United States, bringing to total to 13.

One important incentive for college students to become Lions was passed by the International Board of Directors in October 1999, "to defray membership costs for college students who are often pressed for sufficient discretionary funds." At its April 2004 meeting in Seoul, the board voted to end all charter and entrance fee waivers. Subsequently, at the board meeting the following July in Detroit, the board established a new charter entrance fee of US$10 for students in campus clubs.

To further encourage student membership, an entrance/charter fee waiver and a charge of half international dues was put into effect for all students in any Lions club between the ages of legal majority and 30. Another new initiative is the Leo-to-Lion program. It is similar to the student member program but gives graduating Leos, through age 30, the entrance/charter fee waiver and half of international dues. Additionally, when 10 or more graduating Leos, through age 30, charter a Lions club, the same dues concession is granted.

A Campus Club Web site was established in 2000-2001 and soon faculty advisors and community residents near schools were also encouraged to join clubs. To further emphasize the importance of this growth initiative, in 2002-2003 the position of Campus Club Chairperson was approved. The following year, the Campus Club Chairperson's Manual was developed and translated.

As of July 31, 2008, there were 280 Campus Clubs in 25 countries, with the constitutional areas of India, Southwest Asia, Africa and the Middle East and the United States, Bermuda and its affiliates having the greatest number of clubs. Clearly, the program was taking shape as an effective force for growth.

A prime example is the New York Tribeca Club at the Borough of Manhattan Community College. It was chartered in June 2004 and started service in the fall of that year. At the beginning of each semester, the club makes detailed plans and budgeting. With support from the association, past district governors and Guiding Lions Eugene Wong and Andres Mercado, along with the college's Student Life and Student Government Association which recognizes the club's contributions to the college community and its representation of the college in the greater New York community, this campus club has achieved remarkable results. The young Lions have raised $5,000 for tsunami relief through the sale of New York Mets tickets, enabled more than 500 children to receive eye screenings, helped flood victims in the Dominican Republic and Haiti by working with the District 20-R2 disaster relief committee to ship needed supplies, donated $700 of new books as Christmas presents to a daycare center and presented $1,000 to UNICEF. They also raised $2,300 for a Breast Cancer and Diabetes Walk, conducted a flea market sale with its sponsor club, the Cosmopolitan Lions Club in Chinatown, and volunteered at a number events including Lions Day with the United Nations, Special Olympics, a health fair in the Bronx and Parents of Blind Children. The club continues to expand its involvement in hands-on activities and raising funds for a broad range of causes.

Examples of other campus clubs projects attest to the growing value of this innovative extension program. At the University of Wisconsin-La Crosse, the campus club is a branch club of the La Crosse Lions club and its activities have included a day of bowling and pizza for children who have siblings with physical or mental disabilities. "It's a time for kids to get away for one day to escape the sometimes stressful homelife and to talk with us so we may help them see the benefits of having a sister or brother with a disability," explained Lion Shannon Erickson, a senior majoring in occupational therapy. They have also transported corneas 45 miles away to Tomah where another Lion would relay them to the Wisconsin Lions Eye Bank in Madison.

During a spring break, members of the campus club at Taylor University in Upland, Indiana, joined with Indiana Lions on a mission to Mexico to distribute eyeglasses. One student, Lizzy Moore, a psychology and Spanish major, said, "As I found out later, a few of my words were mixed, but they didn't correct me. They seemed thrilled that I was able to speak Spanish. The interaction with the people was a gift for me. They treated us like royalty. I wasn't really comfortable with this, but just knowing how much we helped and to see this was very satisfying."

A New Millennium Brings Further Expansion

Lions Clubs International prepared to enter the 21st Century intent on expanding the role of "We Serve" throughout the world. As events would show, the association's emblem was destined to be introduced in increasing numbers of new locations, among them the world's largest nation, heretofore closed to active service clubs. From 2000 to 2002 Lions clubs were also chartered in Romania, the Federated States of Micronesia, Serbia, Russia, Lithuania, Ukraine, Latvia, Bulgaria, Croatia, Albania, the Czech Republic and Slovakia, bringing the total number of countries to 189.

During the 83rd International Convention in Honolulu, President James E. "Jim" Ervin. He also expressed his pleasure with the reception of Lions Worldwide Induction day which not only brought in new members, but enhanced the association's image as a global leader in voluntary service. This program would continue over the years in strengthening membership.

The following year would, indeed, prove to be a landmark in the association's expansion.

A total of 683 clubs were added in 2001-2002, two of which being decisive to the prestige of Lions Clubs International as a leader in voluntary service. International President J. Frank Moore III was able to report at the 85th International Convention in Osaka, Japan, the chartering of the first Lions clubs in mainland China. "The China Guangdong and China Shenzhen clubs have been organized with the full support and endorsement of the government of the People's Republic of China," he announced. "An executive order," he continued, "was issued by the Chinese government and countersigned by the Chinese Premier to officially establish the clubs. Prior to this, the Chinese government had recognized no other service club organization. The role of these new clubs, as with Lions worldwide, will be to serve the needs of the community and address sight preservation, youth activities, education, medical services and disaster relief. We are pleased and honored to establish Lions clubs in mainland China and, because one-fifth of the world's blind population resides in China, Lions Clubs International and LCIF will continue to work with the Chinese government to be a catalyst for sight preservation and restoration."

Opening the pathway to mainland China did not happen overnight however. The initial steps were taken in 1997 when Lions Clubs International partnered with the China State Council Coordination Committee on Disability and two of its subsidiaries—the Ministry of Health and the China Disabled Persons' Federation—to launch SightFirst China Action (SFCA). Funding for the program came from LCIF through the SightFirst Program. SFCA thus established a strong partnership between the association and the Chinese government, which illustrated firsthand the powerful impact Lions clubs could make in that nation. This cooperation was augmented with the 2002 extension of SightFirst China Action for five more years. The goal was to complete an additional 2.5 million cataract surgeries and the continued creation of medical teams and training of medical personnel, plus the establishment of permanent training centers in the main regions of China.

Two members of the China Hong Kong Lions Club, Past International Directors Paul Fan and Dr. Tam Wing Kun, served as Guiding Lions for the new clubs. They and the China Hong Kong and China Macau (District 303) Lions provided advice to the new clubs and introduced the objectives, motto and spirit of "We Serve" to the new members.

The extension of clubs in mainland China grew at a tremendous rate and latest numbers show that 81 Lions clubs with 1,786 members are presently active in this vast nation.

In addition to mainland China, two other nations were added during the year: Angola and the former Soviet Republic of Moldova.

New International President Kay K. Fukushima continued to emphasize the importance of extension in the association's growth. He stated at the convention in Denver, Colorado, that latest reports showed that 1,125 new Lions clubs were organized during 2002-2003, bringing to 45,723 the total number of clubs worldwide. "Critical to this success," he told those in attendance, "has been the Area Impact Team, composed of dedicated and energetic Lion leaders, who were charged with organizing clubs in their specific locales."

With the chartering of the State of Vatican City Lions Club, Lions were active in 191 countries and geographical areas. The symbolic target of 200 was definitely within reach.

International President Dr. Tae-Sup Lee announced that 1,020 new Lions clubs had been established during 2003-2004 to bring global club strength to 46,795. In his report to the 2004 International Convention in Detroit/Windsor, the president emphasized the importance of bringing more women into active membership. "The Women's Initiative has proceeded with very positive results," he said. "Latest reports show that a record 42,893 women have joined Lions clubs. An important reason for this success is the *I Am A Lion* brochure which every club president has received. Nearly 167,370 copies of this publication have been distributed, with 1,685 Lions requesting additional copies."

Speaking at the following year's convention in China Hong Kong, International President Dr. Clement F. Kusiak was especially pleased with the growth of the Club Branch, New Century and Campus Lions Clubs. He was also proud that 144 club branches had thus far converted to fully chartered Lions clubs. Concerning the continued expansion of Lions clubs in mainland China, he said, "Perhaps the most exciting and historically important development is the approval of Lions Clubs International as a membership federation in China, which is paving the way for the establishment of clubs throughout the country."

Growth was also emphasized by International President Dr. Ashok Mehta at the 2006 Convention in Boston, Massachusetts. He listed a number of initiatives that promoted the development of new target marketing techniques in order to reach potential members more effectively, such as the North American Baby Boomer Campaign that would be launched at the convention. He viewed as the greatest strategies for future growth the new Family Membership Dues Initiative and the Family Membership Recruiting Campaign. Both were employed under the guidance of the Membership Development Committee. These approaches, he emphasized, could be summed up in one phrase: *Innovative Thinking*. In commenting on these new strategies, he said, "Admittedly, it involved some risk taking and new ways of looking at things to develop this program, but it is the kind of fresh thinking we need to see more of in the future as competition for members and volunteers continues to increase."

International President Jimmy Ross elaborated on these innovative approaches at the 2007 International Convention in Chicago by stating that they were most assuredly paying dividends. "The Family Membership program is a keystone," he announced. "In just the first two months of this calendar year, 96 new family-oriented clubs were formed. The majority of the charter members in these clubs are family members and in January and February more than 5,000 people joined Lions under the family program."

In commenting on the North American Baby Boomer Campaign which is targeting more than 70 million people of this generation, he said, "We're using eye-catching posters and brochures as well as a special Web site to appeal to this highly important age group."

President Ross praised the strengthening of extension activities through the introduction of the regionally-based Extension Workshop Program. As of February 28, 2007, 23 of these workshops were held, resulting in 21 new clubs and nine new club branches. "But more importantly," he stressed, "over 750 Lions have learned first-hand how to charter a new club. These newly trained Lions will be encouraged to continue to support new club development now and in the future. So while the initial results are good, we expect the long-term results to have an even greater impact. We are moving quickly," he added, "to expand the program to South America."

President Ross gave special emphasis to the organization of a Lions club in war-ravaged Iraq. The Iraqi Host Lions Club was chartered on April 1, 2007 with most of the members being young professionals from Baghdad and Najaf. Among the club's primary goals are restoring cancer treatment in their area and providing vision screenings, medical equipment and medical supplies. Before the club could be organized, however, Lions had to secure the approval of the Ministry of Social Affairs in Baghdad. And for safety reasons, organizational meetings were held in Dubai and the charter ceremony conducted in Jordan.

"This is an historic event for Lions Clubs International," observed President Ross, "but, more importantly, it is a sign of hope for the people of Iraq. I commend the 20 charter members of this new club for their personal courage in stepping forward at a time of great insecurity in the homeland and for their desire to improve the lives of people in their war-torn country."

In addition to Iraq and since the establishment of clubs in the People's Republic of China, Lions clubs had been chartered in Timor Leste in the South Pacific; the African states of Somalia, Sudan and Gambia; Kazakhstan, once a part of the Soviet Union; the Indian Ocean island republics of Maldives and Seychelles and finally the United Arab Emirates. With the addition of the UAR, Lions Clubs International had reached its targeted milestone of being located in 200 countries and geographical areas. This global extension didn't stop here. Soon Lions clubs were also established in Montenegro and Laos to raise the total to 202.

As of July 31, 2008, 1,302,527 Lions were reported active in 45,040 clubs, testament to the seed planted back in 1917 in Chicago and then in Dallas when 28 "Founders Clubs" came together to form a new and progressive association committed to community and humanitarian service.

Chapter Nine
Women Energize Lions' Service And Growth Worldwide

Since the founding of Lions Clubs International, women have added a special dimension to the work of the association. Women's auxiliaries have supported and many today still enhance the community programs of their sponsoring Lions clubs and, while the Lionesses clubs program was in effect, these members helped to expand the global "We Serve" image. A number of Lioness clubs have, through the Lioness Clubs Conversion Program, become functioning and efficient Lioness/Lions clubs. The conversion program honors years of service these women have performed as members of their Lioness clubs. And, of course, every year Lions clubs continue to welcome into their clubs thousands of women who have never been Lionesses or members of auxiliaries, but who have expressed a wish to volunteer their skills and enthusiasm in service to their communities.

There are many stories of the growth and services rendered by these women in Lions clubs. Take, for example, the following:

Members of the Lake Wylie Lioness/Lions Club in Lake Wylie, South Carolina, are magicians. They changed used furniture into a week at Camp Leo for a blind youngster. Castoff golf clubs became a computer for a high school student. Used toys, dishes, television sets, power tools, books, or construction equipment are miraculously transformed into support for the Special Olympics, a wheelchair for a disabled adult, medical services for a diabetic child – or a Canine Companion. The magic happens at the "Sweet Repeat" shop and it touches many lives.

Ask Dr. Jane Veith, the stepdaughter of Lake Wylie Lion JoAnn Veith. A clinical psychologist in Redmond, Washington, she and her husband, Michael, were driving to Seattle from the Oregon coast on the Thanksgiving weekend in 1993 when her life changed irrevocably. As they drove through an intersection with the right of way, a car slammed into them from a side street. When Jane regained consciousness, she was a quadriplegic, paralyzed from the neck down, with limited use of her hands and arms.

In August 1994, Dr. Veith completed the detailed application for a canine companion from Canine Companions for Independence in Santa Rosa, California, and was placed on their waiting list. In May 1999, Jane and her husband were invited to Santa Rosa to begin team training. All participants are asked to bring a support person with them to reduce the stress of the two weeks.

"After being paired with the dog seen as the best fit for each of us by the staff, we learned each of the more than 50 commands the dogs were trained to obey," Veith said. "Finally, we completed both the written and field portions of the Assistance Dogs International exam to certify us as team qualified for public access. Ellijay has transformed my life. She gave me a sense of pride and freedom. She's a dog with limitless composure, a Lauren Bacall type. Maybe some of that rubbed off on me."

In June of that year, Veith and her husband visited Lake Wylie, South Carolina, where the Lake Wylie Lions Club hosted a luncheon for her and donated $20,000 to Canine Companions for Independence. The Sweet Repeat thrift shop is the club's primary moneymaker, netting more than $63,000 during the last fiscal year.

The donation from the Lake Wylie members will be used for team sponsorships that will offset the cost of breeding, raising and training two canine companions through the time of placement with individuals with a disability. The dogs are provided free of charge to the handicapped.

"Ellijay has given me the courage and confidence with people that I lost in the accident," Dr. Veith explained. "People focus on her beauty and vitality. In doing this, I think they become less aware of how I remind them of the fragility of the human condition.

"Rather than avoiding me, now strangers come by to share their favorite stories of their beloved pets, to ask to pet Ellijay and tell her she's a beauty, to voice their amazement at her level of training."

The Sweet Repeat shop sells gently used furniture, dishes, toys, electronic goods, sporting goods, and power tools. In fact, they sell just about everything but used clothing. Other beneficiaries of the club's generosity include the Boy Scouts, Girl Scouts, Camp Leo for blind youngsters, a camp for diabetic children, the Leukemia Society, Lions Quest, Special Olympics, and the Leader Dog program. The shop is located in a shopping mall in Lake Wylie and pays no rent due to the generosity of the mall owner, Mark Erwin.

"The mover and shaker behind our club is my good friend, Monique Boekhout," said Lake Wylie Lion JoAnn Veith. "She really did all the leg work to arrange our donation to Canine Companions and get the luncheon for Jane and the contribution in motion."

"The Lake Wylie Lioness/Lions Club began in 1979 with 20 members and now numbers 55," said charter member Ann Sturcken. "We started out small, but very positively, 20 years ago with the objective to always help those with special needs. We now support 16 major service programs and more than 22 other organizations." The club's status as a Lions club came about because of the Lioness Clubs Conversion Program.

Lynn Anthony, another charter member, added: "It's all a labor of love, and work is definitely not a four-letter word for this group." The Lake Wylie Lioness/Lions Club has raised more than $1,000,000 since 1979.

Gudrun Yngvadottir of Lions Club Elk, Gardabaer, Iceland, became a Lion in 1992. Yngvadottir was involved with the association for many years before becoming a Lion, supporting her spouse with his Lions activities. "I learned about Lions clubs when my husband became a member in his early 30s. The club members became our best friends and they still are. When my husband became a district governor, I traveled with him and attended meetings," she said. "Learning about the vision and the strength of this big organization made me a real Lion and I was very happy when I was invited to become a member in 1992."

Yngvadottir has served the association in many capacities on the club and district level. She has focused most of her efforts in the area of leadership development. She has been the coordinator of the Regional Lions Leadership Institute in Iceland since its inception as well as serving as the multiple district Leadership Development chairperson for seven years.

Yngvadottir believes being a Lion helped her become a better person and leader. "Being the member of an international service organization has made me more broadminded, understanding and appreciative," she said. "It has given me an opportunity to face all kinds of challenges. Projects need to be planned, problems have to be solved, new ideas have to be created and members have to be taken care of. If you help your Lions club to grow and be strong, you grow, too. By taking on some leadership roles you develop your skills. My experience with Lions has also been extremely useful in my profession, my career. Being a Lion has made me a better leader."

Yolima Garcia de Paez of Barranquilla Puerto de Oro Lions Club, Colombia, served as a Leo from 1990-1994 and became a Lion in 1995.

When she was 22 years old, Yolima Garcia de Paez met her future husband, Juan Carlos Paez, who was also a Lion. After they married, they founded the Barranquilla Puerto de Oro Lions Club together. She has served as district governor and multiple district council chairperson.

Paez said, "Being a Lion is a way of living, a way of seeing life." She believes being a Lion introduces a person to many valuable personal character traits, including respect, tolerance and feeling valued, and helps develop leadership, listening and friendship skills. "After everything Lions clubs can provide, who wouldn't be interested in belonging?" she asked.

Being a young woman involved in Lions has given her a unique perspective on the association. She has seen changes in her country happen at a rapid pace. "Changes have been seen not just in the role of women but in their number. The increase in women has been dizzying. For example, in Colombia, the number of women almost matches the number of men and our role is now more executive. We already find women district governors, council presidents, international directors, and, within a very short time, international presidents also. It has been a fast and effective learning curve."

For Paez, her Lions clubs membership has helped her fulfill the lessons her father taught. "Since I was small, my father taught me to give the best of myself to others and in Lions I found this – to be able to develop my personal qualities for the benefit of the most needy."

Women Lions are experts at providing care to those in need. Almost instinctively, women reach out to help children, the sick and the elderly. One person at a time, women Lions demonstrate their care and concern. This occurs when they visit pediatrics wards, deliver meals to the homebound, or agree to "adopt-a-grandmother."

The introduction of women into Lions clubs has expanded the reach of Lions activities. Lions now volunteer at shelters for domestic abuse victims and raise funds for breast cancer research.

It was in the 1960s that Doris Cousino joined the Oxon Hill, Maryland, Lioness Club. "We were a strong, hard-working Lioness Club," said Cousino. "There was no reason to believe that we wouldn't be a strong Lions club, too."

From the beginning, the Oxon Hill Friendly Lions were determined to make a statement. They started with a fashion statement. "We didn't feel that the gold Lions vests with purple trim were as attractive as purple Lions vests with gold trim," said Cousino. "So we made our own."

The Oxon Friendly Lions proudly wore their vests as they completed "hands-on" service projects. Twice each month, they delivered coffee and cookies to residents of a local nursing home. "The residents never cared about the coffee," said Cousino. "They just want someone to talk to."

The Lions were – and remain – happy to oblige. For the past six years, the Lions have created a Christmas party for the residents. The party includes a sing-a-long, refreshments, and a visit from Santa. The Lions also present residents with homemade lap robes or bibs.

The Lions work with the local schools, too. They purchase eyeglasses, school supplies and clothing for needy students. Once a year, they visit the schools and distribute drug education information.

Throughout the community, the Lions are well known for their homemade Easter candy fundraiser. "About 15 women spend five 12-hour days making Easter eggs, bon-bons, peanut clusters, and buckeyes," said Cousino. "We take advance orders. We make about $2,500."

A few years ago, the women Lions organized an Italian dinner fundraiser. They decorated a church hall in red, white, and green.

They sold raffle tickets for baskets of bread, wine, pasta, and homemade sauce.

"It was an overwhelming success," said Cousino. "We made far more money than we imagined for a first-time project. You just can't keep good women down."

The Chicago Mayfair Lions Club in Illinois sponsored the Chicago Mayfair Lioness Club. For 23 years, Judy Toft was a Lioness. "Membership in the Lions club was very low," said Toft. "When we [the Lionesses] joined the Lions club, we helped the club stay afloat." Today the club has 21 members, nine of whom are women.

The women Lions continue their service traditions. "We had always performed pre-school hearing screenings," said Toft. "The Lions had always performed pre-school vision screenings. Once the clubs merged, we provided pre-school hearing and vision screenings."

For more than 25 years, the Lionesses had been "adopting" children at Christmas time. "We purchase toys and clothing for eight children each year," said Toft. "We deliver the gifts anonymously to a local community center. The parents pick up the gifts from the office."

Other projects introduced by the women Lions include: collecting used cell phones for a battered women's shelter, organizing a rummage sale fundraiser, and selling discount coupon books for a local department store.

Toft has undertaken personal projects, too. "I send postcards to critically ill children," she said. "A Lions club in England started the project."

"I also took a day off of work to volunteer with 30 other Lions during a recent Special Olympics Opening Eyes event in Chicago. About 100 students from the Illinois College of Optometry screened the vision of 1,200 Special Olympians. It was exciting to watch the kids with their new glasses. Many of them saw clearly for the first time."

Clare Crawford is one of 17 women in the 29-member Knox County North Lions Club, Tennessee. She has been a Lion for the past 16 years and is a Past District 12-N Governor.

"Male-only Lions clubs are diminishing in Tennessee," said Crawford. "Women in this area are willing to donate their time. They're qualified to step into leadership roles. Our club members range in age from the late 20s through retirement."

Club activities focus on a variety of local needs. "We adopted a homeless shelter," said Crawford. "We volunteer for the Remote Area Medical Missions. Several of our members are nurses. They help with the free medical and dental exams. Other members help register patients while still others entertain the children who wait in long lines for hours."

In 2002 the club accepted a new challenge. "The owner of the restaurant where we hold our Lions meetings is a foster mother," said Crawford. "She suggested that we host a Christmas party for all the foster children in the county. So we did."

The Lions contacted the local social service agency. They invited 200 children, their foster parents, and the other children in their households to the holiday event. Eighty-two children and 85 adults attended.

"We had a live band with singing and dancing," said Crawford. "Someone donated the food. The children received a photo of themselves on Santa's lap. They received a wrapped Christmas gift, a backpack filled with school supplies, a bag of candy from the Boy Scouts, produce from a local fruit vendor and a toothbrush from a local dentist." After completion of the successful project, the Knox County North Lions extended a membership invitation to the restaurateur. She accepted.

The year 2007 marked the 20th anniversary of women as Lions. In 1987, after the U.S. Supreme Court ruled that excluding women from service clubs was discriminatory in a case involving a Rotary club, delegates to Lions' International Convention in Taipei, Multiple District 300 Taiwan, officially opened up membership to women. Within two months, 3,500 women in the United States, Canada, and overseas joined Lions clubs. Within five years, 55,000 women joined, and Lions Clubs International ended its official support for the Lioness program for women, which had peaked in 1987 with 157,000 members [though some self-supporting Lioness clubs continue today].

The transition to a mixed-gender association wasn't always smooth. But, overall, the transition has been a rousing success. Female Lions have revitalized many clubs and brought new skill sets to others. Ten female members mean 20 extra hands to get things done and at least 40 new ideas, as a Lion once explained. Some clubs would have folded without the influx of women and others never would have been founded if women were not eligible for membership.

The number of female Lions as of July 31, 2008 was 255,000 or about 20 percent of total membership. That percentage has been climbing. Seventeen percent of the clubs in the United States are all men while one percent of the U.S. clubs are exclusively women. Twenty-five percent of the clubs in Canada are all men while two percent of them are all women, and 22.1 percent of all Lions in Canada and the United States are women.

Lions Clubs International has reached out to women as potential members. In 2003, women's membership chairs were established at the district and multiple district level. To make women feel more welcome, gender-neutral language was adopted for the association. Membership publications targeting women were developed. Worldwide symposiums and workshops on recruiting female members were held. Such efforts continue today.

Lisa Hachicho put in years of community service before becoming a Lion. Her gender was a non-factor when the Alief Noon Lions Club in Houston picked her as its first female president in 2002. Why was she tabbed as president? "I'm a good fund-raiser," she explained at the time.

Female membership upped the talent pool and energy level of clubs. What was once unthinkable was now achievable for some clubs. The Arabi Lions in Louisiana were accustomed to raising a couple of hundred dollars through bingo. After Clare Chauffe became the club's first woman president in 1998, Lions raised $8,000 through a Super Bingo and helped purchase a van, appropriately enough, for a girls' home.

Latest statistics show that the top countries in terms of the percentage of female membership [in nations with at least 250 Lions] are Greece, 52 percent; Jamaica, 52 percent; Trinidad-Tobago,

49 percent; Israel, 48 percent; Barbados West Indies, 47 percent; Indonesia, 44 percent; Venezuela, 44 percent; Colombia, 41 percent; Costa Rica, 41 percent; Cyprus, 40 percent; Ecuador, 40 percent; Turkey, 40 percent; Algeria, 39 percent; and Botswana, 38 percent.

In 2004 the association introduced the Lions Worldwide Women's Symposium Program, which has been very successful and based on learning. It was broadened to include the Family Membership Program in 2007. The purpose of the Lions Worldwide Women's Symposium Program was four-fold: 1) to identify new community projects that are of interest to women; 2) to identify potential members; 3) to promote Lions clubs within the community; and 4) to charter new clubs and club branches and develop community projects identified at the symposium.

Highly successful, this wide-ranging program offers Lions clubs the chance to partner with other service groups in the community, such as:

- Chamber of Commerce
- Red Cross
- Junior Women's Clubs
- Americorps
- Big Brothers/Big Sisters
- United Way
- Girl Scouts
- American Association of University Women
- Association of Trial Lawyers of America
- Parent Teacher Organization
- Nurses and Physician's associations

These partnerships are beneficial to the participating organizations, and combining resources can help the groups plan and hold a successful symposium. In addition to resources, partnering with another organization provides fresh ideas and perspectives on needs within the community.

Clubs and districts are encouraged to add supplementary components to their symposium to further enhance the event such as a community showcase featuring area organizations.

The Membership Programs Department designed a planning guide to help clubs stage a successful event. The guide offers guidelines for selecting a theme, choosing a partner organization, setting a date, finding a location, planning the presentation, inviting speakers, inviting participants, adding additional elements to the event, and publicizing the event. It also contains an event planning timeline/checklist, presentation schedule, sample publicity materials, and an action plan form to help set goals and design programs to meet the needs identified during the symposium.

The enthusiasm of the lady Lions is reflected in the words of Past International Director, Lucie Armstrong from Hamilton, New Zealand. "There is no doubt that women are motivated by causes that are important to them. Since 1987 when women were invited to join Lions Clubs International they have, besides helping to maintain membership numbers, complemented the existing male membership's effort in their projects, programs and the overall environment within individual clubs.

"They have established themselves as a vital, important and integral part of our Association accomplishing broad humanitarian service with enthusiasm and dedication.

"Slowly but surely women are providing quality leaders, working professionally alongside their male counterparts at all levels – Club, District, Multiple District, and on the International Board.

"I value greatly the ideals of our Lions Association and have huge pride in being a Lions member and part of such a WONDERFUL family."

Lucie Armstrong served 2002-04.

In 2003 clubs and districts worldwide embraced International President Tae-Sup Lee's call to recruit more women into Lions clubs. The brochure, "I am a Lion," aimed at potential women members, was in such great demand that the publication was reprinted only a few short weeks after its initial printing. New chairpersons hit the ground running in an effort to build on the momentum that was created when this initiative was officially announced.

Statistics show that women are a largely untapped market for Lions membership development initiatives. Targeting women for membership provides enormous potential for strengthening the association. Those districts that are embracing the initiative are receiving a positive response from both the current women Lions and women in the community.

In Ireland, Gilbert Lee served as the Multiple District 105 Membership and Retention Chairperson. The multiple district's plan is to have each club look closely at itself to make sure it mirrors the community it serves. "It is said that every Lions club is different, as every community is different. It is important that Lions clubs mirror the community in which they serve in terms of religion, gender, race and culture. The female membership of MD-105 extends to some 14 percent of our total membership. Therefore 36 percent of the population within the borders of our multiple district is an untapped source of potential new membership."

A number of districts within MD-105 have chosen not to appoint a specific Women's Development and Participation chairperson, and are having their current membership chairpersons champion the initiative. "We have greatly benefited from recent years' council of governors who totally supported increased female membership. Individually these governors not only encouraged many clubs within their own districts to open their doors to female membership, but they encouraged women to take office at club, district and MD level to the extent that we have two females out of 13 district governors in the current year," said Lee. Lee is confident that his multiple district's efforts will be a success because of this prevailing positive attitude from current and past leadership.

Lee is optimistic about women's roles in the future of Lions. "It remains important that the membership of Lions Clubs International reflect the role of women from whatever position they currently fulfill so that our association and those we serve can benefit from their attributes. It must also be our aim that we will be able to announce, in the not too distant future, that we are truly a dual gender organization with 50 percent of our membership being female."

Female Lions around the world provide a wide range of suggestions:

- Promote family participation: Since women often serve as the primary caregivers for children, creating clubs that encourage participation of the entire family can be very appealing for women who might not otherwise have the opportunity to attend meetings. Family-centered clubs also have the added benefit of demonstrating the importance of volunteerism to young people.

- Partner with existing groups: Working together on a community service activity is an excellent way to introduce others to Lions clubs and interest them in membership.
- Get Involved in youth activities: Many women, especially those with school-aged children, want to be involved with volunteer activities that are directly related to improving the lives of young people. Participating in youth activities such as Leo Clubs, Lions Quest, scouting, the Lions International Peace Poster Contest, etc., will be appealing to parents.
- Target young professionals: Don't overlook young professionals. Lions clubs offer a perfect way for them to become involved in their communities at a time when the demands of family might not be so overwhelming.
- Encourage couples: Participating together in Lions activities is a great relationship-building opportunity for couples. Clubs also benefit from having both adults in the household committed to their projects.
- Participate in relevant community activities: Both women and men want to be involved in groups that truly make a difference in their communities. Clubs that participate in relevant, visible community activities will see their club membership thrive.
- Focus on involvement: Make sure new members are immediately engaged in activities that maximize their talents and interests.
- Foster mentoring: Encourage those with leadership potential who might be a bit hesitant to get involved by fostering a mentoring relationship with an experienced Lion.
- Offer leadership opportunities: Give women the chance to shine by offering opportunities to demonstrate their leadership abilities at all levels.

Female Lions from all over the world have made major contributions to Lions Clubs International:

Polly Voon of the North Vancouver Host, B.C., Canada Lions Club started as a Lioness in 1984 and became a Lion in 1988. Her Lions' experience has grown along with the association as she's witnessed the changes that Lions clubs made in the past two decades. In addition to serving as district governor in 1999-2000, she has been a presenter and group leader at the District Governors-elect Seminar and is currently serving as a mentor to 32 district governors. Voon has served on the faculty of seven Senior Lions Leadership Institutes and has been a presenter at three USA/Canada Lions Leadership Forums.

She became a Lion after attending a Lions club meeting and was impressed by the guest speaker. "Initially, it wasn't by design. A Lion I knew through a cultural organization invited me to a Lions club meeting. It was a club officers' installation dinner and a past international director was the speaker. He spoke about the history of Lions and what Lions do. His speaking ability, style, and content so impressed me that I thought, 'if the organization could give me the opportunity to develop my speaking and presentation skills, I'd be interested in joining'."

Looking back on the past 20 years, being a Lion has helped her gain those skills, and much more. "I don't know what my life would be like without Lions. I enjoy being in Lions. It has given me the opportunity to stretch myself," said Voon. "Lions clubs are a safe environment for people to get involved, to take little baby steps to learn and develop new skills and knowledge in a very supportive and encouraging environment."

The contributions of women Lions are dramatically increasing the reach and effectiveness of Lions Clubs International everywhere as it moves into the 21st Century.

The Zamboanga Preciosa, Philippines, club built a basketball backboard with the Lions logo and a message promoting drug awareness.

The Kelliher, Saskatchewan, Canada, club is helping community members keep physically fit by sponsoring aerobics classes open to the public.

These are but a few examples of what female Lions are accomplishing in terms of meeting some human needs.

"I am so proud of the women in our organization, for I see women as committed to the causes they care about," said Past International Director Beverly A. Roberts. "I view women as desirous of changing things for the better and working as team players as they creatively make changes, contribute to their projects and develop their leadership skills. In addition, women like to see the human side of the results of their volunteering, and they enjoy the satisfaction of their efforts.

"I feel that any organization that has only men or only women as members will become stale and ineffective after a while. Having members of both genders in a club motivates everyone to continuously be better members and put forth better efforts in meeting the mission of our association. Women see things from a different perspective than men; therefore, when both are together in one setting, the organization is better and stronger."

Photo Gallery

1—4. Since its founding, Lions Clubs International has been headquartered at four locations: (1) Insurance Exchange Building,

(2) McCormick Building and

(3) 209 North Michigan building, all in downtown Chicago.

(4) In 1971, the association moved to the modern and eventually
expanded headquarters in suburban Oak Brook.

5. Melvin Jones seldom missed a day in his office at headquarters until shortly before his death in 1961.

6. This is the only known photo taken at the historic first convention at the Adolphus Hotel in Dallas, Texas. Melvin Jones is seated on the far left at the head table.

7. Members of the Chicago Central Lions Club pose for this 1919 group photo in front of one of the lions guarding the entrance to the Art Institute in Chicago. Melvin Jones is shown in the center.

8. (A & B) Helen Keller and her teacher, Anne Sullivan, are shown meeting with Dr. Alexander Graham Bell in this 100-year-old photograph from the archives of the Chautauqua Institution. In June 1939, Helen Keller is greeted by school children upon her arrival in Roanoke, Virginia, where she addressed the Lions state convention.

9. (A & B) Marching bands and the flags of the association's family of nations highlight every parade at the international conventions.

10. Liberty Day Kids quiz adults on the U.S. Constitution upon their arrival for a meeting at the University of Denver.

11. Leos often provide eye screenings for children.

12. In Malaysia, these Leos participate in an "Earth Day" project by making a bin for aluminum cans.

13. Pin trading at international conventions, such as depicted here at the 2002 Convention in Osaka, Japan, is a great way to promote friendship and good will.

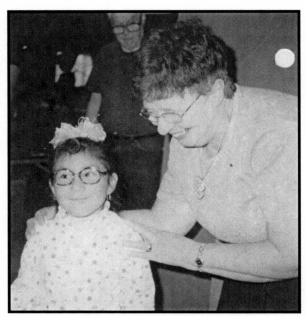

14. This little girl is thrilled with a successful fitting of eyeglasses during a mission of Indiana Lions to Mexico. Lion Mary Deering was a member of the team.

15. Lion Chuck Knight instructs this young archer at the range at Camp Dot-So-La-Lee, sponsored by the Lions of Nevada.

16. A torch signals the beginning of the Games at the Opening Eyes Program, conducted with Special Olympics.

17. Acapulco, Mexico, Lions and their spouses distributed food, clothing and other necessities to people after Hurricane Pauline devastated the city in 1997.

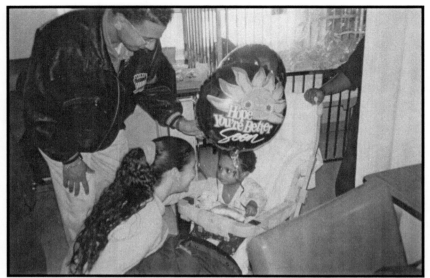

18. Brooklyn Caribe, New York, Leos visit children at the Flushing Medical Hospital.

19. The Dublin-San Ramon, California, Lions Club constructed this playground with special equipment for children with disabilities.

20. This Lion feeds a baby at an orphanage in Lagos, Nigeria.

21. Members of the Akron Goodyear Heights, Ohio, Lions Club
raise the walls for a house they constructed for a family in need
through Habitat for Humanity.

22. Dirty fingers are proudly displayed by RCMP Constable Al Ramey (left),
Lion Peter Thomas and five-year old Dustin Krewenki.
The Nanaimo Hub City Lions Club in British Columbia, Canada, conducted
a free finger painting session at a local child development centre and
donated 250 child identification kits to the facility.
(photo by Glenn Olsen, courtesy of the Daily News)

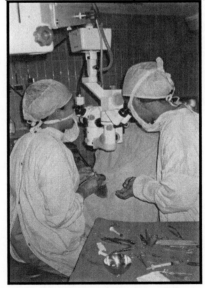

23. This eye surgery in Madagascar is one of thousands to have been
funded through a SightFirst grant.

24. Costumes and dress-up day are part of the fun at the Easter Seal Camp, sponsored by the Lions Society of British Columbia, Canada.

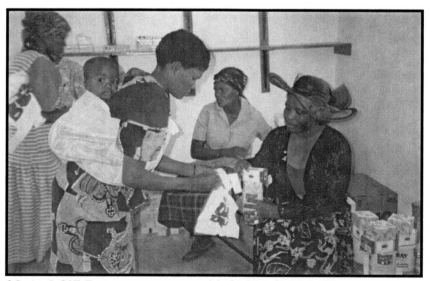

25. An LCIF Emergency grant enabled Lions in Botswana to distribute relief supplies to residents following a flood.

26. Lions from Grand Prairie, Alberta, Canada, gather behind a portion of the used eyeglasses the Lions sent to Sri Lanka.

27. Members of the Four Hills Mobile Home Park Lions Club of Albuquerque, New Mexico, gather around Victoria Gallegos and present her with a new Spinoza Buddy Bear to help give her comfort as she recovers from a bacterial infection which resulted from the amputation of her hands and feet.

28. This girl works on a project at the Georgia Camp for the Blind.

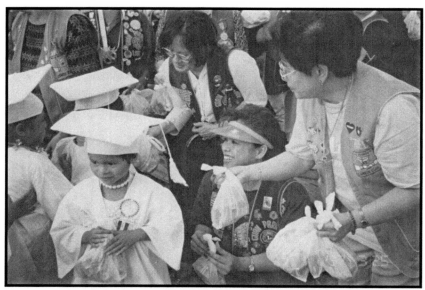

29. Members of the Guam Paradise Lions Club and the Iloilo Integrated
Lions Club of the Philippines present Easter bags to children at the Iloilo
Club's Day Care Center during a graduation ceremony.

30. Bedford, Indiana, Lions (from left) Walt Fishel, Billy Don Baker and Charles Wellman are shown building a ramp for a wheelchair resident. After its completion, the Lions installed carpeting.

31. In Cameroon, Lions distribute ivermectin to prevent the spread of river blindness, a major objective of SightFirst.

32. These Lions enthusiastically celebrate completing the course at a Lions Clubs International Leadership Institute.

33. Lions distribute used eyeglasses at a medical clinic sponsored by the La Union Lions Club in the Philippines.

34. Jill Giovanelli, grand prize winner of the 1992-93 Peace Poster Contest, explains the significance of her winning entry to International President James Coffey and former U.S. Astronaut Dr. Mae Jemison at Lions Day with the United Nations. Dr. Jemison served as spokesperson for the contest.

35. During the parade at the 2002 International Convention in Osaka, Japan, Lions of Multiple District 20 (New York and Bermuda) show their appreciation for the humanitarian assistance Lions provided following the World Trade Center tragedy.

36. Uganda President Yoweri Musevani thanks Past Council President
Steiner Gjertsen of Norway for the leadership role Norwegian Lions
played in building two eye clinics in his nation.

37. Members of the Toyama Jinzu Leo Club in Japan and their
sponsoring Lions held a wheelchair soccer game for disabled youth. The
Leos competed in wheelchairs.

38. In Nigeria, nursery school students are escorted across a street by members of the Akpaburyo Island Calabar Leos as part of a club project to teach the youngsters traffic safety.

39. Lions send food grains to affected areas following the 2001 earthquake in Gujarat, India.

40. Lions Day with the United Nations at UN Headquarters in New York is annually attended by hundreds of association members.

41. In Colombia, these girls celebrate their completion of a Lions Quest course.

42. A SightFirst grant made it possible for Lions in Nepal to provide double cataract surgery for this now happy elderly gentleman.

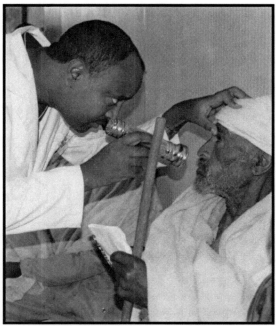

43. SightFirst funding in Africa is providing thousands of eye exams for people who would otherwise have no access to such a service.

44. Responding to the 9/11 disaster, Lions unload tons of supplies at Shea Stadium in New York. From left are Past District Governor Jeff Jerome, District Governor Gloria Burton and Past District Governor Tom DiLorio.

45. In Mali, International President Jim Ervin watches as former United States President Jimmy Carter, accompanied by his wife, Rosalynn, signs an agreement of understanding with that nation in the fight against blindness.

209

46.   A project of the North Sea Lions Alliance was to construct this
Tuberculosis Rehabilitation Center in Katutura, Namibia.

47.   The Branch Lions Club in Reykholar, Iceland, donated books to
local school children.

48. There's nothing like the thrill of catching the "big one" as this youngster shows when participating in the Florida Lions Camp's Reaching Out To Cancer Kids (R.O.C.K. Camp).

49. Lions Worldwide Induction Day was a big hit in Turkey when 57 clubs in District 118-Y inducted 272 members.

50. Ranging in age from 16 to 24, young men and women from 16 nations enjoyed an 11-day International Youth Camp in 1997 in Maastricht, Holland, as guests of the local Lions.

51. Past International Presidents Dr. Jean Behar and J. Frank Moore III present the ceremonial LCIF check representing the second phase of Lions SightFirst China Action to Chairman Deng Pufeng of the China Disabled Persons' Federation. Ma Xiao Wei, vice minister, Ministry of Health, is at left and Wu Jie Ping, vice chairman of the Congress, is at right.

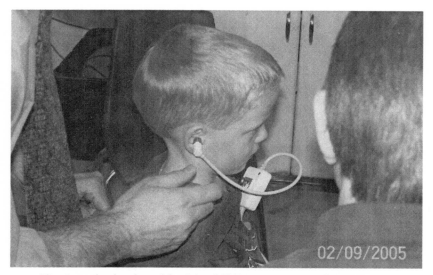

52. A probe is placed in this child's ear as part of the hearing screening program for local preschoolers, sponsored by the Spokane Central, Washington, Lions Club.

53. A child in Bangkok, Thailand, is fitted with a new pair of eyeglasses as part of LCIF's Sight for Kids program which is supported by Johnson & Johnson.

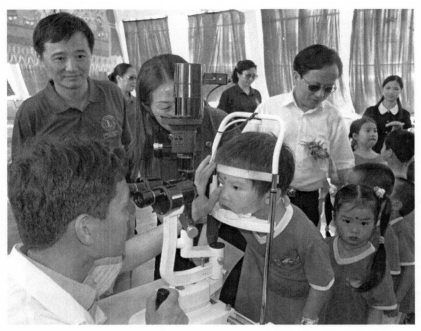

54. Lions assist as a young boy is screened during a program in
Shenzhen, China

55. New members are inducted into the Campus Branch Lions Club
at the University of Wisconsin - La Crosse.

56. District 307-B (Indonesia) Governor Charles Ong Saerang delivers supplies to victims of the Tsunami disaster.

57. Lions unload supplies destined for victims of Hurricane Katrina.

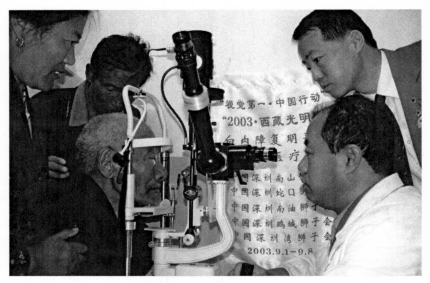

58. This sight screening is held for patients in Tibet, China.

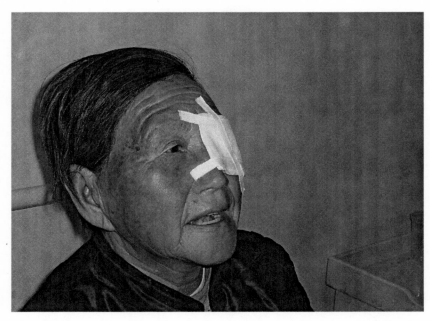

59. This patient has just received cataract surgery as part of SightFirst
China Action.

60. Lions help deliver relief supplies in Thailand in the wake of the tsunami.

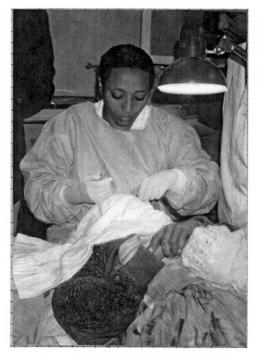

61. An Ethiopian nurse trained by a SightFirst grant operates on a patient with advanced trachoma.

62. "He's the best friend I ever had," says Southeastern Guide Dogs graduate Steven Mercer, taking a stroll with his guide dog, Austin.

63. Dr. Richard Kinney (seated), director of the Hadley School for the Blind in Winnetka, Illinois, studies the world globe. With him are, from left, Past International President Lloyd Morgan and his wife, Ngaire, and Past District 1-A Governor John Massengill and his wife, Diana.

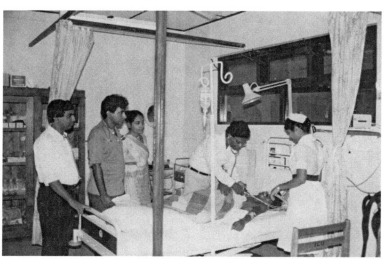

64. The Lions Intensive Care Unit in Baroda, India, a project of District 323-F was, when this photo was taken in 1993, available to more than 500,000 area residents.

65. Lion Polly Letofsky is joined by supporters for a jaunt along the California coast in her successful worldwide walk to raise awareness for breast cancer..

66. Dr. Tae-Sup Lee, 2004-2005 chairperson of the LCIF Executive Committee, sounds the gong to officially launch Campaign SightFirst II at the 2005 International Convention in Hong Kong.

67. Lions celebrate the first year of Campaign SightFirst II by signing banners of support during the 89th International Convention in Boston, Massachusetts.

68. A Japanese Lion leads children in Cambodia to their new school. LCIF provided a US$15,673 International Assistance grant for Lions in Japan's District 333-B to build the school.

69. Nearly 20 retreats for families of 9/11 victims were supported by LCIF in order to help the healing process. At this camp in West Virginia, children were entertained by New York City police officer Danny Rodriguez.

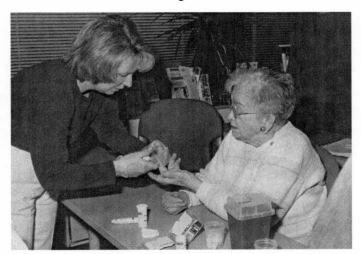

70. Learning to test oneself is crucial to living successfully with diabetes. Patients receive this instruction at the UPMC McKeesport Lions Diabetes Education and Training Center, built by the Lions of Pennsylvania's District 14-B. Lions in District 14-C join with their fellow Lions in 14-B to raise funds in its support and to help low income individuals buy their diabetes medication.

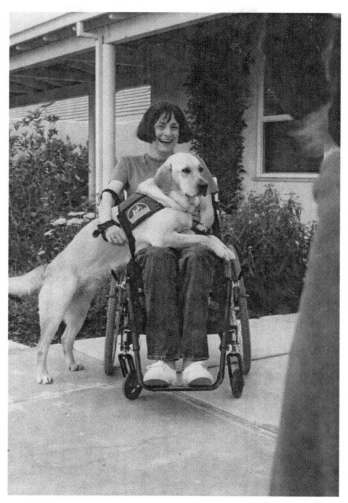

71. Dr. Jane Veith, a quadriplegic and her canine companion, Elijay, enjoy a light-hearted moment. She received Elijay from Santa Rosa, California-based Canine Companions for Independence. The Lake Wylie (River Hills), South Carolina, Lioness Lions Club hosted a luncheon for her and donated $20,000 to Canine Companions where Dr. Veith and Elijay received their team training. Canine Companions for Independence is heavily supported by numerous Lions clubs.

Chapter Ten
Youth Programs

"If you are going to achieve excellence in big things, you've developed the habit in little matters. Excellence is not an exception, it is a prevailing attitude," said former United States Secretary of State Colin Powell. General Powell is quoted from an interview that appeared in the Headquarters edition of THE LION magazine in May 2000.

Born in Harlem to immigrant parents from Jamaica, he lived a rough life in the inner city. He overcame a barely average start in school, then joined the Army and the rest is history. General Powell was a professional soldier for 35 years, and during that time, held myriad command and staff positions. He has received numerous United States military and civilian awards and decorations and has been honored by 18 foreign countries. At the time of the interview he was chairman of America's Promise – The Alliance for Youth, a national crusade aimed at producing a significant nationwide increase in positive youth development support for all children who need help.

In the interview for THE LION Magazine General Powell talked about the history and goals of America's Promise and precisely how members of Lions Clubs International were involved. "The Lions' involvement is very important because of the many thousands of tapes that the Lions have distributed encouraging youngsters to do the fifth part of America's Promise – to give back, to serve the community. Lions can serve as mentors, for example, in a school where kids are in trouble or in despair and where they could benefit most from the kind of talent and commitment to service one sees in the Lions clubs."

Throughout their history Lions clubs have done just that all over the world, serving as effective catalysts in their communities to improve lives. For example, Mexican Lions have been building schools for more than half a century.

Ricardo Morales, 23, is a Mexico City journalist with the newspaper *La Tribuna*. His education began 17 years ago in a grammar school built by the local Lions club. "The Lions got me started in school," said Morales, "and then they encouraged me to go through high school and college. I have a great career today because the Lions were willing to make an investment in me, just as they have done for thousands of other young people in our country. I don't know what my life would have been like without them, but I'm sure I would not be enjoying the career I have or the great future that lies ahead."

Ever since Rodolfo Fernandez founded the Mexico City Lions Club in 1931, the first in that nation, Lions clubs have been a vigorous force in improving the lives of citizens in Mexico.

"One of the major projects of the Lions of Mexico has been building schools," said Antonio Ortiz Vargas, Past District B-6 Governor. A Lion for 23 years, he continued, "We built our first school in Mexico City in 1949 and to date have constructed 13 grammar schools which operate through the sixth grade. We have, in fact, constructed 23 schools throughout District B-6. They include four schools in the state of Guerrero for children who only speak the local Indian dialect. Education is the foundation of the future for the people of Mexico and we value this project highly."

District B-6 includes the popular vacation resorts of Cuernavaca, Taxco and Acapulco. Since 1985, Lions Clubs International Foundation grants to District B-6 have totaled $360,721 and helped build 10 grammar schools and one young adult night school in Mexico City. In addition to this, $60,000 was directed to hurricane relief.

It costs $200,000 to build each school, which operates on two shifts, morning and afternoon, in order to generate the maximum benefit. The Mexican government contributes the running expenses by providing teachers, books and other supplies. The Lions are effective in attracting support to get construction materials and additional services as reasonably as possible.

"By building schools, we help the government and help the children through promoting the objectives of Lions to improve behavior and general attitude," said Edmundo Borraza Robles. "These kinds of projects typify Lionism at its best and enable the people of Mexico to see precisely how the principles of Lions benefit the people, their communities and the entire country."

The Lions of District B-6 raise money for the schools through parties, breakfasts, raffles, beauty contests, donations from individual members, bingo and other activities that draw contributions from local citizens.

The Lions furnish clothing for the children, which includes trousers, shirts, underwear, shoes and a sweater. They also serve breakfast or lunch to the youngsters each day. In addition, the Lions support sports programs such as soccer and basketball by providing equipment for the games as well as instruction.

"We furnish health services for the children," said Enrique Montes Romo, "and see that they have physical and dental examinations and any necessary treatment, all at no charge. We're investing in the future of Mexico by helping these boys and girls get a good education and adequate health care."

He continued, "In Mexico, we are seeing an interesting phenomenon in that the sons of Lions are forming their own clubs. As they become Lions and part of the Lion family, many of them will then start another Lions club, thus ensuring the continuing growth of our association."

One of the many success stories of Lions' assistance is a 22-year-old woman who was crippled by polio when she was a child and became a weightlifter. She bench presses 90 kilos (198 pounds) and holds the women's weightlifting record for her weight. She works for the Olympic Committee, 50 percent of which is composed of Lions clubs members.

She observed, "The Lions made a dramatic impact on my life. They helped me get an education and gave me the needed hope, support and strength that changed me from a crippled girl to a champion athlete. Over and over again, they are making the difference for men, women and children in Mexico and I'm grateful for their presence."

****

Sparked by a $30,000 grant from the Lions Clubs International Foundation, German Lions are giving a second chance to troubled youths with a metal working school in Berlin. More than 120 young people have been put on the right path since the school opened in 1985. It's one of three connected projects of the Berlin Lions.

Andre is a graduate of the project. Now 24, he came to the school after a long history as an incorrigible delinquent. His delinquency began at the age of eight with stealing and truancy and he suffered from many problems associated with his anti-social behavior. Arriving at the shop when he was 19, he spent two years there being trained and showed a genuine gift for the craft. Now employed as a metal working apprentice, he is taking advanced technical training simultaneously.

"I thought my life was always going to be rotten," said Andre, "and I didn't really have much hope it would be better when I came to the school. I had been in trouble with the police all my life and didn't have any place else to go. I was referred there by the church's youth center. I could tell the people at the shop were interested in me but they made sure I understood that I had to behave properly. They didn't put up with any nonsense. I learned that early and also found that I really enjoyed working with metal. The harder I tried, the more they taught me and now I've developed a lot of skill and see that I can develop a great deal more."

There are many other success stories. One of them is Michael, who is 18 and spent a year-and-a-half at the metal working shop after an extremely unproductive, trouble-filled childhood and adolescence. Michael suffers from dyslexia, a learning disorder in which the individual reverses letters and numbers and finds it difficult to comprehend printed material. It is a family trait; his seven brothers and sisters are all dyslexic, too. Through treatment by the social workers and reading specialists, his dyslexia improved somewhat. He learned his trade well and he's now the house mechanic at a large hotel in Berlin.

"My life was going nowhere until I got to the shop," Michael said. "I was always frustrated in school because I couldn't read and the other kids made fun of me. They said I was stupid and I felt stupid. I got into trouble with the law because of anger at the condition of my life. Stealing seemed to be the only thing I was good at. At the metal working shop I found something else I was good at and that was working as a mechanic. The social workers in the program helped me to read well enough to do a good job at my trade. They also taught me the importance of being honest and thorough in my work and being prompt at reporting for a job. Along with working at the hotel I'm taking additional training in the evening and can see now that my life can be very good. When I came to the project I had no hope and my life was bad. The Lions made the difference."

The $30,000 grant from LCIF was an important factor in the success of the project. When it began in 1985, Lions thought the project would cost $20,000; the cost actually ended up at $200,000. As it got bigger, the need also grew for more money for machines and other equipment. The $200,000 includes the contributions in machinery and services by various companies. The LCIF grant helped to attract other money and services and grow to the extent the project is today.

German Lions clubs have grown vigorously since the first one was chartered in Dusseldorf in 1951. Today, more than 27,000 German Lions in 825 clubs improve the lives of those around them. Andre and Michael are just a few.

International Youth Camps

Lions Clubs International came to the Netherlands when the Amsterdam (Host) Lions Club began meeting in 1951. Today, 10,000 Lions meet regularly in 400 clubs. Vigorous and growing, Lions clubs flourish because of such programs as international youth camps.

In June 1997, 25 young men and women from 16 nations spent 11 days in Maastricht, Holland, as guests of the local Lions. Ranging in age from 16 to 24, nine boys and 16 girls composed the group of participants. Each camper enjoyed a private room and an unforgettable experience.

Many of them echo the words of 17-year-old Simone Martinetto, of Italy, who said: "I had read a lot about Holland before I came here. I was expecting a beautiful country, but this is even better than I anticipated. Wherever we went, we saw flowers and plants. I understand they bloom all year long; it was almost like living in a greenhouse."

The list of countries represented at the international youth camp reads like a small United Nations. Included were Japan, Israel, Canada, Turkey, Denmark, Italy, Norway, Peru, Poland, Finland, United States, Sweden, Slovakia, Indonesia, Hong Kong and Belarus.

"Our objective was not to be simply a vacation camp," said Theo Fabius, a founding member of the eight-year-old Eysden-Mergelland Lions Club. "We gathered young people from around the world to foster international cooperation and understanding of culture, trade and industry. I think our 1997 camp was successful on all counts."

The cost of the 1997 camp was $15,000 and was raised by the Lions clubs of Eysden-Mergelland, Maastricht-Euregio, Maastricht-Trajectum, Maastricht-Mondial, Weert and Sittard-Galeen and supported by many Lions clubs in District 110-CO.

The central theme of the 1997 camp was "Unification of Europe." The young people visited Amsterdam, Brussels, Maastricht and Aachen, among other interesting destinations. Maastricht is the historic capital of Limburg, where an ancient bridge links the banks of the river Meuse. It's a city of charming squares, historic buildings and picturesque views. Its history reaches back to the beginning of our era when the Romans founded the settlement called Mosae Trajectum.

"Our program was ambitious and educational," explained Dr. G. J. B. Verbeet, a Lion for 15 years and a member of the Maastricht-Euregio club. "A Dutch girl and boy accompanied the campers as guides on each activity, but the youngsters got tired and had little time to relax. They liked the Dutch people and the Dutch people liked them."

"Unquestionably," emphasized District 110-CO Governor Joop van der Meulen, "this kind of activity is invaluable for enhancing international understanding. When I talked to the group and gave each of the young people the flag of the district, I could see they were all impressed with what the Lions do in the Netherlands and understood that the Lions provide this kind of service in nearly every part of the world. The campers saw Lionism in action."

Along with the organizing Lions clubs, a total of 32 clubs contributed financially to the 1997 Youth Camp.

The participants made an all-day trip to Amsterdam, which has Europe's largest preserved city center with more than 7,000 designated landmarks. It's world famous for the four rings of canals around the oldest part of the city. The Dutch have reclaimed a quarter of their country from the ocean. With dikes, dams and windmills, they have rolled back the lakes and sea and created land where once there was water. Another quarter lies so low that if not for the thousands of dikes and dams, the sea would cover it at high tide.

Nineteen-year-old Tomoko Sagrai of Japan found Amsterdam especially interesting, particularly the Anne Frank house and the trip on a canal boat. "Also," she pointed out, "I enjoyed the museums in Amsterdam because I had read a great deal about the Dutch culture and I found that they have more than 2,000 years of history in Amsterdam and it was my first opportunity to study this firsthand. The camp was very well organized and the Lions certainly worked hard in making sure we had an enjoyable visit."

"I enjoyed the whole camp," said John McCurdy, 17, of Cumberland, Iowa. "The Lions had organized everything very carefully and we used all of our time effectively. I guess one of the things I found most interesting was the American Military Cemetery in Margraten because World War II happened a long time ago – before I was born, but I've always been interested in the history of my country."

"The camp gave me a better understanding of what the rest of the world is like," said Ann Makrinta, 18, of Finland. "I had never been far away from home before and when I arrived, I was a stranger. When I left a week and a half later, I had many new friends and a much greater understanding of the rest of the world. The Lions make the world smaller by increasing people's understanding of how large it is. It helps us see that though we come from different countries, we're all very much alike in important ways."

****

A few years ago at the opening ceremony of the Panama Lions Club Summer Camp, a well-dressed medical doctor gave a speech to the young campers. Speaking carefully in measured tones, he told the boys and girls of growing up in a poor family in the Panama City slums.

"It never occurred to me that my life could ever be any different," he said as the children listened intently. "Then, when I was nine years old something happened that put me on an entirely new road. I was given a chance to go to the Lions summer camp. I didn't know much about it except that it was bound to be an improvement in my life. I spent three weeks in the camp with 300 other boys from the slums. We played soccer, basketball, and I learned how to swim.

"The supervisors taught me manners, they taught me ethics, they talked to me about honesty and respecting my country. These were all ideas that were new to me but critically important in shaping my future life. While the Lions summer camp was not the only factor that played a part in my becoming a doctor, it certainly started me on a different road. The camp gave me hope and direction and the feeling that maybe I could become better than my environment. All of you youngsters today have the same opportunity."

The Panama Lions' story is impressive – they built a facility that brings hope and joy to youngsters who otherwise have little of either. Their history begins on August 24, 1935, when the Colon Lions Club was founded, thus enabling Panama to become the fifth nation to join the association.

The Panama Lions Club, located in Panama City, began on September 25, 1935, and today has 230 members. Presently, there are 52 Lions clubs in Panama with a membership of more than 1,500.

On a pleasant April morning in Panama City, Pedro Rodriguez, Clarence Marquez and Jorge Barnett of the Panama Lions Club talked about the summer camp.

"I'd say as a conservative estimate that the Lions summer camp has helped nearly 40,000 youngsters in the years it has been in existence," said Pedro Rodriguez, president of the Lions Summer Camp Committee 1991-92. "My father was president of the camp 1971-72 and he was a Lion for 32 years. He died in 1989 and had been an extremely involved Lion for all of those years.

"These kids are eight to 10 years old and streetwise," Rodriguez continued. "Our program brings discipline into their lives. It teaches them that they must help others and the older kids must be responsible and help the younger ones."

The camp staff includes 32 teachers, supervisors, monitors and maids. The youngsters from the slums don't have to make their own beds or clean their own dormitories. Maids take care of that. A home economist and skilled cooks and kitchen staff comprise the 18 people providing delicious, nutritious meals three times a day.

The campers play basketball, volleyball, baseball, soccer, and enjoy swimming in a large pool. They participate in field trips to museums, candy factories, folk dancing, and the Panama Canal.

Before starting the camping season, each child gets a free medical, eyesight and dental check-up provided by Lion doctors and dentists. A mobile dental clinic is there throughout the camping period to fix and extract teeth. Since many of these youngsters have never had a dental check-up, the work is very important to their lives.

Colgate-Palmolive donates toothbrushes and toothpaste for the youngsters, some of whom have never brushed their teeth before. The company also provides soap, detergents for washing clothes and cleaning materials to keep the facilities spotless.

Children who have a birthday during their time at the camp are given a party with cake, presents, noisemakers and songs. Understandably, many of these youngsters cry when they have to leave the camp.

High on the list of benefits of the summer camp is the clothing the youngsters receive. Each camper gets five sets of uniforms consisting of shorts and t-shirts, underwear, sneakers and socks, plus a sweater with the Lions emblem. The supervisors receive the same clothing items.

Someone once called the Lions champions at helping others. While not all of the youngsters who enjoyed the Panama Lions Summer Camp have become champions, they are all winners. At least one of them, Eusebio Pedroza, became a champion as well. Pedroza won the featherweight boxing championship of the world in 1978 at the age of 25.

Pedroza attended the Lions summer camp when he was 10. A youngster with neither direction nor opportunity, he got a look at the possibilities of life that he'd never before imagined. Eusebio Pedroza developed his talents and became world famous. The camp has also inspired thousands of other youngsters.

One of the campers, Juan Rios, summed up his experience. "I wanted to stay longer and I love it here, but I know that I have to give other kids a chance to come and enjoy this too."

✳✳✳✳✳✳✳✳✳✳✳✳✳✳✳✳✳✳✳✳✳✳✳✳✳✳

In Denver, Colorado, the spirit of Dominique Savio, the patron saint of youth, is still protecting and guiding his children. But he has taken the shape of a building and the heart of caring counselors, teachers and members of the Lions Club of Denver, Colorado.

For more than three decades, the Lions club has been supporting Savio House in west Denver, which it owns and operates with a single mission: To help children, adolescents and families suffering from violence, crime and neglect. Savio House offers programs to help families overcome destructive behaviors and embrace a quality of life that all children deserve. Since its modest beginnings in 1966 as a home for abandoned youth, Savio House has grown into a multi-service agency with more than 100 employees and a budget of $3.2 million a year.

The Lions Club of Denver has raised more than $3.5 million over a span of 26 years to help more than 6,500 children and families at Savio House, according to Denver Lion William Hildenbrand, for more than 20 years Savio's executive director. In 1974, the Denver Lions took sole leadership of Savio House and have since directed its development into one of the nation's pre-eminent children and family treatment centers. In addition to the club's direct contributions of time and money, Lions work with Hildenbrand and his staff to obtain funds from private foundations and individuals. Funding also comes from local, state and federal agencies.

"The Lions Club of Denver takes a great deal of pride in the success of the Savio House, a major community project for many years," said Hildenbrand. "Our goal is to eradicate violence, substance abuse, child abuse and other destructive behaviors in families. Our programs are designed to instill in a child or adolescent the attitudes and skills needed to be a successful, contributing member of his or her family and community."

Today, Savio House provides residential, education, counseling, day treatment, recreational and in-home services so that boys and girls, most of whom are teenagers, and their families can improve their quality of life. At the same time, the Savio staff protects, loves and cares for its youthful clientele to promote their growth in positive ways.

Savio offers 14 multi-faceted accredited programs to meet client needs. Its residential program, accredited by the Council on Accreditation of Services for Families and Children, Inc., provides round-the-clock shelter and supervision, if necessary. Services range from psychiatric care and therapy to providing education. Savio's day treatment program provides day-time help that combines such elements as behavioral therapy, school, sports and recreation.

"Adolescent clients, who range in age from 14 to 21 years, are considered very high risk juveniles," said Sara Stoner, CBS coordinator. "They have spent time in jail for such offenses as auto theft, burglary and assaults. To graduate from our program, they must successfully transition back into the family and community with no further police contact. And they must stay in school or go to work."

Tim is one such client. Before joining Savio House, Tim, now 16, stole cars and violated his probation. Such activity could have landed him in a correctional facility. "He was beyond the control of his parents, and they had almost given up," Stoner explained. "They wanted him to follow their rules by attending school and ending his gang involvement and substance abuse. Tim was court-ordered by his judge to join our program."

And he did. Savio House counselors and Tim's parents worked together to establish a system of rules and consequences. Over the next five months, Tim's hostility toward his parents diminished and he says he wants to finish school, get a job and stay out of jail, according to Stoner.

Another young Savio client, John, was 14 and considered a depressive with psychotic features when the court ordered him to enter Savio's residential program. John had spent time in a detention facility for stealing car radios. He had also been abusing alcohol and drugs and not attending school. And there was evidence of parental abuse and domestic violence at home, notes Alida Fischer of Savio's residential treatment center.

"John wasn't talking when he entered our program," Fischer recalled. "He cried a lot. It took a lot of patience to work with him, but he began to explore more acceptable behaviors."

At Savio House, John got plenty of attention and no longer had to "act crazy" to get noticed, said Fischer. He began attending school at Savio and adhering to its rules and structures. Eventually, through a process that included family involvement as well as cognitive behavioral therapy (which helps patients connect their thoughts to behaviors), John began to make better choices. He now attends regular school and recently received a job promotion at a popular Denver amusement park.

"We work with families to give them better parenting skills," explained Fischer. "And we encourage pro-social attitudes and values in their kids."

Swedish Lions of Multiple District 101 sponsor a Lions Folk Music Camp in Jamtland, Sweden, for boys and girls from 16 to 23 who can play the violin.

In August 1988, 16-year-old Anthony Millar traveled from his home in River Forest, Illinois, to Sweden to take part in the Lions International Camp for Diabetic Teenagers. Then a student at Oak Park-River Forest High School, Anthony enjoys lacrosse, water skiing, and snow skiing. He became a diabetic at the age of four.

"The camp is about an hour and a half from Stockholm and it was great," he said with a smile. "It really helped me with my diabetes. I used to eat candy even though my mother told me not to. These kids just amazed me because they wouldn't go near it. We had a doctor there who is an expert on diabetes, Dr. Johnny Ludvigsson. After breakfast we'd go to the conference room and discuss topics. He talked about self-control, fibers, diet, meal planning, alcohol, and other subjects that affect the diabetic. I learned a lot that I hadn't known before, including different types of insulin techniques."

"After the morning discussion we played games until lunch," Anthony continued. "The afternoon was free time and we'd spend it canoeing, swimming, or playing soccer or volleyball. I'd never traveled to a different country before. I flew from Chicago to Copenhagen and then to Stockholm and then took a train the rest of the way. They have great trains. I was sponsored by the Berwyn, Illinois, Lions

Club. They filled out my application for the camp, sent it to Sweden, and I was accepted. It was an outstanding experience."

Anthony was the only American among the 30 boys and girls attending. Others came from England, Denmark, Germany, Switzerland, Austria, and Sweden. All the campers spoke English, the official language of the camp. Anthony spent two weeks before the camp visiting with District Governor Lars Lundstrom. "His family is really nice," said Anthony. "They went out of their way to be hospitable. They have a 17-year-old son and a 15-year-old daughter. Lars and the other Lions took us to see Stockholm and other points of interest in their country. They were very thoughtful hosts."

The aims of the camp are fourfold, explained Dr. Ludvigsson, the specialist in diabetes. "The camp is designed to: 1) reward and encourage diabetic teenagers; 2) stimulate international contacts between youngsters; 3) provide education about modern active treatment for diabetes; and 4) spread ideas about active treatment of diabetes in different countries."

Rose Ann Millar, Anthony's mother, called his experience in Sweden "wonderful." She added, "I think seeing that there are so many other kids with diabetes gave him a feeling that he wasn't the only one who had to take shots on an outing and be careful of his diet. He met great kids that he really liked and learned a great deal about diabetes and its management. Finding out that he can travel by himself gave him confidence. He's happier and more outgoing than he was before going to Sweden. The experience has been very, very positive for him."

The Iowa Lions Youth Camp in Madrid, Iowa, is another example of how Lions as citizens of the world are promoting a world without borders and fostering international understanding among the future leaders of the world.

The camp is 100 percent supported by Iowa Lions clubs. Campers pay nothing for the time they spend in the camp's 1,100 acres of woods, river, meadow, lodge and comfortable dormitory housing.

As campers, visitors from several countries participate in activities such as swimming, archery, skeet shooting, Frisbee, golf, volleyball, softball, soccer, canoeing and dancing.

"It may be that ours is the only Lions camp in the world which offers campers the chance to soar into the air aboard a hot air balloon for a bird's-eye view of the countryside," Orlin E. Buck, the Iowa Lions Club youth coordinator pointed out. "Dedicated balloonists interested in our project frequently bring in their balloons and launching equipment and take our kids for a ride," Buck explained.

"Each of the nine districts in Iowa is asked to provide a boy or girl as a counselor, and all meal preparation and other work in the camp is handled by volunteer Lions, Lionesses, and spouses (or family members)," Buck continued. "We also assign two or three foreign youths to help campers having problems with language or cultural differences, so the camping experience usually goes very smoothly for every camper."

There is a drug abuse program where campers describe drug or alcohol problems in their home countries. There are also some strictly enforced rules. "No drinking or drugs, no boys in girls' quarters or vice versa, and we discourage smoking."

A highlight of the one-week camping experience is when foreign youths explain their flag and their country to other campers.

Does the camp really break down the barriers and bring youths from many different countries closer?

"You just have to believe it does on the last day of camp when you see how close these new-found friends have grown and how reluctant they are to part," Buck said. "Our camp motto is 'We met as strangers, but leave as friends,' and I can see the motto has become a reality. When these boys and girls leave us they are friends."

Another testament came from Kare of Denmark who attended the camp in Mount Brydges (Districts A-1/A-2 Lions Clubs International Friendship Youth Camp, Canada). "I came to the camp with quite a lot of fear and skepticism. I was afraid of being shy and not being a part of the group. Usually, I don't make friends easily.

"In this camp I met some wonderful human beings whom I am going to keep as my dearest friends forever. All 34 of us became friends in spite of culture, religion and opinions. We took the first giant step toward the happy and absolutely necessary reunion of all the people on this earth. I have gained belief in a global understanding and peace; a peace growing out of happiness and joy, thanks to all

Lions and Lionesses. I wish with all my heart that this was more than a one-time experience."

The Norwegian Lions camp is dual purpose in that it allows able-bodied youths to volunteer to assist the disabled campers and learn camp management. The primary purpose, of course, is to help the disabled young people develop their own possibilities and establish relationships with other disabled people of their own age from many different countries.

In only a year of organizing, the Lions Club of Lofoten, Norway, with help from clubs in District 104-A, organized a very successful camp that promoted "international friendship north of the Arctic Circle."

"We definitely did not want it to be a vacation camp," explained Ame Christoffersen, club president. "The intention was to gather youths from around the world with an interest in international cooperation and understanding, culture, trade and industry." In all, the two-week camp attracted 28 persons from Norway and 14 different countries in 1986, its first year. Participants also spent another week in the homes of host families.

Campers visited commercial and industrial companies, schools, and museums, heard presentations about one another's countries, and went fishing and climbed mountains.

"We got many reports that many of the participants were getting together privately in several countries for discussions similar to those fostered in camp," said Christoffersen. "That was proof that the camp was not a vacation camp and had achieved the objectives we had set for it."

****

Sixteen-year-old Meagan Daniels is looking forward to another summer at Lions Bear Lake Camp in Lapeer, Michigan, about 50 miles northeast of Detroit. She enjoys climbing the 40-foot wall, navigating the rope courses, playing baseball, trying archery and making bead jewelry and crafts with pipe cleaners. She has been attending the 160-bed camp for the past seven years.

Fiercely independent, Meagan has been blind from birth because of complications from a premature delivery, but she doesn't let the disability limit her enjoyment of the camp. Her favorite event is the talent show when campers in each cabin get together and perform a skit on the final night of camp.

Her parents, William and Linda Daniels, are as fond of the camp as she is. "If you could have dreamed of a camp you wanted to go to as a kid, this is it," said William Daniels.

Linda Daniels added, "With all the campers together, their visual impairment becomes invisible. It's a wonderful opportunity to be with friends who have similar problems."

Campers come from all over Michigan and everything is free. There are no fees or costs to the campers and their families. The camp is supported by the Lions clubs of Michigan and is under the guidance of Dennis Tomkins, of Lapeer. He has been the director for two years and is currently spearheading a campaign to raise $800,000 for a new dining hall. The Lions camp was founded in 1982 by Past District Governor Al Kassin, a member of the Lake Orion Lions Club.

The camp has grown steadily in the last 20 years and in 2003, the summer schedule was increased from two weeks to eight weeks. Many Lions' camps are founded initially for a single purpose – to help blind youth, or deaf young people, or those with some other physical disability. Often, the clubs operating these single-purpose camps have found it an easy and natural step to broaden their operations to include various other disabilities. This is true of the Lions Bear Lake Camp.

According to Tomkins, "The program at the camp is designed to meet the needs of the special campers that it serves. The aim is to help children become self-reliant, self-confident and independent while having loads of fun."

Camper Laura White, 14, has been coming to Bear Lake Camp since she was seven. She is blind, and says she loves to camp because it gives her just the right amount of independence that any teenagers needs.

"It's not like we're helpless because we're blind," she emphasized. "In the city, people are like 'your shoe is untied, want me to get it for you'? But we don't need that. Here, they don't act like that."

April Thurston, 16, agreed. "Yeah, there are a lot of things that we can do here that we can't do anywhere else. Here, we're with a crowd of our own. Nobody makes fun of you."

Bill Walling has been a Lion since 1974 and he and his wife, Dorothy, volunteer at the camp each summer. Dorothy worked as a special education teacher in the Lake Orion School District before retiring.

Bill Walling is always looking out for ways to help the campers. He rigged up his special bus to assist many of the campers with their luggage and give them a ride to the cabins from the parking lot.

"The kids are happy and grateful," Walling said. "There's a great deal of satisfaction in having my wife volunteer her time at the camp with the two of us working side by side. We're a team."

The camp enjoys an international flavor. Several years ago, of the 22 camp counselors on duty, three were from Australia, one from England, one from Sweden and one came from South Africa.

Children enjoy different aspects of the camping program. Telling scary stories at night really was the high point of the camp for 11-year-old Mike Borowicz, of Lake Orion. For Marc Henninger, 12, "The best part of the camp so far is the swimming, boating and soccer. The cabins are great and the counselors are the best," he said enthusiastically.

Each young camper takes home a different perspective. Joy, laughter, a sense of wonder – campers enjoy them all during the exhilarating experiences they share at Lions Bear Lake Camp.

****

Bear Lake Camp is one of numerous Lions-sponsored outdoor facilities that provide youngsters having disabilities with the opportunity to enjoy themselves in activities that before would not have been possible. Consider this scenario:

The children are divided into small groups. Some are playing baseball, others, volleyball. The clank of horseshoes can be heard not far away and, indoors, ping pong, bowling and less strenuous games such as dominoes, chess and checkers are occupying the interest on kids. The place: a summer camp in Texas. What's so unusual about boys and girls taking part in myriad activities at a summer camp? Let's take another look. Every child here displays some type of handicap. Some are on crutches or in braces; others in wheelchairs. Many are blind. The camp is in Kerrville, in the hill country northwest of San Antonio, and it is a normal day at this, the Texas Lions Camp. Opened in 1953, it is one of the oldest and largest Lions-sponsored camps for disabled children.

It began as an idea of the Kerrville Lions Club to provide a place where crippled youngsters could be taught skills that would make them less dependent and, by associating with other children with disabilities, show that they are not alone. The idea grew until it became a statewide project of the Texas Lions. Eventually, blind and deaf boys and girls joined the physically disabled at the camp. Blind adults also attend special classes, September through May, and are taught a variety of vocational skills, techniques of daily living and mobility training. During the summer, special camping sessions are even held for children with diabetes.

Since it opened, the Texas Lions Camp has provided thousands of children with an opportunity, at no cost to their families, to rise above their disabilities to become independent and confident in their ability to live happy, fulfilling lives.

Kerrville does not stand alone in the world of Lions Clubs International. A number of other camps and other facilities, sponsored by Lions clubs, districts and multiple districts are providing youngsters with disabilities with a *chance of a lifetime*...certainly a "hand up" that they find priceless and rewarding.

Leesville, Louisiana, is another site where handicapped children participate in a variety of outdoor camping activities. Sponsored by the Louisiana Society for Crippled Children, boys and girls learn that braces and wheelchairs need not be barriers to enjoying a full and rewarding life. The generous support of Louisiana Lions provides facilities whereby children can participate in activities they never before dreamed available to them. Again, Camp Tatiyee in Arizona, sponsored by the Lions of Arizona, is yet another example of the ways Lions are opening new frontiers for youngsters with disabilities. Located in the scenic White Mountains, Camp Tatiyee opened in 1961. It is aptly named, for in the Navajo language, the word, "tatiyee" means "handicapped." Here, youngsters from seven years of age who suffer a variety of crippling conditions, are able to enjoy sports, fishing, swimming, train rides, parties, sing-a-longs, crafts and a variety of outdoor adventures. Modern dormitories, a craft building, dining hall and a trained staff assure them of a memorable camping experience.

Such camps are worldwide in scope. In Nairobi, Kenya, Lions sponsor an athletic program for physically and mentally handicapped youngsters, and in Japan, in 1966, Lions and their wives in an entire region "adopted" children at a camp for one day, bringing them food and presents.

These and many other camps, organized and financed by Lions, continue to give this *hand up* to young people who are blind, deaf, physically disabled, mentally challenged or diabetic, or who live in circumstances that deprive them of chances to enjoy the great outdoors.

In Antigua, Guatemala, Juan Hernandez is smiling because of the Lions. Born with a cleft lip and palate, when Juan was six years old, a Guatemalan medical team working with the SmileTrain repaired the disfiguring condition and the boy's life dramatically changed for the better. Suddenly, the youngster looked like everyone else.

"Before, the other kids wouldn't play with me and I had no friends," said Juan. "The operation only took about 45 minutes and when I healed, I looked just like all the other kids. If anybody ever had a cleft lip and palate, he knows how important that is. Sometimes kids can be cruel and now I have a new life."

Juan's life was transformed by the SmileTrain. Headquartered in New York City, the SmileTrain provides free cleft lip and palate surgery for boys and girls in more than 50 countries. Even though the cure for clefts was developed decades ago, very few children in developing countries can afford it. More than a billion people exist on less than $1 a day while the costs for surgical repair of a cleft in the United States can run more than $10,000.

However, the SmileTrain provides cleft surgery that is safe, effective and affordable for tens of thousands of children. In as little as 45 minutes, they help end the suffering of children born with clefts. Since the SmileTrain began in 1999, surgeons around the world have surgically repaired the clefts of more than 125,000 children. Because the SmileTrain works with hundreds of locally trained doctors, it costs $250 on average to repair the smiles on these children.

Bob Drews, a Melvin Jones Fellow and past president of the Greendale, Wisconsin, Lions Club, pulled his fellow members aboard the SmileTrain in 2004 with a personal donation of $1,250 which his club matched. "At 85 years old, I don't work much anymore," Drews explained. "But," he added, "I do volunteer and in 2004, I earned $1,250 volunteering and gave it to the SmileTrain and our club matched it.

"This year, I'm going to donate $1,500 to the SmileTrain and the club will contribute $500," he said. "I think it's an outstanding project because when a person looks at the 'before and after' photos of these little kids, he sees how Lions are changing lives all over the world. It's a powerful experience."

"The SmileTrain is unique because 100 percent of all donations go toward activities that directly help the children and nothing goes toward overhead expenses," pointed out Michele Sinesky, Special Projects Coordinator of the SmileTrain. "We have a generous Board of Directors who pay for all non-program and administrative costs. So as a consequence, for every $250 we receive, we are able to provide free cleft surgery to a child who would otherwise not receive it. Although it takes as little as 45 minutes, this cleft surgery has an impact that lasts a lifetime."

A Lion for 11 years and past president of the 50-member Greendale Lions Club, Ron Steffes explained, "The SmileTrain is only one of our projects. We have 17 activities in our community and among other things, we aim at a younger membership with scholarships for children here, children's playground equipment, parades and those kinds of things. We give $25,000 a year to various organizations to meet our obligation of serving others. The SmileTrain is a great project because it transforms a child's appearance and his life. It's right on target in serving others."

The SmileTrain inspires support from Lions and Leos alike. In 1982, the West Babylon, New York, Lions Club chartered the Leo Club of West Babylon High School. Very active, the club has contributed to an extensive range of programs and projects. "We got interested in the SmileTrain several years ago," said Tracy Dobie, who is now a junior at Princeton University. She served as president of the club during her junior and senior years at the high school.

"I enjoy community service work," Dobie explained, "and when I saw the before and after pictures from the SmileTrain, I was inspired. I got into community work in junior high school and have been in it ever since.

"My junior year, we had an '80s dance at the high school and raised $1,400 for the SmileTrain. The next year, we had a teacher talent show that raised $3,000 for the SmileTrain.

"The SmileTrain makes a huge impact when you look at the dramatic effect that it has on people's lives. It made me grateful that through the Leo club, I had a chance to participate in something like that," Dobie emphasized.

Far away in Antigua, Guatemala, Juan Hernandez would agree.

International Youth Exchange

Since it began in 1961 the Lions Clubs International Youth Exchange Program has had a long and resilient life. Lion Marty Strauss of the Hayward, California Lions Club put it this way. Speaking on November 14, 2006, he said, "In 1977 I was chairman of the Foster City Lions Club Youth Exchange Program and this past year I was the MD-4 Chairman responsible for the hosting of the Japanese students. Little did I know that 29 years after my first experience with the program it would all come together again. It's youth exchange at its best."

This story that appeared in the *San Jose Mercury News* on August 26, 2006, explains what he was talking about. "Terry McIntosh sat transfixed in Foster City's Community Center, watching 21-year-old Yohei Iga haltingly give a speech in English about his home town in Japan and his appreciation of the Lions club. 'It's like deja vu,' she said, shaking her head at the young man in the bright blue blazer standing at the podium. 'He looks just like his mother.'

"Twenty-nine years ago McIntosh hosted a young Kyoto woman named Chieko Sakuma for the Lions clubs youth exchange program, starting a very special trans-Pacific relationship. 'She fell in love with us, and we fell in love with her,' McIntosh said. McIntosh and Iga's mother forged a relationship that has endured nearly three decades."

McIntosh is called "American Grandmother" and never misses a birthday of her "Japanese grandchildren." Yohei Iga remembers his one visit to the Bay Area with his parents when he was a little boy, and eating lasagna at McIntosh's Peninsula home. Now he attends Keio University and is the same age his mother was when she was a youth exchange participant.

"Both my parents were young exchange students, too," he told the 70 members of various Lions clubs at the Foster City dinner Tuesday night. His parents' first visit to the Lions club was indeed special, he said, "because they met in California in 1977."

Chieko Sakuma married Masanori Iga five years later. They honeymooned in California, the place that had brought them together, visiting McIntosh and her children and deepening their friendship. Yohei was born in 1984, his sister Azusa a few years later, and the family settled in Maghimeji near Kobe. His parents took one more trip to California when the children were ten and seven, playing for hours with McIntosh's first grandchild and teaching each other how to count in Japanese and English.

Photo albums and old newspaper clippings were passed around. One relic stands out, in an August 17, 1977, newspaper photo his mother, Chieko, is standing in a kimono with four other youth exchange participants from Japan in Finland, along with McIntosh and Marty Strauss, who still heads the Lions district youth exchange program.

Yohei Iga had the time of his life, fulfilling much of his wish-list for his three-week trip to California. He saw Barry Bonds bat during the Giants-Dodgers series, sailed on San Francisco Bay, tagged along with the Los Gatos Police. He shot a .457 magnum at a shooting range, showed off pictures in his digital camera of him in a Habitat for Humanity project in Santa Clara Valley and of a police officer stopping a speeder during his ride along the previous week. These exchanges happen all the time all over the world. Young people often write and visit their host families in subsequent years. "This one is unusual even by Lions club standards," said his San Jose host mother, Mary Kelley.

246

The Lions Youth Exchange Program has been a glowing success from the start. It allows young people to do what few adults get to do—live under one roof as part of a family with people of another country.

The genesis of the program came out of a Lions meeting in Kobe, Japan, according to Joseph Saito of Sacramento, California, past chairman of the Multiple District 4 Youth Exchange Committee.

He said the idea first surfaced in a conversation between the president of the Kobe East Lions Club and two Lions from California/Nevada Multiple District 4. They talked about an exchange of youths during the summer vacation period. The youths were to stay with Lions families in the host countries.

That summer nine youths from Japan spent the summer with California families while 13 youths from California went to families in Japan. That exchange was apparently organized independently of the association program and arranged between Lions in California and Japan.

"This small exchange was so successful that the International Board of Directors decided to make it a worldwide Lions' activity," Saito said. "When the Lions Youth Exchange Program was adopted, the Board of Directors concluded that this program could contribute significantly to a greater understanding among people throughout the world."

The resolution to create the program was formally adopted at the international convention in Atlantic City, New Jersey, in June 1961. The first official exchange took place in 1961 when 16-year-old Lorenzo Calabrese, sponsored by the Bari, Italy, Lions Club, was hosted by the Sam C. Verdi family of Detroit, Michigan.

The idea spread swiftly among Lions. By April 1962, 457 Lions clubs and 89 district leaders had requested information. Eighty-six clubs said they would serve as host clubs, and 60 as sponsor clubs. Applications flooded in. They included 118 young French men and women and 85 students from Sweden who planned to visit Minnesota.

The Downtown Lions Club of Long Beach, California, set aside several thousand dollars to participate in the youth exchange program. They paid round-trip transportation costs for four area youths chosen from candidates selected from local high schools and colleges on the basis of an essay written on why each student felt he or she would best represent the United States and Lions ideals in other countries. Of the four winners, one went to Mexico, two to Germany, and one to Denmark.

The St. Petersburg, Florida, Lions Club arranged for a one-for-one exchange between their club and the Lions club in Arequipa, Peru. The Lions club of Vandalia, Ohio, sponsored five young women. One went to France, one to Switzerland, and three to Canada.

From the very first—and there were 131 exchanges reported to the International Headquarters Office in the first year—the program has accomplished what Lions hoped it would.

Those objectives as expressed by Past International President Kaoru Murakami were "to bring young people of the world into contact with the youth and adults of other countries, to share family and community life of another culture, to promote international understanding and goodwill throughout the world of Lionism . . . and to contribute to the attainment of world peace."

The program has enjoyed spectacular growth.

By 1971 more than 1,500 young people from 36 countries were participating annually. Ten years later annual participation had more than doubled with 3,548 exchanges involving 53 countries. During the Youth Exchange Program's first 25 years, more than 50,000 young people from 80 different countries shared their cultures and developed friendships with families in participating nations.

"I think the Youth Exchange Program of Lions clubs gives the world a chance to unite in friendship. It's the most beautiful thing anyone could experience," said one exchange youth from the United States.

Lori Gail Anderson, another exchange youth from the United States wrote that living abroad with a family is "an education that is impossible to get in any school."

Youth exchanges can be arranged between two Lions clubs or two districts. Usually they last from four to six weeks and the program is open to all young men and women between the ages of 15 and 21. Each young person should have a good reputation in the community and an above average academic record. Sometimes applicants are selected through essay or speaking contests conducted by the sponsoring Lions club or district.

At the first district screening for the youth exchange program in Japan, the district governor explained to the participants what the Youth Exchange Program is and what is expected of them as representatives of Japan. A language test and individual interviews follow. The committee interviewing young people evaluates health, character, motives, and knowledge of the Youth Exchange Program and Lionism. Even the parents' attitudes toward the exchanges are noted and weighed. When an applicant is found to be not prepared or suited for the exchange, the sponsor club is notified. It is up to the individual sponsor club to decide whether a youth will participate.

About six months before the actual exchange date, orientation begins for both the young people and their parents. During the following months the youths meet between once a month and once a week to learn about Lions Clubs International, the objectives of youth exchange and the customs and traditions of the country to be visited.

The young men and women participating are encouraged to study the country they are visiting. They are urged to learn about the host country's history, national heroes, sports and entertainment figures, educational system, geographic features, principal religions, and other information designed to give them an understanding of the nation's culture.

At the same time, it is suggested that they bring with them photographs and digital photos of their families, home, school, community, friends, and other material that will help the host family understand them better. Digital photos, in particular, are suggested because often the young men and women are asked to give a presentation to the host Lions club. Frequently, the sponsor club provides a banner, pin, or other memento to give the host club at that time.

While the sponsor country is preparing its young people for the experience of living in a foreign land, Lions of the host country are making careful and elaborate preparations to find and prepare host families. Lion Barry Crowther, Youth Exchange Chairman for

Multiple District 14, Pennsylvania, explained that "the most important part of hosting is finding and preparing the host families."

To recruit the families, Multiple District 14 sends a form letter to each district youth exchange chairman and district governor requesting a projected number of host families, a list of desired countries for exchanges, and suggestions for the program. Youth exchange chairmen from each Lions club and a representative from each Lioness club gather to review goals and share suggestions.

"It is important to build up a reserve list of host families," Crowther said, "in case an assigned family is forced to withdraw because of unexpected circumstances." Another practical tip: "Discourage phone calls from parents during the first week of a youth's visit because it complicates the young person's adjustment to his new family. Most calls from parents are not because their sons or daughters are homesick but because the parents miss their child."

Despite the endless hours the job requires, Lions continue to shoulder the job of youth exchange chairmen and find in it a great sense of contributing to international understanding.

"I have thoroughly enjoyed and am continuing to experience tremendous satisfaction from this portfolio, especially when I welcome youths on their return from their participation overseas," said Lion Eric Fernandez of District 201-S2, Australia.

An indication of how well the program works is watching young people who have finished their visits to Australia and are departing. "The tearful, unhappy faces of those bound for their native lands and who are unhappy to part with their hosts is a clear indication that the first Purpose of Lions Clubs International—'To create and foster a spirit of understanding among the peoples of the world'—has certainly been achieved."

Lions sponsoring and hosting a visitor are responsible for:

- All financial matters related to the exchange
- Travel arrangements, passports, visas
- Local transportation, arrivals, departures
- Insurance
- Supervision of the exchange
- Liaison with parents and host families
- Emergency situations

Members of several Lions clubs in New Zealand learned a lot about the United States when Diane Hillman of Northwood, Iowa, was sent to that country under the Lions Youth Exchange Program. According to Lowell Gangstad, the Northwood club's exchange program chairman, Diane prepared a slide show about her life in Northwood which she showed to several New Zealand clubs. "The New Zealanders were amazed at the size of the tractors and other farm machinery we use in Iowa," Diane told the Northwood Lions Club when she returned.

Other surprises: "When Lions saw slides of my home, they always remarked that the windows were smaller than in New Zealand. They didn't realize how cold Iowa winters were or that we heated our houses all winter long." The family of Lion Peter Ryan with whom she stayed at Gladfield, a tiny farm community on New Zealand's South Island, "heated only one room of their house and that only one month out of the year," she told the sponsoring club.

She liked the fact that New Zealand students, even those in high school, wore uniforms. "Here it would be unthinkable to wear the same clothes two days in a row or even twice in the same week. With uniforms you wouldn't have the pressure. It would be easier for families on a limited income."

Among other notable successes of Lions is their sponsorship of Boy Scout units, Liberty Day and the Peace Poster Contest.

Lions And Scouting

Since the founding of the association, Lions clubs have been deeply involved in sponsoring Boy Scout units: Cub packs, Scout troops and eventually Explorer posts. It has been especially rewarding inasmuch as the Lions know they are helping to mold the character of tomorrow's leaders. Lions clubs have, in fact, been the largest single non-sectarian sponsor of Boy Scout units.

In June 2003, Lions Clubs International entered into a Memorandum of Understanding with the Girl Scouts of the United States of America. The purpose of the memorandum is to establish a cooperative alliance between the two organizations, with a salient feature being to establish liaisons, one at each organization's headquarters, who will serve as primary contacts concerning collaborative projects and activities involving Girl Scout councils and Lions clubs or Leo clubs.

Among the many mutual benefits of the Memorandum of Understanding that will accrue are identification on their respective Web sites with instructions on how members and volunteers can become involved. It was also agreed that the Girl Scouts of the United States will be invited to participate in Lions Clubs International conventions, the USA/Canada Forum and other association events and activities, as feasible. Lions Clubs International will also participate in special Girl Scout events and activities, as feasible. And the Girl Scout organization will educate its staff, volunteers and Scouts about the association and Lions youth programs, including the Leo Club Program.

A Unique Civic Class Venture

A program that is gaining in popularity is Liberty Day. Initiated in 1996, Liberty Day projects are sponsored by Lions clubs throughout the United States to reach young people with facts about the nation's two founding documents, the Declaration of Independence and the Constitution. Andy McKean, a member of the Denver, Colorado, Lions Club, is the founder and international coordinator of Liberty Day and stated, "What spurred me to become involved was realizing how little both young people and adults know about these documents." This observation was seconded by Hernando, Mississippi, Lion Faye Daniels who lamented, "More children could identify Bill Gates than James Madison. I thought it would be a nice way to give them a little history lesson."

"Booklets printed by the Lions that contain these two documents are given to students in cooperation with school districts. On the day chosen, Lions schedule speakers, very often elected officials, to address assemblies and classrooms. Students are then given assignments related to the Declaration of Independence and the Constitution.

The most visible part of Liberty Day is when the students— Liberty Day Kids—8-12 years of age, prepare a list of questions relating to the Constitution and, with adult escorts, usually Lions, travel to locations such as state capitols, post offices, universities, municipal forums, etc., to quiz adults. They are always warmly received and those quizzed are at times somewhat embarrassed that they don't know the answers.

What may some of the questions be? "Name two freedoms guaranteed by the First Amendment. Which Amendment abolished slavery? Which Amendment introduced the income tax? What are the first three words of the Constitution? What did the 19th Amendment provide? Presently, how many Amendments are there? What are the three qualifications for being a U.S. Senator?" Sometimes the questions get harder, but it is all done in the spirit of fun and good will, and the adults enjoy the sparring as much as the kids.

To further emphasize the importance of Liberty Day, both the United States Senate and House of Representatives issued a resolution in 2000 declaring March 16 as Liberty Day. It marks the birthdate of James Madison, the country's fourth President, who is considered the "Father of the Constitution" for his decisive efforts in its preparation and passage.

Artistic Visions Of Peace

One of the most successful and popular programs on behalf of youth and in promoting strong community relations is the Lions International Peace Poster Contest. Initiated in 1988, it presently involves the annual participation of more than 325,000 youngsters, 11-13 years of age, from nearly 100 countries who create their personal artistic visions of the particular year's theme to create lasting peace around the world.

Participating in the contest enables Lions clubs to build a solid relationship with young people in the community while also impacting the views of children, teachers, parents and fellow Lions around the world. The Cebu Centennial Lions Club in the Philippines viewed it quite eloquently: "Through this contest, the Lions have found that seeing the world through a child's eye can be an enlightening experience."

One grand prize winner is selected each year along with 24 merit award winners. All are asked to describe the significance of his or her poster. In describing her 2007 grand prize winning poster, as it related to the year's contest theme, *Celebrate Peace*,

13-year-old Min-Ji Yi, whose poster was sponsored by the Tarzana, California, Lions Club, said, "My poster represents the harmony of all the countries in the world coming together as one. Just as music creates a peaceful melody, the world should be able to also." And she added, "Keep sponsoring the contest and remind kids about peace. Let them express what peace means to them. Until every last hint of suffering is eliminated in the world, I think that our efforts to create world peace should not rest." Min-Ji Yi, who speaks fluent English, is president of her debate club and participates in a number of school activities, moved with her family to California from the Republic of Korea six years ago.

Past merit award winners were also proud to explain the reasons that inspired their artistic creations. For example:

> "Peace is a feeling that is inside us. To have peace in the world, we must transmit that feeling to each other through gestures of brotherhood and love." — Maira Fassoni, Ribeirao, Brazil, 2003.

> "Children think about peace. We realize there is still a lot of war, violence and injustice going on in the world. People have to respect other ways of living, other cultures and other people." — Klara Thein, Germany, 2004.

> "I was hoping to convey that if we all work together, we can get along and live in harmony. We are the foundation on which this peaceful world must be built." — Jason Messina, United States, 1996.

> "The boy in my poster has an artificial leg because he stepped on a land mine. The girl lost her mother and is carrying her younger brother on her back. They are very skinny because of the lack of food. I don't want people to go to war. I want everyone to live equally." — Yuika Sasaki, Japan, 2001.

Grand prize winners and their sponsoring Lions clubs have been:

1988-89: Moustafa Tawoukji, Beirut, Lebanon — Beirut Lions Club

1989-90: Ugo Ciocchetti, Biella, Italy — Biella Bugella Civitas Lions Club

1990-91: Jean-Michel Pain, Fort De France, Martinique — Fort De France Madinina, Lions Club

1991-92: Yuki Nakajima, Miki, Japan — Miki Chuo Lions Club

1992-93: Niken Ayu Murti, Depok Utara, Indonesia — Jakarta Dian Mas Pumama Lions Club

1993-94: Jill Giovanelli, Richeyville, Pennsylvania — Scenery Hills Lions Club

1994-95: Zeynep Gulec, Sirinyer, Izmir, Turkey — Sirinyer Lions Club

1995-96: Danielle Hernandez, Peoria, Arizona — Phoenix Phil-Am Lions Club

1996-97: Don Nemesio Miranda III, Taytay, Rizal, Philippines — Taytay Pag-Ibig Lions Club

1997-98: Cinthya Vanessa Villacorte, Tumbes, Peru — Tumbus Miguel Grau Lions Club

1998-99: Andre de Villiers, Strand, Republic of South Africa —Somerset West Lions Club

1999-2000: Satoko Nakadate, Tokyo, Japan — Tokyo Ebara Lions Club

2000-2001: Delphin Tiberge, Saint-Barthelemy, Guadelupe — Ile de Saint-Barthelemy, Lions Club

2001-2002: Hei Man Lau, Hong Kong, China — Hong Kong Mandarin Lions Club

2002-2003: Sittichok Pariyaket, Samutsakhon, Thailand — Sakornburi Lions Club

2003-2004: Vittoria Sansebastiano, Novi Ligure, Italy — Novi Ligure Lions Club

2004-2005: Cheuk Tat Li, Hong Kong, China — Hong Kong Metropolitan Lions Club

2005-2006: Cleverson da Silva Rosa, Cidade Gaucha PR, Brazil — Cidade Gaucha Lions Club

2006-2007:   Min-Ji Yi, Los Angeles, California — Tarzana Lions Club

2007-2008: Ming Yang Soong, Bidor, Malaysia — Bidor Lions Club

This contest provides an outlet for young people to express their peaceful vision for the future, sharing their thoughts and ideas with millions of people the world over. Past International President Dr. Tae-Sup Lee, in observing how the contest inspires the leaders of tomorrow to share their feelings on promoting a peaceful world, observed, "It's truly amazing to see the end result when the world's children use their imagination."

Chapter Eleven
Leos Reach Out Around The World

"How wonderful it is that nobody need wait a single moment before starting to improve the world." Those words were written by Anne Frank while in hiding from the Nazis and can easily be applied to the spirit of the Leo Club Program. "That desire to make things better," observed Pamela Mohr, associate editor of THE LION Magazine, "whether by small steps or giant leaps, has for five decades defined the young men and women who call themselves Leos. The world is indeed a richer place for their commitment to making a difference."

The movement took root in 1957 when Bill Graver, a high school student in Abington, Pennsylvania, asked his father Jim Graver, a member of the Glenside Lions Club and baseball coach at the high school, why there wasn't a Lions-sponsored service club for young people. Jim Graver saw the wisdom and feeling in his son's question and, together with fellow Glenside Lion William Ernst, thought that such a youth group would be an excellent way to involve teens in a meaningful opportunity for community service.

The members of their Lions club agreed and went on to organize the world's first Leo club at the high school. It consisted of 26 players from the baseball team and nine other students — 35 in all. Using the acronym Leadership, Equality (later changed to Experience), Opportunity, the Abington High School Leo Club was established with young Bill Graver, also a member of the baseball team, as the charter president. "It remained the only Leo club until 1963 when the Tamaqua, Pennsylvania, Club was organized," reported Mohr in her magazine article. "As an appropriate charter gift, the Abington High School Leos presented a banner to the new club. The next year, there were 27 Leo clubs in the state and one in New York."

Three years later, Lions Clubs International adopted Leo clubs as an official program and today membership stands at more than 140,000 young people in 5,400 clubs in 134 countries and geographical areas.

And it all began with a question posed by a high school baseball player.

Bill Graver married Louisa, the daughter of William Ernst, and is now a Lion in Manchester, Connecticut. "My dad died in 1969," he said, "and Bill Ernst died a couple of years ago. Right up until the end, my father-in-law was actively promoting Leo clubs. I think he was their number one cheerleader."

"Now retired as an educator and counselor," said Mohr, "Bill believes strongly in learning by example." "You get involved with people and issues at an early age and learn problem solving," Graver remarked about his early years as a Leo. "You are inspired by the people you look up to."

Thousands of former Leos have continued their service as Lions. Anne Katrin Peters, for example, now in her 20s, was a member of three different Leo clubs in Germany and is a member of the Munich Karl Valentin Lions Club. She is presently the editor of the German edition of THE LION Magazine. "In all these years," she said, "I learned a lot about getting people to work for the benefit of others. I also learned about real friendship across borders and ages since I've met so many Leos and Lions, people I would really miss if I hadn't first joined a Leo club." Several other former Leos are members of her club, all wishing to actively keep the spirit of volunteerism going that had been sparked during their earlier years.

June Palmera Vasquez, the 2005-2006 president of the Bataan Host Leo Club in the Philippines, believes that joining the club brought about "the moment that defined what true service and purpose mean. I found my role in making a difference and touching lives." Vasquez went on to state in THE LION Magazine article that "being a member and leader of my Leo club was a great privilege, with challenging experiences and yet fulfilling opportunities. Giving service to the community, especially the children and less fortunate, paved the way in defining what responsibility, discipline and commitment mean. Leo clubs empower young people to make a difference and to go beyond the limits to inspire, touch lives and serve."

In still another endorsement, Mike Hall, a past president and current advisor to the SALSA (Serve & Learn Student Association) Leo Club in Sioux Falls, South Dakota, numbering more than 500 young people from four area public high schools, said, "These students recognize the need to volunteer and feel an obligation to give back to their community through service learning projects." In fact, during 2005-2006 SALSA Leos contributed more than 5,600 hours to various community agencies.

These and thousands of other testimonials could be cited to tell what being a Leo means to the young members. In the year 2007, Leos stood for a half century of understanding and celebrating the value of voluntary community service throughout the world.

Leos in many countries echo the words of Paulo Caceres, 22, "Before I joined the Paijan Leo Club (Peru), I was a lonely person. I didn't have a lot of friends. I was selfish and egotistical. I worried about myself – about new clothes and new shoes. I never cared about people in need. I always said, 'It's not my fault that they're poor.'

"Then six years ago, the Paijan Lions invited me to become a Leo. I have now found the thing that was missing in my life. Now, I care about other people's needs. I care about the world. I'm a better person now. I can express myself in public – without being afraid. Many people say I'm a leader. Others say that I should be my town's mayor. My Leo club has given me all of these things."

Paulo is a leader. He's a Leo. In January 2004, Paulo became a member of the Paijan Lions Club.

Membership in a Leo club provides opportunities to:

- develop local, regional, and international friendships
- organize community service projects
- belong to a team
- cooperate with community groups including Lions clubs, Leo clubs, schools, social service agencies, hospitals, homes for children, and homes for the elderly
- develop leadership skills
- earn awards and other recognition
- attend local, regional, and international meetings and conventions.

From its 1957 beginning in Glenside, Pennsylvania, the Leo Club Program and its purpose have expanded on every continent. By the end of 2006, Leo clubs numbered 5,536 throughout the world. The United States led with 1,476 clubs and 39,900 members, India ranked second with 471 clubs and 11,775 members, Brazil third with 410 clubs and 10,250 members and Italy was fourth with 397 clubs and 9,925 members. With their global view of responsibility and service, Leo clubs change lives on every continent.

"In Jamaica, the Leos are active in giving vision tests, glaucoma screening, and working with the disabled," said Patsy Henry, a member of the Spanishtown Leo Club in St. Catherine, Jamaica. "We learn sign language so we can communicate with the speech and hearing impaired. We teach them mathematics, English language, sewing, and cooking. We also hold a Special Olympics for handicapped youngsters."

Twenty-four years old, Patsy Henry has been a Leo for three years. Her club has 15 members and is one of 18 Leo clubs in Jamaica. Average club size is 20 to 25, with one club of 46 members.

"We're working very hard to battle drug use in our area. We're active in schools, not only high schools but grammar schools and working with the four, five, and six year olds. We go to schools with little tots and tell them, 'Say no to drugs.' They draw pictures about it and then take this message home to their parents. We try to be consistent so at our Leo functions nobody smokes or uses alcohol. Being a Leo has made me a better human being. I thank God for making it possible for me to touch someone."

Does Patsy Henry plan to become a Lion when she grows too old for her Leo club? "No," she said with a smile, "I'm going to be a Lioness."

Members of the Leo Club of Bintulu Kemena, Malaysia, have dedicated themselves to helping the less fortunate members of their community. They have, however, also realized that those living outside their own community also need help, and for that reason, embarked on a project to help people living in a rural area located nearly two hours away. Leos had to travel by car and then be transported by boat over the water to reach a small town in which 81 families were displaced by a "long house" fire.

According to Leo Anica Ko Ing Hung, 2002-2003 club president, a "long house" means that there are 81 doors terraced along this residential area and is occupied by at least 500 people, including 54 children. "The villagers living in this long house lived peacefully until the night of the fire disaster," she explained.

"Since then," she added, "We continue our generous support along with our sponsoring Lions club, the Lions Club of Bintulu Kemena, to donate food, clothing and medicine. We have also helped an elderly man receive the eye surgery he needed and helped a young man continue his schooling after he had to leave because his parents passed away.

"Besides donating items, we also come to visit them and do continuous follow-up on what they need. We try to help them with daily things they needed after this disaster.

"After the fire, the villagers were living in a temporary plywood shelter that could protect them from the sun and rain. After an appeal to the state government and help from Lions and Leos and also a private company that donated wood and building materials, they have now rebuilt their long house."

Twenty-five-year-old Saiful Bari Khan, a Leo for six years, is a graduate of the University of Bangladesh and is working toward a master's degree in political science.

"I was looking for some way to help the people in my country," he said, "and a friend asked me to join the Leos. He said that I could learn something about leadership and serving the needs of my fellow men and women. My friend was right. There are more than 100 million people in Bangladesh and there's plenty to do to make life better for them.

"We raise money and make sure it goes to work where it's needed. For instance, we saw that a farmer who had been using his cow and plow to cultivate other people's land had been put nearly out of business because his cow died and he couldn't afford another one. He and his son began to play the role of the cow and pull the plow themselves. We saw this in the newspaper and contributed some money for another cow and then presented it to the farmer. I've never seen a more grateful human being when he saw the cow and realized it was a gift for him.

"More than 75 Leos became eye donors. We have a large eye hospital in Bangladesh and the number one eye specialist is a past district governor of Lions Clubs International. The death rate of children in our country is very high and we sponsor immunization programs against polio, along with general vaccination programs and dental camps."

A serious, thoughtful young man, Saiful Bari Khan continued, "We had a big flood in Bangladesh a few months ago and during this time there was no food. Mothers sometimes could feed their children, but had no food for themselves. We'd find out about that and take food to the mothers, and anything else they needed. Our Leo district slogan is 'Drug Free Society' and we've been making a major effort in the fight against drug addiction. It's an ongoing activity with us and we can see progress, even though it's slow. Whether it's food for flood victims, buying a cow for a farmer, or donating corneas, we keep busy."

Led by District Governor Clarence Templeton in 1964, the District 14-K Lions joined with the Glenside Lions and created Leo Clubs, Inc., of Pennsylvania. The Leo Program was made an official District 14-K project. Momentum grew as a number of other Leo clubs sprang up in larger high schools in the area. The publicity generated lively interest in other districts in the state and Leo clubs were organized throughout Pennsylvania.

As awareness grew of the program's accomplishments, the Leo club idea spread rapidly. In the spring of 1967, Leo Clubs, Inc., held the first statewide Leo Clubs Convention. Lions who learned of the program returned home enthusiastic about the possibility of carrying the Lions service message to young people.

In the first 10 years of Leo clubs the concept grew steadily in effectiveness and popularity. In 1967 the Youth Committee of Lions Clubs International studied the possibilities of developing a youth club program that would operate in conjunction with The International Association of Lions Clubs. At the October 1967 meeting of the International Board of Directors the members voted to implement the Leo Club Program.

By October 1968, 200 Leo clubs had been organized. By October 1969, there were 918 clubs in 48 countries. By 1974, there were 2,000 clubs, with 50,000 Leos hard at work in 68 countries. Today there are clubs in over 100 countries. Leo clubs continue to expand because they fill a need.

Club twinning is a popular Leo activity. Members of Leo clubs correspond with each other and share their experiences with different kinds of projects. Sometimes members of twinning clubs visit each other in exchanges to learn first hand about the other's country.

In an effort to fight illiteracy in their country, every member of the Canaan City, Nigeria, Leo Club served as a volunteer. For a three-month period, Leos worked at nine literacy centers with people needing assistance. Other ways in which the Canaan City Leos are helping include: donating educational materials to the centers and sponsoring an essay competition.

In Malaysia, members of the Alor Setar Leo Club collected used clothing for over 300 people whose homes were lost to a fire that swept through their community. It is estimated that over 5,000 pieces of clothing were collected by Leos, who personally delivered their donation to the fire victims.

The Leo Club of Kathmandu Downtown, Nepal, joined with the citizens of the village of Belkot in a tree-planting project. The area chosen was a one-hour walk from the road, accessible by foot. Leos report that they planted 1,200 plants of different varieties, which will be tended by the villagers. In another activity, Leos helped the Downtown Lions Club with a blood donation project, during which 47 pints of blood were collected from volunteers.

Members of the Leo Club of Penang (City) in Malaysia organized a cruise ship party for residents of various local institutions. Invitations were extended to those living in a variety of homes designed to meet the special needs of the elderly, physically and mentally disabled and orphans. In addition to a dance band, guests on the cruise ship enjoyed refreshments, games and a singing contest. Following the cruise, equipment was presented to the administrators of a home for the elderly.

Leos operate in the real world. They solve problems with courage and imagination. In Peru, the Leos in Tingo Maria are battling the drug scourge. A relatively small town of 25,000 persons on the edge of the jungle, Tingo Maria has a Leo club with between 20 and 25 girls and boys as members.

"Most of the Leos are young people around 16 or 17," explained a Lion from Lima. "They are very effective in programs opposing drug abuse. That includes drug education. That's a tough, dangerous job because there are many drug dealers and terrorists in that area. However, these Leos are fearless and are working tirelessly to combat the drug epidemic. They don't seem to be having any problems with the drug dealers or the terrorists.

"District T-3 in Chile also has a very strong and active Leo district. They work very closely with the Lions because Lionism is very active in Chile. In Chile most of the Leo clubs, especially the big ones, have clubhouses in which they also perform such activities as helping people with dental service, medicines, glaucoma screening, providing eyeglasses, and other health aids."

After being absent from the community for 25 years, the Mattituck, New York, Leo Club was reorganized in 2001 and has since been thriving.

Leos have raised more than $3,000 by sponsoring the sale of tree seedlings, a golf tournament, a dunking tank and pie throwing activity at the Lions Strawberry Festival, face-painting at a Lions Fall Festival, a dance and other projects.

Among the recipients of Leos' generosity are local food banks, community theater, Guiding Eyes for the Blind and the World Trade Center Disaster relief fund. Leos also have purchased school supplies for children in need and donated more than $800 for breast cancer research by sponsoring a dance.

Leos are highly visible in their small town and actively seeking new members. According to Arthur Tillman, Leo club advisor, "We had a recruiting drive for new members at Mattituck Junior-Senior High School and our Leos visited the English classes to tell the students about the rewards and fun of being a Leo.

"Those interested were invited to an introductory meeting held at a local pizza parlor. A whopping 50-plus prospective members showed up. Currently, our club has 27 members. This is a tremendous response for our small town. We have T-shirts with the Leo logo on front and are now ordering Leo sweatshirts. In the spring induction to the National Honor Society, 12 of the new inductees were Leos. A number of our girls are on the high school softball team that made it to the state finals last year."

Tillman pointed out: "We also have many students who have not been active in school life, so our club has provided constructive and character building activities for all types of kids. Written on the back of our shirts is our club motto, 'It's Possible.' Our Leos have learned so much and are now familiar with the joys in planning, hard work and giving to others and the community.

"I always tell them," he emphasized, "that when you give of yourself for others, you will get back so much more, and so it has been for them and for me."

Abraxus High School Leos in Poway, California, devote much of their attention to the children of homeless families in their area. Abraxus Leos hosted a Halloween party for the children, complete with games, crafts, dancing and pizza and sponsored a Christmas party for them.

The Christmas party featured festive holiday decorations, an arts and crafts table, a special "makeover for Moms" by Rancho Bernardo Lions affiliated with Mary Kay Cosmetics, and Christmas gifts wrapped by Leos.

Additionally, Leos have also provided and assembled bag lunches for Interfaith Community Center's homeless clientele and collected clothing and food for orphanages in Mexico.

This active club has also helped Rancho Bernardo Lions host a World Service Day luncheon at the San Diego Center for the Blind, assisted with White Cane Day collections, flower deliveries and decorating the Lions' Rose Parade float.

Activities that Leos may support in connection with the literacy and culture program are extensive:

- Book collection and distribution.
- Teaching or tutoring students in accordance with local regulations.
- Conducting fundraisers to buy books and materials for schools or students.
- Offering scholarships and grants as incentives to area students, with the help of local businesses and schools.
- Sponsoring concerts to raise money for literacy projects.
- Corresponding with or meeting with clubs in Club Twinning to exchange ideas, materials, and culture.

- Teaching basic job and work skills to the functionally illiterate and then helping them find employment.
- Working with literacy organizations and foundations in common efforts to promote literacy.
- Sponsoring Braille sections in local libraries and providing Braille literature for this purpose.
- Improving library environments by cleaning desks, books, and study areas, painting walls and replacing light bulbs.

In the Philippines, members of the Bataan Host Leo Club are keeping the spotlight on children as they serve the less fortunate in their community.

One project involved collecting and distributing toys and used clothing to children; another was the establishment of a nutritional program for children living in two remote areas.

Leos packed soup, fruits and other foods with a high nutritional value to bring to the children. Additionally, they stayed to play games with the kids and distributed prizes to youngsters. More than 200 children benefited from this project.

Leos are actively involved in helping the less fortunate. They recently visited the Bataan General Hospital to bring fruit and flowers to patients. Club members also visited the nursery and general ward to distribute their gifts and cheer the patients.

One of the largest projects ever undertaken by Leos in District 306-C, Sri Lanka, was designed to rebuild and refurnish school libraries.

In coordination with the Prefects Guild of Mahanama College, Leos launched the "Donate a Book or Brick" project. A total of 21 schools benefited from this service endeavor and Leos also constructed a children's park at a tsunami-affected school. Two severely damaged school libraries were also totally repaired and restocked with books.

A massive publicity campaign was conducted with the help of the media, mailings, banners and door-to-door collection. One of the leading radio stations in Sri Lanka provided sponsorship of the project.

Several international donors also provided financial contributions to Leos. Among them were several Lions and Leo clubs in the United States.

The Seki, Japan, Leo Club collected recyclable used milk cartons throughout the year, which amounted to 8,338 pounds of material. Leos cleaned the cartons and cut them up for recycling, earning a sizeable amount of money for their efforts. The funds were donated to a local welfare society.

In Malaysia, members of the Poi Lam High School Leo Club collected funds from their fellow students to help rebuild a local fireworks factory which was destroyed by fire.

The Eyup, Turkey, Leo Club sponsored one main project last year, the furnishing of a local neurological clinic. Leos were able to purchase and donate to the clinic enough furnishings for three complete rooms.

Members of the Leo Club of Tallinn, Estonia, have "adopted" the youngsters living in a community orphanage. Leos organized a party for the children, took the youngsters into a nearby forest on an excursion and on a river trip. Additionally, Leos helped the orphanage administration with gardening duties at the facility.

In 1995 Lions Clubs International sponsored "Reality, Risk and Response," a national symposium to address the problems facing young people in America today. Held in Chicago, Illinois, it called upon leaders of service and community organizations, teen-age leaders and experts on youth issues from across the nation to work together to solve the problems facing America's youth.

"Those of us who work in the community can have a dramatic and positive impact on America's future," said 1994-95 International President Prof. Dr. Giuseppe Grimaldi. "And," President Grimaldi added, "Lions has a responsibility to take a leadership role."

Keynote speakers, former U.S. Secretary of Education William Bennett and former Atlanta, Georgia, Mayor Andrew Young, offered their thoughts on the roots of today's youth problems and offered feasible solutions. "The dissolution of the family is the number one problem facing our country today," Bennett said. Young agreed, but also felt that Americans need to devote more time to finding solutions to the problems facing youth and cited the symposium as a step in the right direction.

"Our policy and attitudes about young people are often formed by 60 second soundbites," Young said. "And, unfortunately, many of our solutions to the problems that are plaguing us tend to be treated in the same quick and easy manner."

A panel of teens at the symposium discussed personal triumphs and disappointments they have experienced growing up in the '90s -- living in neighborhoods plagued by gangs, drugs, crime, unemployment and inadequate housing.

"Who you are in life and who you become depends on what you are taught at an early age," said youth panelist Karr Narula, the 15-year-old founder of "Kids Helping Kids," a program that encourages young people to help other children.

Bennett, Young and the panel agreed that what children need most is an adult willing to play a role in their lives and a safe haven to learn in, such as a home, school or community center. "It is clubs like the Leo clubs and the (Off the Street Club) that are there for the kids and are taking positive steps to save kids today," said panelist Shauna Gambill, Miss Teen USA 1994. "It is the kids who have someone to make a difference in their lives, whether it be a parent, a friend or an organization; who don't need drugs, who don't join gangs and who stay in school."

In Germany, members of the Frankfurt-Hochst (Mainline) Leo Club sponsored a fundraising activity to aid the victims of the cholera epidemic in Peru.

Balloons with pictures of cartoon characters were sold in a local shopping mall to people who then entered their balloons in a contest to measure those that flew the farthest. A business in the community donated a watch for the first prize.

Members of the Ogbe, Nigeria, Leo Club sponsored a recent lecture on drug awareness for local secondary school students. A prominent doctor and nurse spoke out about the effects of illicit narcotics on the body.

Lions and Leos in Port Shepstone, Republic of South Africa, joined together recently in sponsoring a kart race through the streets of their town. For five hours, karts and motorcycles roared through downtown streets. While the motorcycle racing attracted adults, the kart competition was geared to youngsters between the ages of eight and 12. All the funds were donated to helping needy children.

In Nairobi, Kenya, members of the Leo Club of Nairobi City are helping feed residents of a local orphanage. Leos buy food on a weekly basis for the orphanage, and deliver the groceries personally, so that each Leo takes a turn visiting the home.

In another activity, the club spent over $210 purchasing milk for a group of Somali refugees living in a camp provided by the government.

In the Republic of South Africa, members of the Leo Club of Tableview sponsored a Dog Walk for the Blind. Dog owners were invited by Leos to parade their proud pets at a local mall and then automatically be qualified for a dog show which featured many prizes. All the money raised was donated to helping equip the ophthalmology clinic at a new hospital.

In Louisiana, members of the Delta Leo Club donated $200 to the Crippled Children's Wish List, gave $60 to the Lions Journey for Sight and another contribution to a local nursing home.

Another activity included babysitting for children from low-income families. Leos also provided nearly $100 worth of groceries for an elderly widow in need.

Members of the Leo Club of Flintridge Prep, California, sponsor multiple bake sales throughout the year to raise service activity funds. The club recently gave $500 to the Nazoo Anna Education Centre in Peshwar, Pakistan, to provide relief to 700 refugees.

The club also devotes time and money to Elizabeth House, a shelter for battered women. During the holidays, Leos helped decorate the shelter, prepared dinner with them and helped celebrate Christmas with the mothers and their children.

A cultural exchange in Oregon was sparked by a request that appeared on the Internet. It started in October 2000, when Susan Li, of Lake Grove, Oregon, a member of the Laker Leo Club, discovered a posting on the Leo section of Lions Clubs International's official Web site. China Hong Kong and China Macau District 303 Leo Pina Lo had posted a message that Chinese Leos were trying to locate a country to visit for a cultural exchange to take place in June

2001. They also wanted to be of assistance to their host country by participating in some challenging environmental service activities. Li brought this unusual request to the Oregon Lions District 36-O Cabinet, which approved the project, calling it to the International Youth Cultural Experience.

According to Lion Susan Grant-Higgins, who served as both International Youth Cultural Experience and District 36-O Leo chairperson, "A proposed itinerary for the visiting group was augmented and flexed to fit various schedules. On June 14, 2001, 16 Leos aged 18 to 30 years old arrived from China to spend a busy nine days in Lake Oswego and neighboring areas.

"After some time to get used to a different time zone," Grant-Higgins said, "the visitors began the first of their requested environmental service projects. With help from some Laker Leos, they removed ivy and cleared paths at Tyron Creek State Park.

"The next day," she said, "the group, now composed of Laker Leos, China Hong Kong and China Macau Leos, and their Lion chaperone-tour guides began an overnight tour around Mt. Hood. After sightseeing, the group was hosted by the Mt. Hood River Lions and Leos to an excellent barbecue dinner."

Following an overnight stay at Nanitch Scout Lodge and time to explore some of the mountain, the group went to the Oral Hull Camp for the Blind, where they participated in a work party to clear and make paths for the sight impaired to hike.

The next outing was to the Oregon coast, where Seaside and Astoria Lions coordinated the lodging and transportation of the group, and helped take them sightseeing. After touring the coastal area, Leos pitched in and went to work cleaning a beach as their service activity before returning to Portland.

The whirlwind nine days of the exchange were so successful, Grant-Higgins emphasized because of the work of the District 36-O Cabinet, Lions Youth Outreach Committee and the Astoria, Greshman (Breakfast), Hood River, King City, Lake Oswego, Lake Grove, Seaside and West Linn (Riverview) Lions and the Sherwood, Upper Valley (Hood River) and Laker Leos.

The evening before leaving for home, the visiting Leos presented a program of Chinese cultural dances, songs and martial arts to honor their "homestay" families. Grant-Higgins reported, "The northern Oregon Lions and Leos and the Chinese Leos had the time of their lives. Experiences and friendships were made that will last for a long time."

In Newfoundland, Canada, the Goulds Leo Club organized a community weekend Halloween celebration to keep children safe and happily entertained. The events consisted of a dance on Friday night, and the following evening, several Halloween-themed movies were shown to participants.

Members of the Samana City, India, Leo Club organized a diabetes screening camp, gave 20 school uniforms to students in need and planted 50 trees at a school for boys.

In Malaysia, members of the Leo Club of SMK Batu Lintang visited a home for disabled children and cooked for them. They introduced the children to spaghetti, which was a big hit.

The Leos, who also brought along a film to show children after dinner, contributed most of the ingredients themselves. Before they left for the evening, they gave the home a 500-piece puzzle for the children to enjoy.

Reaching out to youth is the essence of the Lions Opportunities for Youth Program. Lions — many of whom are senior citizens — work with young people and share their knowledge of community service. Youth within the community benefit from this assistance. As an end result, they continue the legacy of Lions community service.

By virtue of their community involvement, Lions are civic leaders. Whenever they interact with youth, they become mentors as well.

Mentors are adults who serve as positive role models for youth. For more than 75 years, Lions have successfully fitted this image. Lion mentors serve as teachers, coaches, cheerleaders, confidants and friends to youth. Such interactive connection with youth sends this message, quoted from *One-on-One Mentoring: A Guide for Establishing Mentor Programs* published by the United States Department of Education:

"You are worth my time and effort because you are a valuable human being. And I can offer you — by my word or deed, or by the example of my life — ways to expand your horizons and to increase the likelihood that you will achieve success."

"At-risk youth" are influenced in a positive way by Lions. In addition to serving as role models, Lion mentors reinforce parents' messages to avoid negatives such as gangs, drugs, and early sexual activity.

Mentoring develops a youth's self-esteem and academic skills according to the Creative Mentoring Program of Creative Grandparenting, Inc. Mentors also provide cultural enrichment as they expand a youth's awareness of potential career opportunities. Likewise, interaction between the older generation and the younger guarantees the preservation of time-honored traditions. For Lions, the key tradition is humanitarian service.

Service-learning combines community service projects with classroom learning. Service-learning is recognized worldwide as a valuable training method. Of course, the method is incomplete without a trainer, and that's where experienced Lions are needed.

In Illinois, the Elmhurst Evening Lions Club contacted their Lions Quest class for aid in completing a Lions Quest fundraiser. The school offered the students extra credit for their participation; the Lions raised funds for Lions Quest.

Service-learning occurs regularly in Flagstaff, Arizona. Every year, the Flagstaff Sunrise and Flagstaff Noon Lions clubs organize Rose Day. The Flagstaff Lumberjack Leos participate by helping sell and deliver 700 dozen roses.

"In Flagstaff, I can honestly say that the Lions and Leos work well together," stated Kathryn Peavy, Leo Chairman for District 21-C. Every November, the Leos help the Lions during their annual Gift of Sight Day. Then the tables turned. When the Leos needed financial help to sponsor someone for Leader Dog School, the Lions were there. And after the Leos organized a clothing drive, the Lions transported garments to Mexico.

Around the world, Lions and youth work together. In India, the Palakol Leos helped their Lions club during a medical camp. In New Zealand, the Waitangirua Leos helped the Lions paint the tunnel doors to the Aotea Railway. In New Brunswick, Canada, the Island View Leos helped their Lions clubs with a craft show.

In Europe, 1993 was designated as the European Year of Older People and Solidarity Between Generations. European research revealed that 75 percent of Europeans over age 65 are in good health and are active. The same is true in the United States. The Intergenerational Child Care Demonstration Project Act in Pennsylvania serves as an example. This potential law encourages the eldest generation to become caregivers to the youngest -- an excellent opportunity for Lions.

The Lions of Multiple District 105 (the British Isles and Ireland) understand and are actively recruiting Leos. "It's almost unfashionable in (MD) 105 not to have a Leo club, stated Philip Nathan, multiple district Leo chairman and a past international director.

As mentors, the Lions guide the Leos toward successful community service projects. Working hand-in-hand, they have participated in the annual Children in Need telethon, bed push race, duck race, stationary bicycle marathon, air shows and mobile van diabetes screenings.

Their investment in youth pays off. "The more involved Leos become Lions," stated Nathan. "We've encouraged it enormously." Leaders quickly surface. "It doesn't take too many years for the Leos to become Lions club presidents."

In Bermuda, members of the Bermuda High School Leo Club volunteered at the "Dunking Stool" at a local fair to earn money for the "Make a Wish" Foundation. A total of $250 was raised for the foundation. Additionally, Leos donated $600 towards the purchase of a hydraulic bed for a traffic accident victim now confined to a wheelchair.

The Leo Club of Chartiers-Houston, Pennsylvania, worked with the American Cancer Society during their Relay for Life event. Leos prepared the field for walkers, which included themselves, and worked all day unloading vans and cars, running children's games and selling luminaries.

Preceding the Relay for Life, club members sponsored an Italian dinner and all-school talent show that featured students in grades 7-12 performing a variety of acts from singing and dancing to impersonations. Leos raised $2,160 for the American Cancer Society with their efforts.

The Trafford, Pennsylvania, Leo Club sponsored a bake sale to raise funds for the family of an out-of-town patient hospitalized for several months at the West Penn Burn Trauma Center. Leos served a picnic lunch to the patient's family and presented them with the club's contribution.

In another activity, Trafford Leos baked 72 plates of cookies for Meals on Wheels.

In California, members of the Seal Beach Leo Club undertook their largest service project ever – the construction of a new archery range at the Lions Camp at Terrestita Pines. The range was finally completed after Leos made three trips to the mountains. The club also supplies new bows and arrows for the new range, and has pledged to maintain the range for an additional three years. The new range has been named in honor of the Seal Beach Leo Club for members' hard work and commitment to the project.

During his term as international president, Harry J. Aslan spoke of the development of leadership qualities and experience among Leos. President Aslan said, "It may very well be that 15 or 20 years from now these Leos will be our legislators, mayors, business and industrial executives, school and hospital administrators, and other governmental and civic leaders. The training they received in their Leo clubs will help them make rational judgments and decisions. Being Leos has given them the opportunity to learn sensible values about those most important qualities of life – decency, honesty, and respect for others. Their membership in Leo clubs provided this opportunity to become good and useful citizens. They learned to enrich their own lives through community service and aid to the less fortunate."

Chapter Twelve
Far Reaching Services

Leprosy is a terrifying diagnosis.

"I knew something was wrong back in 1973," said a man we'll call Bob, "but nobody knew how to diagnose it properly. The doctors called it peripheral neuropathy. I'm 40 years old now. Back in those years, I used to play baseball and basketball and I started to experience trouble with my coordination. I was working in a furniture store in Texas and began to have numbness in my fingers. I couldn't do what I wanted to do. For instance, if I dropped a coin and there were people watching, I couldn't pick it up, and rather than fumble I used to laugh and say, 'Well, I'll leave that to the sweeper.'

"The condition continued to get worse and I couldn't find out what was wrong. I went to visit my brother in Salem, Oregon, and while there went to a hospital in Portland. I was there a week and they, again, told me I had peripheral neuropathy. A Japanese doctor was visiting and he asked to check me. He made an incision in the calf of my leg and took out a section of nerve. Three hours later the doctor called me in and said, 'We've got good news and bad news. The good news is we know what's wrong. The bad news is you've got a form of leprosy.' He told me about this hospital and I came directly to it."

Bob is a member of the Point Clair, Louisiana, Lions Club and a patient at the Gillis W. Long Hansen's Disease Center in Carville. On the Mississippi River, Carville is 25 miles south of Baton Rouge and 75 miles north of New Orleans.

The word "leper" and "leprosy" are now in medical and social disrepute and the disease is referred to as Hansen's disease, named for the Norwegian physician, G. Armauer Hansen, who discovered the bacillus in 1874. To contract the disease a person must have low resistance and live in contact with a person whose body contains large numbers of the germs. Hansen's disease develops in only about 5 percent of those persons married to Hansen's disease patients. It is rare among doctors and nurses who care for patients with the disease. It is not hereditary and almost never fatal.

Hansen's disease usually affects the peripheral (end) nerves near the surface of the face, arms and legs. Nerve damage causes a loss of feeling in the skin. Hansen's disease patients may injure or burn themselves without realizing it and severe nerve damage may cause paralysis.

Between 200 and 300 patients are at the Hansen's Disease Center at a time and they stay anywhere from two weeks to a year. It is estimated that there are 5,000 persons with this disease in the United States and about 20 million worldwide. Most U.S. patients were living in Texas, Louisiana, Florida, New York and Hawaii when diagnosed.

The Hansen's Disease Center provides comprehensive care for its patients, prepares the patient to return to his community, serves as a major research facility, and works to improve public understanding of Hansen's disease.

"The Bible mentions leprosy, but describes a very different disease and this has contributed to the misunderstanding and stigma," explained Dr. John Trautman. "For example, it is not highly contagious. Exposure to the disease rarely causes it. The second point is that it doesn't cause fingers, toes and noses to drop off as many people continue to think. When treated, the disease becomes inactive, but people must be careful of their hands and feet."

The Point Clair Lions Club was chartered October 4, 1950. Sponsored by a Lions club in Baton Rouge, it was started for the patients and later staff members were also invited to join. The club meets once a month in the library.

Along with providing help for patients at the hospital, the club contributes to a number of other activities such as the Lions of Louisiana Camp for Crippled Children and the Louisiana Eye Foundation. Recently the Lions bought a specially equipped electric bed for a 31-year-old handicapped woman in New Orleans.

A staff member, Bill, has been at the hospital for 25 years. Now 58, he said, "I got Hansen's disease in Puerto Rico at the age of 9 and at that time there weren't any remedies. In 1946, I began to get effective treatment but by then I had developed what's called disseminated Hansen's disease and this causes disfiguration. I came to the hospital in 1962 and have been here ever since.

"Clinically, the disease is not our problem. The stigma and fear of being rejected is: We have to hide the disease. Today, it's a little better, but most people are still frightened; they don't understand the disease. I think social aspects of Hansen's disease have not been scratched. One of the things I'd like to see in my lifetime is for people to accept us the way we are, as human beings with a treatable condition.

"I joined the Point Clair Lions Club here at the hospital in 1970," he added, "and this has had a major impact on my life. It gives me a chance to serve those who are less fortunate. It's a chance to put something back into life. One of the best ways to forget my own troubles is to look at someone else's and help that person. Lionism gives my life a purpose and friends to help me fulfill it."

Healing means "to make whole." Drugs, therapy, recreation, good food and pleasant surroundings combine to bring physical health to the patients at the Hansen's Disease Center.

However, that's only part of the prescription. Understanding and meaning are also essential. Reaching out with principles refined over seven decades, the Point Clair Lions Club holds out a fresh and hopeful vision of lives grounded in giving and serving.

Lions Battle Drug Scourge

In his best selling book *Reality Therapy*, William Glasser, M.D., wrote: "People who are not, at some time in their lives, preferably early, exposed intimately to others who care enough about them to love and discipline them will not learn to be responsible. For that failure, they suffer all their lives."

Dr. Glasser, a California psychiatrist, created a stir with his analysis of dishonest, irresponsible behavior as the root cause of many mental and emotional problems including drug addiction and alcoholism. Three hundred miles north of Montreal in the center of Quebec, Lions have put Glasser's ideas to work in a successful drug treatment facility for adolescents called Havre du Fjord (HDF) in the town of La Baie.

Spearheaded by an LCIF grant of $45,881 received in October 1995, 12 Lions clubs are working together to upgrade and expand the facility. The clubs include La Baie, Alma, Roberval, Chicoutimi, Metabechouan, Clermont La Malbaie, Baie St. Paul, La Baie Nord, Jonquiere Metro, Dolbaur, St. Felicien and Jonquiere.

"Including the LCIF grant, Lions have contributed $125,000," said Jacques Tremblay, Past Governor of District U-2 and a member of the Chicoutimi Lions Club. A Lion since 1978, Tremblay continued, "The center treats adolescent drug users between the ages of 12 and 17. These young people have been using cocaine, marijuana, hashish, mescaline, crack and PCP and many of them drink alcohol. While many use both drugs and alcohol, 80 percent use only drugs and the center is designed to house nine people, both male and female, for a 12-week program."

The recoveries make moving stories. Jacques began sniffing cocaine when he was seven. All of his family used drugs. He was detoxified in a hospital and then came to Havre du Fjord from Montreal in 1993 at the age of 14 with a real desire to kick the drug habit. During his 12 weeks in the facility, he went to school and received tutoring to improve his marginal reading, writing and mathematics skills. He was sent to a foster home in Montreal where he lives today, goes to school, is free of drugs and works at a part-time job.

Now 17, Jacques said, "I'd be dead if it weren't for Havre du Fjord. I never knew anything about living until they showed me how to make some sense out of my life. Sometimes I still get tempted to use drugs, but I remember the lessons they taught me and it reminds me of what that life was like and I never want that again."

Irresponsibility is the hallmark of drug abusers and alcoholics and for that, they suffer unless they are fortunate enough to find a structured environment in which they can learn to live responsibly.

At Havre du Fjord they find such an environment. In an atmosphere of compassionate toughness, understanding, discipline and responsibility, each resident learns to grow up and function as a mature adult. Demanding but fair, it combines work, recreation, training, group therapy, education; all of these in a climate of loving concern. For some of these youngsters, it's the only family they've ever known.

The facility includes five bedrooms, five baths, eight meeting rooms, a kitchen and dining room. There are only seven residential drug treatment centers for adolescents in the province of Quebec and most of them have only limited space for housing long-term patients.

In 1994, 17-year-old Marie arrived at the center from Montreal trying to kick a six-year cocaine habit. Her family didn't use drugs, but she became addicted and is now HIV positive and suffers from Hepatitis B. She said, "I was just waiting to die when I came to HDF. They changed my direction and gave me hope. I don't know how long I'm going to live, but I know that I'm going to use all the time I have left as wisely as possible."

Frequently, addicts come from homes lacking discipline and the controls needed to produce responsible individuals. With knowledge born of successful experience, HDF provides the kind of disciplined love that rebuilds addicts into men and women equipped to live drug-free.

Adolescent alcoholics and drug addicts are recovering at Havre du Fjord because Quebec Lions reached out and said, "How can we help?" With an inspired blend of their time, energy and money, the Lions are transforming lives day after day.

Although not all the youngsters who come to Havre du Fjord are successful, some of the stories are dramatic. In 1992, 16-year-old Yvonne arrived at HDF from Chicoutimi with a bad drug problem, a damaged liver and severe depression. Her father was dead and her mother a drug user.

"I wanted to quit but I didn't know how," she said. "The counselors at the center were very patient and showed me how to change my attitudes and habits so that I didn't have to use drugs. I had been a rotten student, but I went back to high school and today I'm 20, working as a waitress and going to college at night. My thanks to Havre du Fjord."

The Federal Republic of Germany is one of the many nations in which Lions have made a difference in the drug problem with a program to stop addiction before it begins.

"One of the problems with a prevention program is that people generally don't believe that evil will come," said Dr. Herbert Schafer. "Parents invariably feel that drug addiction won't strike their child, and if it happens, cannot understand how it happened."

Director of Law Enforcement for Bremen and Bremerhaven in the Federal Republic of Germany, Dr. Schafer is one of the Lions in District 111-0 who developed the addiction prevention program that has taken hold in the country. He is a member of the Bremen (Hanse) Lions Club.

"Prevention means working with hope in the future," Dr. Schafer continued. "It takes time and patience, but if we persist, we can be sure that we'll save some of our young people from the misery of drug addiction. We can see some results already. For instance, where marijuana is concerned, there was a powerful movement 10 years ago in Germany to legalize it. There was endless talk about its not being harmful. Today, that has turned around. People are aware of its dangers and at least some of that awareness results from the Lions prevention program."

Dr. Schafer's remarks are supported by data from the National Institute of Drug Abuse in the United States. This shows that, aside from alcohol, marijuana is the first drug most young people try. If they are buying marijuana on the street, as most of them must, then they will be exposed to the rest of the drugs, too.

The Bremen program got its start in May 1981, at a district meeting in which more than 700 Lions participated. The program was adopted unanimously by the group. The project cooperates with all appropriate agencies but does not receive any financial support from the government. About 50 percent of the Lions clubs in Germany take part in the program.

The addiction prevention program aims at stopping *all* drug abuse, including such prescription drugs as tranquilizers and sleeping pills. Ambitious and specific, it is designed to provide information and motivation to young people to avoid *any* chemical dependency.

Herbert Baumgarte, of the Delmenhorst Lions Club, is chairman of the prevention program. "We've prepared a workbook that is the backbone of the program," he explained. "This was developed by several Lions, including Bernd Isler, Dr. Horst Liebig, and me. The age of drug abusers is getting younger and younger and our aim is to prevent young people from experimenting with drugs. Drug abuse cuts across all social and economic classes."

"We've directed our program at schools and teachers," Lion Baumgarte continued, "and the workbook gives the teachers factual information on the problem and what to do about it. It also includes tips on the best ways to use the information. In many schools in Germany there is a teacher responsible for informing other teachers and the students about the drug problem. This is the person we concentrate on with our prevention program because he or she will be most influential and best qualified to use our material."

The effectiveness of drug prevention programs is often hard to measure. However, there are many cases like a young man we'll call Karl. Karl lives in Bremen and said, "I heard one of my teachers talk to our class using the workbook the Lions provided. Then, as part of the program, I heard a former addict talk about what had happened to him as a result of drug abuse. He was in his 30s and had been down a rough, rough road created by his addictions. I knew that he knew exactly what he was talking about.

"I had been smoking marijuana and treated getting high like a joke. I was 16. Suddenly, it wasn't funny anymore. There just wasn't any way I could ignore what had been said. Several days later I went to see the teacher who had talked to us and told him about my marijuana use. He put me in touch with a small group of people my own age who had been experimenting with drugs. The leader of the group was a former addict who had recovered and I haven't used drugs since. That was nearly three years ago. I finished high school and am going to college. That talk several years ago was a major turning point in my life."

Lions' approaches to the drug problem take varied forms. In Japan, 10 Lions clubs in District 333-A sponsored a citizen's rally against drugs. It was followed by a parade during which Lions handed out leaflets.

Finnish Lions in Multiple District 107 work with the "Free of Drugs" organization to toughen laws on abuse of alcohol and other drugs. Tasmania, Australia, Lions of District 201-T1 erected a drug information center in Hobart while the Tall Ships were docked there.

Between 30,000 and 40,000 persons visited the exhibit each day of the four-day period.

The Turkish Ministry of Health assigned the Lions District 118-T Drug Awareness Committee to coordinate all their drug awareness programs.

Special Camping Opportunities

An ecology camp is the project that the Lions Club of Zvishavane, Zimbabwe, has chosen to offer young boys a chance to learn the basics of the flora and fauna of the Zimbabwean bush country.

"Knowing that there are children we never leave the towns and most often some who cannot afford the pleasure and valuable knowledge that an ecology camp can offer," said Lion Glenys Morgan, "the Lions pressed on and this camp is now run successfully on an annual basis."

He explained, "The first camp was run for only three days, but has now been stretched to 10 days so more time can be spent in getting to know the boys. Their itinerary has also been spread out, making comprehension much easier." The camp is designed to give the boys a working knowledge of their surroundings. They participate in group activities and are encouraged to mix with other children from all levels of society to help them become future leaders in their communities.

Morgan pointed out: "Their days are filled with walks in the bush, during which experienced guides lecture on plant life, birds, and the follow-up on animal spoor. They are also taken on game rides, where the boys see elephants, lions, and a variety of wildlife."

At the end of each ecology camp, he noted, the boys are asked to write about their experiences and what they had learned during the camp. "Some of the accounts are very informative, showing that the boys took note of everything and learned quite a lot," he added.

"On the last night, a public speaking contest is held in which each boy may talk on any subject he chooses. On arrival back in Zvishavane, a floating trophy is presented to the winner of the contest. Parents are invited to attend the presentation," Morgan said.

"One of the notable factors of the camp," he explained, "is the inter-service club relationship between the two Lions clubs of

Zvishavane and Triangle. The fellowship experienced among the Lions creates an atmosphere of security and togetherness," Morgan emphasized, "giving the boys greater confidence so that they return home with a new outlook on life."

In an article in *The Lion* in 2001, writer Mike Hernacki told an engrossing story of a camp founded by the San Diego, California, Lions in 1995.

It began in 1994 when Lion Jack Wyatt was watching a documentary that told the story of a Brooklyn police officer who on his own time took poor urban kids to upstate New York to experience the great outdoors. Jack, who has been District 4-L6 Governor in 1991-92, was at the time Director of PAL, the Police Athletic League. It occurred to him that there were probably plenty of kids in San Diego who were as needy as those in New York. He thought, "Why not do something like that here?"

He presented the idea to PAL and the San Diego (Host) Lions Club, and got an OK. He set a goal to send 100 underprivileged and at-risk children to a one-week camp in 1995. Then he learned that many years before, the mother of a long-time Lion had donated land for a camp in the mountains 60 miles east of San Diego. Camp Wolahi is owned and operated by Campfire Boys & Girls, who offered to make the camp available for 100 kids at $180 each. The total amount needed would be around $20,000. Wyatt secured grants of $5,000 from his own club, $5,000 from the Boys & Girls Foundation, and the rest from other area Lions clubs and charitable organizations.

Since PAL was co-sponsoring that first camp, children were identified and selected with the help of law enforcement and probation officers. The County Probation Department provided the buses to take the kids to camp and Campfire Boys & Girls provided the counselors and other personnel needed to create a complete camp experience. As the organizers were hammering out all the details, someone noted that the camp had to have a name. After trying and rejecting dozens of possibilities, a committee member said, "It was Jack's idea. Let's just call it Camp Jack" — and the name stuck.

"That first year was great," Jack Wyatt recalled. "We had kids out there who had never smelled a pine tree, never went on a hike, never sat around a campfire. But we knew that if we wanted to make any kind of lasting impression on them, we needed to get them back a second and third time."

So the second year, Camp Jack hosted 200 urban kids — 80 from the year before and 120 new ones. The 80 percent retention rate was considered a major victory. The youngsters liked their camp experience enough to come back again. This time the bill was $40,000, about half of which Jack got from his and other Lions clubs in the area. In the third year, the camp drew 300 kids — 100 new and 200 repeaters. Camp Jack had become an institution.

Camp Jack now annually hosts 100 campers per week for three consecutive weeks each summer. The main sponsors are still the San Diego (Host) Lions Club Welfare Foundation, Boys & Girls Foundation, and PAL. A number of other sponsors have come aboard, including several foundations whose mission it is to protect children who are abused or whose parents are in jail. PAL still provides camper candidates, law enforcement volunteers, and transportation.

The annual price tag is up over $60,000, with all funds going for camperships. Camp Jack pays for:

- The camp facilities, which include dining hall, recreation room, sleeping cabins, swimming pool, arts and crafts rooms, plus use of nearby Lake Cuyamaca.
- Trained counselors and camp staff, provided by Campfire Boys & Girls
- Food and beverages
- Health and liability insurance
- A T-shirt for each camper
- $5.00 in-store credit for each camper to buy candy, gum, etc. The children are allowed to hold no cash.

Even with a well-trained and paid staff, Camp Jack would not be possible without the help of 125 volunteers who come from area Lions clubs and from city, county, and federal law enforcement agencies. The Probation Department provides incarcerated teens to do kitchen work and clean-up around the camp. These teens work voluntarily — they get no time off their sentences for their work.

Wyatt explained, "A program like this takes three elements —— people, money, and ideas. If you have any two of those, the third will come. And it will come naturally, with the synergy that results when people see they're in a win/win situation."

Indiana Lions Battle Lung Cancer

"In the fall of 1999 I was diagnosed with lung cancer," said Jack Richards, a service station attendant in central Indiana. "For years I had emphysema and other respiratory problems no doubt related to many years of smoking and now I had a golf-ball-size cancerous tumor in my right lung. Because of the other lung problems I wasn't a candidate for surgery and didn't have too many choices. One of my doctors told me about a new clinical trial at the Indiana University Cancer Center in Indianapolis and after talking it over with my wife, Millie, and son, William Gene, we decided to give it a try.

"I started the trial in June, 2000, and received three treatments over a 10-day period. There were no side effects and I always felt fine afterwards. The tumor shrank to the size of a marble and today I visit the Cancer Center every three months for a checkup where the doctors and staff evaluate my health. I heard somebody once say that cancer is a word and not a sentence. I am 50 years old and hope there are many good years ahead of me thanks to my treatment at the Cancer Center at Indiana University."

One of the nation's leading cancer treatment centers, the Indiana University School of Medicine in Indianapolis, has worked with the Indiana Lions since 1946. Since that year the Indiana Lions have raised more than $4,500,000 for the Department of Radiation Oncology at the Indiana University School of Medicine and have provided funding for 30 major pieces of equipment. Most of the money has been used to buy treatment equipment, but some funds have been spent to educate physicians and therapists while other donations have been directed toward cancer research.

Despite steady advances in treating cancer, it remains the second leading cause of death among Americans, behind heart disease. According to the American Cancer Society, lung cancer is the leading cause of cancer death for both men and women. This year officials say, about 169,500 new cases of lung cancer will appear in the United States. An estimated 157,400 people will die of lung cancer: About 90,100 men and 67,300 women.

Since the Lions began contributing to the Indiana University School of Medicine's Radiation Oncology Program, more than 60 residents have been trained on the most up-to-date equipment available. In addition, numerous research projects and protocols have been developed and results have been published in more than 85 articles in leading medical journals in just the last five years.

"Lung cancer patients frequently have numerous other health problems such as emphysema or heart disease that weakens their reserves, making them poor candidates for major lung surgery," said Pulmonologist Mark D. Williams, M.D., Clinical Assistant Professor of Medicine and principal investigator of the trial. "If the results of our trial are as promising as we hope, this will provide an exciting new treatment option for these lung cancer patients."

The new procedure, Stereotactic Body Radiotherapy, uses intensity modulated photon radiation, 3-D imaging and Stereotactic body mapping. It employs treatment concepts similar to those used in Gamma Knife radio surgery, a non-invasive technique which has been very effective in treating brain tumors. The Stereotactic Treatment Plan involves three outpatient treatments. This trial is for patients with early-stage lung cancer who are not candidates for surgery due to significant related medical problems. These patients typically have limited treatment choices.

"Stereotactic Body Radiotherapy is a promising technology," said Robert D. Timmerman, M.D., Assistant Professor of Radiation Oncology and co-principal investigator in the trial. "In 1997, Indiana University did the first treatment in the United States using this technology for a patient whose cancer had spread to the lung. This trial is unique and exciting, though, because it is for cancer that originates in the lung, a much more common problem affecting cancer patients."

Results are promising. A 77-year-old retired Indiana State Police Trooper was the first to use the Stereotactic Body Frame treatment for lung cancer. He was diagnosed four years ago and lost part of one lung to cancer surgery and was not able to tolerate another surgical procedure. He was also concerned about the side effects from radiation therapy. However, with the new treatment he underwent only three radiation treatments rather than the traditional 31.

"This can revolutionize the way medically inoperable, early-stage lung cancer is treated," said Dr. Robert Timmerman.

Elburn Lions Promote Healing

Let's hear it for the Elburn, Illinois, Lions Club. In a community with a population of only 3,300, the Elburn Lions Club numbers 200 members and that includes 42 Melvin Jones Fellows. Founded in 1928, the Elburn Lions Club funds and supports an extensive range of activities at every level.

Among many projects, twice a year the Elburn Lions host a hyperbaric oxygen chamber in the 26-acre Lions Park in the center of Elburn. A major asset in community activities, the Lions Park features about 70 events a year.

"Lions help has been priceless," said Carrie Capes of nearby Maple Park. "We learned of the benefits of hyperbaric oxygen therapy for our son Max from a parent support group. He's four and a half and has a genetic condition called mitochondrial metabolic disorder. This manifests itself with neurological symptoms that include shakiness, low muscle tone, poor motor planning, speech difficulties and mild hearing impairment. After 164 treatments, Max has made rapid strides.

"By hosting the mobile hyperbaric unit in the Lions Park, the Elburn Lions have made a major contribution to the health of many of us in the area. They provide the space to park the mobile chamber, bathroom facilities for the patients and community contacts for free generator fuel. We have people come from as far away as Kenosha, Wisconsin; Kankakee, Illinois; and even South Dakota. Parents have reported improvements in their children with reduced seizure activity, better speech, stronger muscle tone, reduced spasticity, improved walking and thinking ability. We could not have done this without the Lions."

Hyperbaric oxygen has proven effective for treating stroke victims, diabetic gangrene, burns, crushing injuries, osteomyelitis, multiple sclerosis, lyme disease. It is particularly potent in helping children with brain injuries or cerebral palsy.

During hyperbaric oxygen therapy (HBOT), the patient breathes pure, 100 percent oxygen under increased atmospheric pressure.

(The air we normally breathe contains only 19-21 percent of this essential element.) Concentration of oxygen normally dissolved in the blood stream is thus raised many times above normal (up to 2,000 percent). In addition to the blood, all body fluids including the lymph and cerebrospinal fluids are infused with the healing benefits of this molecular oxygen. It can reach bone and tissue which are inaccessible to red blood cells, enhance white blood cell function and promote the formation of new capillary and peripheral blood vessels. This results in increased infection control and faster healing of a wide range of conditions.

When administered by highly trained professionals, HBOT is extremely safe and effective. It is used, usually as part of an overall medical treatment plan, for a variety of conditions. While increasing in popularity in the United States, it is still far more common in Europe and the Orient. In fact, in some areas of Italy, a physician may have his or her license revoked for neglecting to utilize this therapy. The results reported by Capes are routinely seen.

Scientific research has shown that in children or adults who have been brain injured, the brain tissue surrounding the injury contains cells that have not been killed but only stunned. These idling or sleeping cells lie in a dormant state between the damaged and the healthy parts of the brain. Hyperbaric oxygen can revive these cells and this is where the improvements come in the treatment.

For example, Carrie Koenig's son Tyler is six-and-a-half and has received a hundred treatments in two years. "Tyler is mentally impaired," said Koenig. "He was developmentally delayed with poor muscle tone and delayed in speech, reading, and writing. After the first round of 40 treatments we saw better speech improvements than he was getting from speech therapy at the time. He took a three-month hiatus from the therapy for the hyperbaric treatments and the speech therapist said he made nine months of progress through the hyperbaric therapy. Without the Lions we would not have been able to do this. They have changed our lives."

"That's what we like to hear," said Doris Klomhaus, a past president of the Elburn Lions Club. "My husband Tim is club secretary and keeps busy. We have a strong club. That includes our

Leos. They raised $25,000 for a three-year-old girl with multiple disabilities."

"The Elburn Lions have made a huge difference in our lives," said Tracey Weaver of nearby Sycamore whose four-year-old often shares treatment sessions with Max Capes. "We've noticed a big improvement in Jake's muscle tone after his HBOT sessions and the treatments help prevent his epileptic seizures as well."

Human beings can live without food for weeks, without water for a couple of days, but without oxygen for only a few minutes. Twice a year the Elburn Lions bring oxygen and healing to their neighbors. "The Lions brought us hope when we had very little," said Carrie Capes. "I knew nothing about Lionism before my experience with the Elburn Lions Club and it's wonderful to see that there are men and women who will reach out to perfect strangers and change their lives."

Chapter Thirteen
How Lions Meet Special Needs
– Part One

When a human being needs help just about anywhere in the world, the Lions find a way to provide it. Whatever the need, the Lions tailor a program to meet it. Special needs require special efforts. Here's an example from Jamaica.

Denise Pinnock is a charming woman who might not be alive today if it were not for the Lions of Jamaica. A fitness enthusiast, Pinnock walks four-and-a-half miles a day, as well as working out in the gym regularly.

"I started the exercise program several years ago," said Pinnock, "when the Heart Foundation screening showed that I had high blood pressure. The regular exercise and attention to my diet brought my blood pressure down to where it belongs and I'm probably the healthiest 66-year-old in Jamaica." She is a regular participant in the Heart Health Fund Run sponsored by the Lions; her last jaunt covered 22 laps at the National Stadium.

"Our club started the Heart Foundation of Jamaica in 1971 to help prevent heart disease in our country," explained Peter Bangerter, a Lion since 1965 and a founding member of the Kingston, Jamaica, Lions Club. "Heart disease is a major problem in Jamaica," he pointed out. "As an example, in 1993, 13,354 blood pressure checks showed that 38.2 percent of the individuals tested suffered from hypertension. Nearly half of these persons were unaware of their conditions."

Jamaican Lions include nine Melvin Jones Fellows among their membership. Peter Bangerter is one and another is Rufus Chang, a Lion for 23 years. Chang is the uncle of Deborah Chen, who is a registered nurse and general manager of the Heart Foundation.

"Heart disease is the Number One killer in Jamaica," Chen said, "and 30 percent of the people in our country suffer from the disease.

The Heart Foundation nips these problems in the bud and saves the lives of many, many Jamaicans. We do everything as inexpensively as possible. For instance, we provide medication at a small charge and if a person cannot afford it, then we find a way to provide it for nothing."

The annual budget of the Heart Foundation is $145,000. That includes $80,000 in cash and another $65,000 which is donated in goods and services. The Lions contribute 20 percent of the yearly budget and work effectively in generating support for the foundation.

The Netherlands Embassy donated $4,500 to the foundation, which was used to open a pharmacy. Three pharmaceutical companies then donated drugs to help the pharmacy get started.

The British High Commission in Jamaica has donated an EKG machine, stethoscopes, blood pressure measuring machines, and other necessary equipment for checking circulatory system health.

George Manley, a 61-year-old retired farmer in Montego Bay, said, "I had no idea there was anything wrong with my blood pressure until the Heart Foundation van came to our area and I was screened and found it was 190/120. I hadn't any symptoms of ill health and they gave me medication which brought my blood pressure down to manageable levels. I was at high risk for a heart attack or perhaps a stroke and the Heart Foundation examination probably saved my life. The lady who did the screening also taught me how to change my diet. I began getting more exercise and relaxing a bit more."

Stephanie Brown, a school teacher in Ocho Rios, is another whose life was changed by the Heart Foundation. She said, "My granddaughter told me about the Heart Foundation screening and almost dragged me over there. I'm 58 years old and always felt well, but she said I ought to be checked out anyhow.

"It turned out that I have an irregular heartbeat that the doctor said could have been serious. I had noticed a shortness of breath and they gave me a prescription for some medicine, which I take and now I have no problems with the heartbeat. It probably would have become more severe in the next couple of years," she noted, "so I'm grateful to deal with a health problem now that I didn't even know existed."

The foundation employs 24 staff members, including six registered nurses. Originally, the Heart Foundation of Jamaica aimed at raising funds to purchase diagnostic, surgical, and intensive care equipment for the treatment of heart patients. The bulk of the equipment was given to the University Hospital of the West Indies, where open-heart surgery was, at the time, being performed and the catheter laboratory was functioning for diagnostic purposes. However, the Heart Foundation of Jamaica's priorities have since changed to prevention.

"Initially, the foundation was involved in paying for surgery," said George Bullock, who served as 1994-95 president of the Kingston Lions Club. "For example, rheumatic heart disease is still a severe problem in Jamaica. This damages the heart valves, each of which costs $3,000 to repair in surgery. For that amount of money, we could screen 600 people.

"Obviously," Bullock pointed out, "we're better off screening and preventing heart disease. I found out about the Lions because my father is nearly blind and I learned about the Lions' mission in helping the visually handicapped." Bullock joined the club in 1988.

Diet counseling is an important part of the Heart Foundation's mission. Obesity has now reached epidemic proportions among Caribbean females and that includes adolescent girls. The problem is growing among young males as well. This is a major factor in high blood pressure and hypertension as these young people get older.

"I never knew anything about Lions until recently," said Mary Wilson, a 63-year-old retired Kingston school teacher. "Two years ago I was in a supermarket and the Heart Foundation was checking blood pressure there. Just on a whim, I asked them to check mine and to my amazement, my blood pressure was nearly 200. They told me I was at high risk for a heart attack or stroke and sent me over to a heart specialist at the University Hospital of the West Indies. I was extremely overweight. The doctor gave me a complete physical examination, put me on a diet and prescribed some medication, which fairly soon brought my blood pressure down to normal. I also lost 65 pounds.

"In Jamaica," emphasized Wilson, "we say 'boonoonoonoos,'" which means 'super,' and what the Heart Foundation has done for me is certainly 'boonoonoonoos'!"

In British Columbia the Canadian Lions are building new lives at the Child Development Centre.

"Without the centre and the help from the Lions we'd have been lost," said Joy Kerr. "Brendan is five years old and he's been going to the centre almost his whole life. He's epileptic and has fairly severe developmental delays. That was diagnosed when he was about nine months old and he's been attending here full-time and receiving physiotherapy and speech therapy, and generally working with the team to address his delays. The Child Development Centre is the only facility around here geared to helping youngsters like Brendan who have special needs.

"I can only speculate on how far behind Brendan would be at this point without that early intervention. My husband and I feel that we can control Brendan's epilepsy and prevent the seizures from happening. It's the delays we're concerned about. He can live a productive life with epilepsy by applying the help he has received at the centre. Brendan's whole life is going to be better than it would have been without it."

Brendan is one of 3,500 children helped by the Comox Valley Child Development Centre in Cumberland, British Columbia, Canada, on Vancouver Island. Operating on an annual budget of $500,000, the centre opened in 1974. Presently, a staff of 23 serves the needs of 183 children. Ages range from newborns to 19, and special needs children are treated without charge.

Local Canadian Lions play a major role in the facility's success. The Comox Valley Child Development Centre is a joint project of the Lions clubs of Baynes Sound, Comox Valley, Courtenay, Qualicum Bay and Royston. Much of its operating costs result from fundraising activities of the Lions with the net total over the years in excess of $250,000. Funding also is received from the Ministry of Health and the Ministry of Social Services.

"The main objective of our mission is to help each child referred to us rise to his or her fullest potential," said Glenda Lake, the centre's administrator. "We want children to become as independent and functional as possible, given their individual resources.

"I began here as an assistant in 1975," she continued. "Then the centre was nowhere near what it is now. We only served seven or eight children. We have since had two expansions and presently have 15 rooms, excluding bathrooms. These include a small gymnasium, a physiotherapy treatment area, an occupational therapy treatment area, and a speech and language area."

The centre was opened originally to serve children with cerebral palsy. The scope of its operation has grown steadily over the years and, today, it uses 15,000 square feet for its various programs.

Therapy is available to infants and school-age children while the classroom programs are primarily for children who are functioning at a preschool level. Each approach has proven effective in correcting a variety of problems.

"Our club has been involved with the Child Development Centre from the beginning," said Wayne Lawrence, past president of the Comox Valley Lions Club. "One of our projects in helping to finance the facility is raffling a fishing boat every year. We raise from $8,000 to $9,000. As an example of what the centre is able to do, one youngster who recently moved into the area has muscle problems resulting in a lack of coordination. Therapy has helped him tremendously. We've just bought him a tricycle and he's able to ride. He never could have done that without the centre's treatment."

Since 1974, the Child Development Centre has worked with children suffering disabilities such as muscular dystrophy, cerebral palsy, autism, blindness, deafness, Down syndrome, cleft palate, speech and language delays, infantile seizures, assorted learning disabilities, and brain damage, along with those who are paraplegic and amputees."

The centre employs a treatment team approach. All staff members including the medical advisor work together in planning and implementing individual programs for each child. Parents are encouraged to become a part of the team to heighten effectiveness of the treatment.

The Lions Clubs International Foundation provided a $50,000 grant for the Child Development Centre in 1989, bringing total contributions from Lions to more than a quarter of a million dollars.

"The LCIF grant was a shot in the arm," said Lake, "because knowing the money was coming provided the impetus to raise the additional funds needed for expansion. Together with money from other sources, we were able to reach the $430,000 necessary for this expansion. The funds also helped to purchase new equipment.

"The involvement of the Lions is at the heart of what keeps the centre going," she continued. "Their interest has been consistent. Their support is unwavering and they develop projects of their own. They sell raffle tickets and hold horseride-a-thons. A bike-a-thon is also being planned which will see participants pedaling from the northern tip of Vancouver Island to the southern. The Lions are not only there for specific occasions, they are there all the time."

The preschool programs at the centre are integrated for children with special needs and those who are developing normally. They may be as young as 16 months and as old as six, and are enrolled two-to-four days a week. Parents, therapists, teachers, and others pool their skills to design the most helpful intervention for the special child. Assessment and continuous evaluation and communication are part of each process. Individual needs may range from mild to severe, including speech problems, behavioral, motor or learning disabilities, and specific conditions or diseases.

The preschool program uses four classrooms and teachers in each one provide a separate program tailored for that group of children. All these teachers are certified Early Childhood Educators and some have Special Needs training. Therapists often work with children and teachers in the classrooms to provide additional support for the students.

Activities are arranged to provide a balance of:

- Group and individual involvement
- Organized play and free choice
- Quiet periods and active periods of play

The program is designed to make learning and developing skills fun. It provides an opportunity for the children to accept those who are different with participation aimed at enhancing and reinforcing their family life experiences.

The Speech and Language Department is designed to aid in the development of each child's ability to communicate, either verbally or through alternative systems such as sign language, picture boards or electronic devices.

The ages of children enrolled in this program range up to eight and function at various levels of development. Because of the requirements of some of the children, the speech therapist is also involved in developing feeding programs for children with neurologically-based problems.

Therapy may be conducted on either a one-to-one or group basis depending on the child. Designed to be fun and motivating, therapy may include art, music and play to help the child deal with some of the emotional stress or frustration that accompanies the communication delay.

A Lion for 30 years and past president of the Courtenay Club, Tom McNee speaks from personal experience when he said, "The program really works. I have a granddaughter who goes there. She's four and has been attending the centre since she was eight months old. She was a little slow in her speech, but now she's running around and talking a mile a minute. Why? Because she received speech therapy and it made an immense difference. It's meant a lot to many of us who have been Lions for years to see something we worked so hard to support help so many people."

The physical and occupational therapists are part of a united team which, along with parents, are involved in the coordinated program and management of their children. Each therapist brings a sound knowledge of normal and abnormal development to the job. Special techniques encourage each child's development while discouraging abnormal movements and deformities. The emphasis of all treatment is to provide the experience of progressive, active, normal development upon which the child can build.

"During the years I've been here I have seen endless inspiring examples," said Glenda Lake. "We had one little fellow who was referred to us soon after birth. He was born with a cancerous tumor on his leg and the leg was amputated when he was five months old. He was with us for three and a half years before the family moved away. He wouldn't let anything stop him. You would see him running up and down stairs with a peg leg. He had a great disposition and a wonderful attitude. When he left here he still had that peg leg and will, of course, graduate to a proper prosthesis. He was a marvelous boy and you just knew that this was a kid who was going to make it."

"When my daughter was nine months old she was diagnosed with cerebral palsy and the doctor recommended the Child Development Centre," said Phyllis Baudais. "At first we would come in once a week and Amy would receive therapy and when she was 18 months old, she was eligible to be enrolled. She's five years old now and has made outstanding progress. Not only is she walking, but she has a talking computer and the help of a speech therapist. Learning how to use the computer has really added to her self-confidence. The people at the centre have worked very hard with her and she's made wonderful progress. Amy was so proud when she was selected to cut the ribbon at the centre's expansion ceremonies in 1990. So was I."

After little Amy Baudais and Travis Hudson cut that ribbon on September 22, 1990, a troop of Brownies came bursting through the paper behind the ribbon carrying balloons and plates of cake. A jazz combo added to the happy celebration.

The results speak for themselves. The centre has enabled children to break out of the prison caused by their handicaps. The Lions of Vancouver Island, however, do not intend to stop here.

"The Comox Valley Child Development Centre is a fine example of Lionism in action," said Bob Pearson of the Royston Lions Club. "I'd like to see these kinds of facilities in every community in the world. They're a necessity. The Lions in our area are now putting the funds they've raised toward another child development centre near Abbotsford, east of here. Where there's a need, we'll try to meet it."

In Europe in a magnificent display of combined initiative, 500 Lions clubs with more than 15,000 members in four different countries banded together to transform lives in developing nations. They call themselves the North Sea Lions and include 10 European districts.

- Denmark – 106-C
- England – 105-M
- Germany – 111-N and 111-NB

- The Netherlands – 110-AN, 110-AZ, 110-BZ, 110-CO and 110-CW

The concept of the North Sea Lions cooperative program originated in Great Britain in 1979 with District 105-M. Each year one country proposes a project and all work together to make it successful. The North Sea Lions Federation breathes life into the First Object of Lions Clubs International: "To create and foster a spirit of understanding among the peoples of the world."

"The North Sea Lions established contacts with friends in Bangladesh, Swaziland, Kenya, India, Indonesia, Namibia, Sri Lanka, Rwanda, Tanzania and Thailand," explained Past District 111-MD Governor Dr. Wolfgang Griese. "The contacts are steadily expanded by continuing activity in the projects."

The first North Sea Lions program in 1979-80 was spearheaded by the English Lions in District 105-M and provided advanced X-ray equipment for a children's hospital in Bangladesh. Working closely with the Bangladesh Lions, the North Sea Lions bought, delivered and installed the X-ray equipment, paid for in part by a $10,000 LCIF grant, and then trained local technicians in its correct use.

One of the most populous and poorest countries in the world, Bangladesh has more than 80 million people living in an area slightly larger than New York state. The nation has been torn by war and is plagued by nearly annual cyclones and floods. Severe floods in 1974 left 70 percent of the country flooded, millions homeless and widespread starvation.

Against this background of poverty and natural disasters, the North Sea Lions stepped in to provide up-to-date, high tech X-ray equipment for disease diagnosis.

The medical director of the hospital reported: "We treat many different health problems in children ranging from infants up to adolescents. The new X-ray equipment enables us to make an accurate diagnosis quickly and far more accurately than we could before. As a result, we've had children come here for treatment from all over Bangladesh and have been able to dramatically increase the recovery rate for many illnesses."

The following year, the Lions of the Netherlands in MD 110 designed and implemented a North Sea Lions project of programs for handicapped children in the capital city of Mbabane, Swaziland. In cooperation with the Swaziland Lions, the project provided instruction and training to help the workers function effectively and as independently as possible. An LCIF grant in the amount of $6,384 helped provide laundry facilities for the school for the disabled.

The Danish Lions of District 106-C led the way with a similar project for handicapped youngsters in Nairobi, Kenya, in 1981-82. They, too, worked closely with local Lions clubs. Programs for handicapped children in Third World nations aim at total rehabilitation. Any necessary surgical and medical care is available to correct physical problems. Medical care includes all types of therapy required to bring maximum physical mobility to each child.

"I never had much hope when I came to the Lions program seven years ago," said one of the students, a 22-year-old male. "However, I learned a great deal through the training and have been able to support myself since then."

In Ranipur, India, men, women and children enjoy clear, cool water because of the North Sea Lions. Clean water is nearly impossible to find in many parts of India and a large segment of the population lives in villages where the nearest water is more than a mile away. In many communities where there is water, it is frequently an open pond and may be used for drinking, washing clothes, bathing, and other needs and is often polluted. In summer, many of the ponds dry up completely. In at least one Indian community, the North Sea Lions solved the problem with deep wells in a program spearheaded by English Lions.

A shortage of housing is frequently a major source of misery in developing countries. In 1984-85, the Danish Lions selected Wajir, Kenya, for the North Sea project and built 80 homes for its inhabitants. The spotlight fell on housing again in 1986-87 when the English Lions led the way in building 100 native homes and one large community house, this time with the assistance of a $14,285 LCIF grant, in Sri Lanka.

"Due to population growth there is major need for new and larger schools to teach Africans academic work and trades," explained Thomas Seidensticker, past president of the Storman Lions Club in Germany. "At this stage of Namibia's development the need is urgent

300

and the construction of the schools can be met within the Lions' principles of understanding and peaceful coexistence."

In the farm schools, children from poor families are taught the basic skills of reading, writing, and arithmetic. The schools include courses in manual skills as well as arts and crafts. Students are also trained for such careers as carpenter, blacksmith, weaver, saddlemaker, metalworking, and construction.

Karl Lemp, a Lion for 10 years and a past president of the Storman Lions Club, explained, "We expect to develop our third project in Namibia in 1993-94, which will be the construction of more schools for young people. We built hothouses that raise cucumbers, tomatoes and carnations that some of the children of farm workers sell in town. Thus far we've built five large schools, four smaller ones, and a facility that teaches 500 students. The workers make their own bricks for building the schoolhouses."

Fred Huck, a founding member of the Harburger Berge Lions Club in Hamburg, added: "We've developed and implemented a wide range of projects and find it a highly effective program. We work with the Lions clubs in developing countries. Literally tens of thousands of men, women, and children have been helped by the joint activities of the North Sea Lions."

Proposed by the English Lions, the 1990-91 North Sea Lions Project was carried out in Pakponong in southern Thailand. Under the slogan, "Fresh Water in Thailand," a desperately needed fresh water reservoir was provided with the help of the local Buddhist Temple Lions Club. The reservoir provides all the water needed by some 2,500 people. Until the North Sea Lions became involved, the villagers had only received fresh water once a week and that very sparingly. It had to be delivered in tanks fastened to motor vehicles and the residents often found it necessary to walk more than a mile to gather precious supplies. Those unable to make the trip relied for survival on the help of their neighbors. The inhabitants are poor fishing families and many suffered from diseases caused by polluted water. Now, however, the villagers' health is better and lives made somewhat easier because of the massive water reservoirs.

In the Thailand project, the North Sea Lions provided the initial financing and worked with World Vision — England in its implementation. Thai officials continue to educate their citizens about the dangers of polluted water and about ways to improve sanitation, and Thai Lions remain involved. This enabled the villagers to start developing their own programs and has created other improvements in living conditions.

In 1991-92, Dutch Lions took the lead in a project based in Rwanda. North Sea Lions built a new medical center near Satinsyi, an area with about 40,000 inhabitants. Multiple District 110 also received an LCIF grant for $49,029 for the center. Until then the people had no medical center and no facilities for surgery, X-rays, dentistry, maternity or rooms for the ill. Working together, the Lions built a 30-room center which includes: operating room, laboratory facilities, dental offices, pharmacy, library, nurse's office, two delivery rooms, an isolation room with a 12-bed intensive care section, a 37-bed hospital ward, two kitchens, and a power station and warehousing space.

In addition, there are baths, showers, sterilization facilities, waiting rooms and other necessary facilities for the modern clinic.

The president of Rwanda, Juvenal Habyaramana, enthusiastically supported the project. He emphasized: "Our country fully backs this new medical facility built by the Lions and will continue to supply all necessary support for medical, domestic and maintenance staff. This represents a major step forward in safeguarding the health of my people."

Dr. Wolfgang Griese observed, "It is more and more important that we realize one of the most vital goals of Lions Clubs International: To work for peace and understanding among people. The North Sea Lions program puts that goal into action. Obviously, it's easy to formulate such a goal, but working out a specific program to reach it is much harder. The North Sea Lions Federation has done this."

The involvement of Lions is not limited by language, customs or national borders. Wherever there is a need, Lions will find a way to meet it. For nearly two decades the North Sea Lions have demonstrated generosity and compassion to residents of developing nations thousands of miles away.

British Columbia's residents are proud of the beauty of their home. The province's 6,000 Lions take great pride in an organization known as the British Columbia Lions Society for Children with Disabilities.

Since the Lions Society also owns the provincial franchise for Easter Seals, it is often recognized as the Easter Seal Society of British Columbia. Under both names, the Society's mandate is to enhance the lives of children with disabilities.

The origins of the Lions Society date back to 1947, when a handful of Vancouver (East) Lions Club members volunteered to use their own cars to transport children and adults diagnosed with polio and tuberculosis to hospital appointments. In 1949, other clubs in Vancouver joined the cause and purchased three buses to serve the city. These buses marked the beginning of the Lions Society's Easter Seal Bus Program, which still exists today.

In 1952, the British Columbia Lions Society for Children with Disabilities was officially registered as a provincial nonprofit charitable organization. Today the Society is among the largest nonprofit organizations in Canada. It raises nearly $8 million annually, and employs a full-time staff of 40 people. With the exception of two members, the Society's entire Board of Directors are Lions.

The primary objective of the Lions Society is to focus on the abilities of special-needs children and to enrich their lives by emphasizing those abilities. The Society is committed to introducing these youngsters to new experiences that will help them achieve greater independence and self-esteem. Most of the services are provided at minimal or no cost to the children's families.

The Lions Society functions on the belief that special-needs children should be able to enjoy the same recreational pursuits as other kids their age. Every summer, Lions Easter Seals Camps provide a fun-filled camping adventure for 1,300 children with disabilities. At Easter Seals Camps, the children swim, hike, canoe, perform skits, sing songs around a campfire and sleep overnight in a tent.

"Many mornings my six-year-old son, Kyle, refused to go to school," remarked his mother, Susan. "He complained that kids at school said he talked like a baby. Finally, I took him to a speech pathologist at the child development center. Now, a year later, Kyle speaks much more clearly and with more confidence."

The Lions Society funds three Child Development Centers located in Abbotsford, Dawson Creek, and Smithers. These facilities offer programs in physical and occupational therapy, speech pathology, infant development, and family support and counseling. They also provide preschool and day care services which fully integrate special-needs children with other kids the same age.

In 1992, the Lions Laser Skin Center at Vancouver Hospital was founded with a $720,000 grant from the Lions Society. Prior to the establishment of the Center, thousands of children and adults in British Columbia endured the emotional trauma that disfiguring birthmarks can cause.

"My daughter, Danielle, was born with a purple port wine stain that covered half her face. I'm convinced that if left untreated the stain had the potential to cause devastating harm to her emotional well-being," said Kathleen, her mother. "After four years of laser treatment, my daughter's stain is reduced to a healthy pink glow."

Hundreds of young patients like Danielle now face the world with renewed self-confidence and self-esteem, thanks to the Lions Laser Skin Center.

Horseback riding has multiple benefits for physically disabled children. In one treatment known as hippotherapy, experienced physiotherapists incorporate the rhythmic swinging motion of the horse's gait into a therapeutic, physically enhancing program for special-needs children.

Recognizing the value of hippotherapy, the Lions Society purchased 43 acres of farmland in 1990. Located in a suburb of Vancouver, the land now contains the Valley Therapeutic Equestrian Association. Children who rely on mobility aids such as wheelchairs and crutches gain a tremendous sense of achievement and freedom when they are able to control the movement of their horse.

Though the Lions Society can look back on its achievements with pride, it will continue to implement additional services for an increasing number of special-needs children in British Columbia. As always, their programs will focus on encouraging kids to have fun, experience new activities, and generally feel good about who they are and, just as importantly, what they can accomplish.

The following chapter further investigates the myriad ways that Lions meet special needs.

Chapter Fourteen
How Lions Meet Special Needs
– Part Two

Historically, the Portuguese have been fearless sailors, skilled navigators and courageous explorers. Fueled by the seamanship and genius of Prince Henry the Navigator, Portugal's swift 15th Century expansion placed it in the lead in Western Europe.

Against this rich historical past, the Portuguese Lions work tirelessly in the present to carry their message of hope and help. Lions Club International came to Portugal with the Lisbon (Host) Club in 1953 and today numbers 108 active clubs and nearly 3,000 members in the country.

The Portuguese Lions' membership includes more than 60 Melvin Jones Fellows, the first of whom was Past International Director Rui Taveira, a retired army colonel who became a Lion in Mozambique.

"We have many outstanding projects in Portugal," Rui Taveira said, "and have a home for the elderly in the town of Oeiras, a major project of the Oeiras Lions Club. We received a major boost with a $65,000 grant from LCIF for the project which cost a total of $2 million. The Portuguese government contributed half, the county gave 35 percent, the parish gave most of the rest, and the local Lions contributed $40,000 plus the $65,000 LCIF grant."

Oeiras is a community of 30,000 people about ten miles from Lisbon and the Lions club numbers 39 members, including five women.

Called the Parish Social Center of Oeiras, the facility was dedicated on November 15, 1997, by His Eminence the Archbishop of Lisbon, D. Antonio Riberio. Construction on the center began on October 30, 1993, and was completed in April, 1998. The facility has been a major emphasis project of the Oeiras Lions Club for ten years when they began raising money for the complex. The director of the center is Father Fernando Martins who is an active honorary member of the Oeiras Lions Club.

The center includes 30 sleeping rooms with baths, a large kitchen, cheerful dining room, rooms for recreation and handicrafts as well as the Lions Pavilion. Thirty employees cook, clean and handle social services.

Said 72-year-old Maria, "My children live several hundred miles away and as I've gotten older and less capable of caring for myself I wondered what would become of me. This beautiful center solved my problem because I have friends here, good food and medical care if I need it. I really don't know what would have happened to me without it but it has become a very pleasant home for me. The meals are good, we have lots of activities and my life is far more interesting that it was a year ago before I moved in here."

The day's activities at the center are extensive and include exercise, handicrafts, singing, card games, bingo, parties and medical assistance wherever needed. The residents and day-care clients receive excellent food, clothing if they need it, and enjoy books, movies and other entertainment. They have friends with whom they can share the rest of their lives. The Lions Pavilion in the center seats 400 people and is a multi-purpose auditorium. It's used for church services, films, lectures, parties and any activity that the staff schedules.

Maria Avelina Angeiras was governor of District 115-CS, 1997-98. "One of the many wonderful things about this center for the elderly is that the people won't be alone anymore. Some of them have no family and no one to turn to but us. Without us they would have been all alone."

A member of the Costa Do Sol Carcavelos Lions Club since it was founded ten years ago, she was the first secretary, the second president and every year has had some job in the club. A middle-school principal, she finds her teaching background useful in working with others.

Eighty-one-year-old Antonio was a watchmaker until his diminished eyesight made it impossible for him to work at his trade, but he still sees well enough to read, play cards and enjoy movies. "This home has been a lifesaver for me and in some ways is the best time of my life," he said. "I don't know how long I'm going to live but I'm going to have a good life because since I moved in here I have many new friends and realize that every day when I get up I will no longer be alone. I have everything I need."

Zaragoza Lions Help The Elderly

Lions Clubs International came to Spain in 1964 with the chartering of the Madrid Lions Club. In that year, there were three-quarters of a million Lions in a little over 19,000 clubs worldwide. The association has enjoyed a steady growth in Spain and currently there are 102 clubs in the nation with a membership exceeding 2,500.

In 1969, the 40-member Zaragoza Lions Club was founded. Historically, Zaragoza has been a city of great strategic importance. Caesar Augustus made it his headquarters while carrying out the campaigns that were to end two centuries of struggle necessary for Rome to subdue Spain. Charlemagne arrived at its walls in the year 777 but despite fierce fighting was unable to capture the city. It was liberated from the Moors in 1118 and immediately became the capital of the kingdom of Aragon. Centuries later, in savage battles with the legions of Napoleon in 1808-09 the heroic resistance of its defenders is a dramatic example of courage and endurance.

Today, the Zaragoza Lions are bringing the same resolve to enriching lives with the Melvin Jones Center for the Elderly. The total Lions' contribution since the facility opened is $200,000, including an LCIF grant in 1989 for $50,000.

"The LCIF grant enabled us to dramatically improve the quality of help we are able to give to the elderly in this facility," said District 116-A Governor Jesus Soriano Uriel.

"This is a cultural center for the elderly in Zaragoza," added one of the city's Lions, "and fills a real need in our community. We did not have a center of this kind until our Lions club stepped in and provided it."

The building was donated by the mayor of Zaragoza and features one huge 900-square-meter room. The mayor wanted a facility for the elderly and presented the building to the Lions as a gift. The Lions then began an intensive remodeling job. They painted, plastered, donated carpentry work, installed plumbing, and upgraded electrical and other services required to put the building in top condition. They also purchased tables, chairs, billiard tables, games of all kinds and giant-screen TV sets. As a personal touch, they visit with the elderly clientele and organize parties and other weekend activities.

The center has dramatically improved the quality of life for the elderly living in the community. Many of them echo the words of 60-year-old Pedro, a retired plumber: "The Lions facility gives me something to look forward to every day. Before this opened there really wasn't too much for older people to do here in Zaragoza. I go over there during the day and may play cards or billiards, or watch a movie in the evening. I get a chance to visit with old friends and have made many new friends since I started going there a few years ago. I especially look forward to the parties on the weekends. Before there wasn't much of anything happening in my life, but now there's as much activity as I want."

Maria, a 70-year-old retired nurse, added, "While I still spend time with my children and grandchildren, I don't feel that I'm a burden to them now because I have plenty of enjoyable activities at the Melvin Jones Center. There wasn't anything like this before the Lions opened it. It fills a need and gives the older men and women something to look forward to each day. I probably go there three or four times a week and the rest of the time I have other activities with friends. In some ways, however, it has become a focal point for activities for retired persons in Zaragoza."

"The LCIF grant has been a major factor in the success of the Melvin Jones Center for the Elderly," said Past District 116-A Governor Francisco Quintas Vicente, who also served as 1993-94 Multiple District Council Chairman. "This, along with additional funds raised by the Lions themselves, enabled the members to remodel and buy furniture and equipment for the building. The Lions did a great deal of the work themselves and stretched the money available much farther than it would have gone otherwise."

The center includes kitchen facilities for snacks, coffee and soft drinks, as well as capabilities for preparing large amounts of food for special dinners, fiestas and parties.

Francisco, a Lion for 18 years, said, "I didn't know anything about the Lions until a friend of mine who is a member suggested I join my local club and help in the community. My membership now gives me many chances to assist my fellow citizens in Spain. The Zaragoza Lions Clubs' Melvin Jones Home for the Elderly is a continuing example of our motto, *We Serve*, in action."

Home For Troubled Girls

"I was eight years old and couldn't read, write, add or subtract. I cried all the time and couldn't learn anything the times I would go to school," recalled Maria Garcia. "My mother was an alcoholic and my father abandoned us when I was two years old. I was hungry and frightened and cried myself to sleep most nights."

Then Maria's life made a dramatic improvement. The local police brought her to the Melvin Jones Home for Girls in Elche, Spain. Supported by the Elche Lions Club, the facility is home for girls between the ages of eight and 16 who come from families in which there are problems with alcohol, drugs, poverty, abuse, prostitution and other conditions that make childhood intolerable. Founded in 1975, the 45-member Elche Lions Club has made this a major project.

Fifty girls live there fulltime in four dormitories, operated by six nuns who also serve as teachers. Because of the emotional trauma suffered while growing up, most of the girls have learning problems when they arrive at the school. The nuns work with them to improve learning skills and give them lessons in cleanliness, courtesy, good manners and correct speech.

Diego Agullo, president of the Elche Foundation for five years, explained, "Generally the children come to the home from child welfare or the police because they have been in trouble with the authorities, or neighbors have complained about the family. We have seen many tragic cases and lives that have been turned around by the Melvin Jones Home for Girls."

The objective is for all the girls to receive at least a grammar school education. Some attend high school and a few go on to college or business school. After leaving the home many of the young women go to work as maids in hotels or private homes in the area. Some are employed as clerks in stores or in business or government offices. A few go further.

"The home certainly changed my life," said Maria Garcia, now 22. "I learned typing and shorthand and, when I finished, got a good job with a firm that manufactures plastic products in Elche. I had a natural aptitude for typing and shorthand and did well at all the rest of my studies after a year or two at the school. When I graduated at the age of 16, I went to work for a company and started at the bottom. Now I'm office manager and as the company grows, I can see my responsibilities grow, too."

Understandably, many of the girls have mental and emotional problems, such as depression, anxiety, hostility and other conditions. Some are alcohol and drug abusers. They are treated for these conditions, in addition to receiving a high school education and job training. When they leave at the age of 16, they are able to work as seamstresses, chefs, factory employees, nurse aides or secretaries. Occasionally, a few students go on to college.

About 100 miles south of Valencia, Elche is a popular vacation destination overlooking the Mediterranean on Spain's Costa Blanca (the "White Coast"). On many road signs, the town name is Elx, as the Moors called it. Centuries before the Muslim occupation, Elche was famous for its date palm trees, introduced by the Carthaginians, who later were evicted by the Romans when Hannibal was defeated in the Third Century B.C. in the Second Punic War. During holiday season, hundreds of thousands of tourists come to enjoy the city and beautiful surroundings. Unfortunately, for some of the young people, life is not so beautiful.

"These days in Spain, there are many children with personal and family problems," said Past District 116 Governor Francisco Quintas Vicente of Madrid. "In the Melvin Jones Home, we learned it's important to separate the child from the family where many of the problems originate. We give the young girl stable surroundings and a good education, because otherwise the youngster might follow the family example and be in trouble with the law and perhaps live in the street.

"We just received an LCIF grant of $35,000. That will enable us to build eight more rooms housing four girls each, buy more equipment and expand the kitchen and laundry."

Members of the Elche Lions Club have stimulated interest in the project, and donations from Lions as well as community and business sources have totaled more than $350,000. Additional fundraisers recently have brought in more than $38,000 from the Elche, Madrid, Elda and Crevillente Lions clubs. The parish of Santa Maria is responsible for administrative costs of the facility. The Elche Lions Club hosts annual fundraisers for the home, and club members serve as volunteers in the facility.

The school has produced stirring examples: one of them is Luz, a nurse at a hospital in Elche. She was able to continue her education after leaving the school, though in general the students go right to work when they graduate at the age of 16.

"I was lucky," emphasized Luz. "The nuns arranged a scholarship for me at one of the local nurses' schools, and I went on from there to study, graduate, and become a full-fledged nurse. I enjoy helping the sick because one thing I learned from the Lions is that all of us are supposed to help others. When I went to the school at the age of eight, the nuns gave me hope, along with direction, discipline and stability, which I never had in my life.

"My father left when I was three years old and my mother struggled to support us," continued Luz. "She had a problem with drugs and was often in trouble with the police. The nuns took me in and gave me the home I never had. The nuns encouraged me, and I found out I was a good student and could learn when people took the time to teach me. I go back to the school often to encourage other young girls who probably have doubts as I did about ever succeeding. My example shows them that they can succeed. The Lions' commitment is helping the school to grow and expand its services to the young people in our town. This is tremendously important."

One of the Elche Lions added, "I've been a Lion for 12 years and didn't know too much about the association when I joined. A friend of mine suggested I come to a meeting, and when I saw what the Lions accomplished, I decided that's what I wanted to do, also.

"I've been involved in a number of projects through the years, but the Melvin Jones Home for Girls is the most effective I've seen in really changing lives of young people. We see young ladies who graduate and then come back to the home to visit after many years.

They come from impossible family backgrounds; now they are married with children and are raising their boys and girls in ways that will not duplicate the terrible problems that they encountered growing up. This kind of project shows the people in Elche exactly how Lions build a better world."

Twenty-three-year-old Luisa is one of these young women. Luisa found she had a gift for languages while she was at the Melvin Jones Home. "I graduated from the school when I was 16," said Luisa, "and went to work as a secretary and studied languages in my spare time. Today I can speak Spanish, English, French and Italian and have worked as a tour guide for the last three years. I've traveled all over Spain, France, Italy and Switzerland and hope to take tours to the United States in the next few years. If I get to the United States, I certainly want to visit the headquarters of the Lions in Oak Brook, Illinois, because of the support LCIF gave the home where I grew up. My life was a total disaster before I got there and now it's great."

No Dream Is Impossible

Twelve-year-old Tim had a dream. He wanted to fly in the sleek, supersonic jet helicopter featured in the popular television series, "Air Wolf." The action thriller starring Jan-Michael Vincent and Ernest Borgnine was a top-rated TV favorite.

Tim also had leukemia. A doctor at the Alberta Children's Hospital recommended the young boy as a candidate for the "Make a Child's Dream Come True" project of the North Hill Lions Club of Calgary, Alberta, Canada. Tim's dream began to come into focus.

"We got in touch with Universal Studios in California and told them about Tim's dream and they told us we had a problem: the 'Air Wolf' helicopter was a mock-up," remembered Jack Rooksby, a North Hill Lion and 1995-96 District 37-E Governor. "They told us to send him anyway. Our club sent Tim, his parents, and his brother and sister to southern California for two weeks. The club paid everything – airfare, hotel, car and spending money and made certain that Tim had medical supervision while he was gone."

"We were met at the airport by Jan-Michael Vincent and Ernest Borgnine," recalled Tim. "They took us on a tour of Universal Studios and the next day I flew by military helicopter from Los Angeles to the

San Diego Navy base. I spent a day and inspected the base with the base commander and then flew back to Los Angeles that evening. We went to Sea World, Disneyland, Knotts Berry Farm and everywhere I wanted to see. It was the best two weeks of my life."

Lions' involvement began in January 1982. Jack Tennant, a Calgary Sun columnist, wrote about a television show in the United States that he had seen which provided special dreams for terminally ill children. Tennant thought it was an excellent idea and suggested that some service club might consider such a project for the Calgary area. One of the North Hill Lions felt the same way and brought the column to a meeting. A committee was then created to study the project and report back to the club.

"We realized that the project could be quite expensive," said Jack Green, a 35-year member of the club. "So, that spring we implemented a telephone canvass of the city of Calgary and raised about $100,000. We selected Alberta Children's Hospital as the logical place to find the right candidates. Dr. Zyph at the Pediatric Oncology Clinic liked the project, but was hesitant until we assured him that we would not be using the families and the children for publicity. We do everything anonymously."

Green, who has served as president of three different Lions clubs, talked about one boy who was diagnosed with inoperable cancer. The parents came to a meeting of the North Hill Lions Club after their son died to tell members what fulfilling his wish had meant to their son and them. They felt it extended his life more than a year and brought joy to the family in an otherwise hopeless situation.

Added North Hill Lion Ron Nugent: "The program is medicine for everybody. It gives the parents a chance to relax because there is so much stress that quite frequently the family breaks up when there is a terminally ill child. It creates so many problems in the family that the marriage cannot withstand it."

The club averages about seven or eight dream fulfillments a year and the cost runs as much as $4,000 each. The Lions pay for everything and get excellent cooperation from airlines, hotels and other services.

"Lionism grows by attraction," Green pointed out, "and we've had many, many new members join the North Hill club as a result of this project."

A terminally ill 16-year-old girl from Powell River, British Columbia, had just one dream — and that was to ride Big Ben, a famous national show-jumping horse owned by Ian Miller. After Big Ben won the lucrative Chrysler Classic Derby, Miller led the horse around the field with the ecstatic young woman on its back. "We don't think of tomorrows because we have so many of them," Miller mused. "This meant a lot to her."

Children referred to the project by the Alberta Children's Hospital staff, by their own medical doctor, or by a friend or relative are considered by the Selection Committee. All referrals are accompanied by a written outline of the child's dream. This may take the form of a chance to meet a sports hero, a television star, a trip to Disneyland or some such place -- or perhaps a simpler dream, such as a ride with a police or fire chief. The identity of the child and family are always kept in confidence. They are never publicized, Lions emphasized.

Throughout the years, the corporate community has been cooperative and helped in many ways. Airlines charge their lowest possible fares. Theme parks provide VIP status and passes free of charge. Travel agencies are always on the lookout for free events that can be used as part of a dream, and professional sports teams go out of their way to make a child feel special.

While the most commonly fulfilled wish is a trip to Disneyland, they can be varied:

- A 12-year-old girl with cancer wanted a large deck on her house so she could go outdoors and enjoy time with friends. North Hill Lions undertook the project and completed the deck themselves.
- A terminally ill teenage boy had a dream of playing hockey with the Calgary Flames. He was able to join in a practice session with the Flames and received pictures, a Flames jersey and an autographed hockey stick.
- A teenager with cancer who was also in the Sea Cadets wanted to visit a naval base to see the Navy in action. With the cooperation of the Canadian Armed Forces, he was able

to travel to Victoria, British Columbia, where he was met by the base commander. Arrangements were made for him to visit a navy vessel, lunch with the captain and then fly on an armed forces helicopter to another base and visit the major submarine base on the West Coast.

• A teenage boy confined to a wheelchair with muscular dystrophy had lived in the hospital for the last half of his life and dreamed of an ocean cruise. His dream came true on a two-week Caribbean cruise during which he was accompanied by an attendant from the Children's Hospital.

Austrian Lions Expand Lifesaving Goals

Known for its handsome palaces, stunning museums, impressive art galleries, classical and jazz music, lovely rivers, forests and parks, Austria attracts visitors from all over the world. None go home disappointed. Seasoned travelers who've been everywhere often say that Austria and its capital, Vienna, are among their favorite destinations.

Against this background, Austrian Lions are improving the quality of life for their countrymen and others. Grants from the Lions Clubs International Foundation are playing key roles in expanding two Austrian service projects: the St. Anna Kinderspital in Vienna and the Center for the Handicapped in Baden.

St. Anna Kinderspital: This 160-bed children's hospital was founded in 1837. About 45 of the hospital's beds are used for children with cancer. The largest pediatric center in central Europe, it draws many patients from eastern European nations.

In 1987, Multiple District 114 received a $40,000 grant from LCIF to purchase a chromosome analyzer, a sophisticated diagnostic tool, for the hospital.

Dr. Andrew Zaumschirm, a specialist in pediatrics and intensive care medicine, has been at the hospital for six years. "The chromosome analyzer is a major advance in determining the type of cancer, the stage and aggressiveness of the tumor, and the type of treatment necessary. It is faster and far more accurate than equipment we used previously. With the chromosome analyzer, we have a much higher cure rate than before the Lions grant made its purchase possible."

Dr. Oskar Haas is director of the laboratory and an associate professor. "I'd say conservatively that the chromosome analyzer gives us an accurate diagnosis in one-tenth of the time we used before. With the new equipment we don't have to go into the darkroom anymore for diagnosing cancers.

Kinderspital patients range from newborns to adolescents. The staff treats a full range of cancers including kidney tumors, neuroblastoma, bone tumors, leukemia and lymphoma. Brain tumors in young people are diagnosed and treated at another hospital in Vienna. The hospital is full most of the time and mothers stay in the rooms with the young children while they are there.

Dieter Kneissel, 1991-92 District Governor of 114-O (East) said, "Since the Lions became involved in 1986 we have contributed about $250,000. Lionism continues to grow at a good rate here in Austria. We feel this hospital is an excellent example of putting the principles of our association into action. Many, many children have been helped and continue to be helped. The $40,000 grant from LCIF represents money that Lions from all over the world contribute to the foundation.

Said Dr. Zaumschirm, "In 1880 to 1890 deaths from diphtheria had been epidemic. Thousands of children died all over the world and St. Anna Kinderspital became a treatment center for the disease. Thousands of children were treated and a great deal of research was done on the best forms of treatment early in the 20th Century. Today the approach to cancer research and treatment in this hospital is similar. We have a number of children coming from eastern Europe for treatment because they don't have the facilities in their own countries."

Said Vienna Lion Hans-Dieter Tacke, "Our objective is to see that this hospital continues to grow and continues to improve its services so that greater numbers of children can be saved from cancer. Obviously, we Lions have plenty of work ahead of us because the hospital is becoming so famous that more and more doctors want to send their patients here for treatment. We'll keep working at it."

The Center for the Handicapped is in Baden, a beautiful city about 20 miles from Vienna. Twelve years old, the center is a project of the 31-member Voslau-Baden Lions Club. The Lions decided the next step would be a home where some of the center's clients could live.

"When First International Vice President Don Banker came here in October 1991, he thought the home would be a great idea," said Fritz Baldt, president that year of the Bad Voslau-Baden Club. The $48,107 grant from LCIF to District 114-O was forwarded to the club in May 1992 and was put right to work. The money from LCIF gave us a running start on the living quarters which are now open and in use."

The 14-room house opened in May 1992 and includes baths, showers, a dining room and living room for relaxation. The atmosphere is warm and comfortable. "The idea is to help the workers live alone and as independently as possible," explained Wolfgang Rubl, director of the home. "Each resident is allowed to furnish his or her room as desired. They are responsible for keeping their quarters clean and orderly. That is part of the overall training philosophy of the center. The home is ideally suited to making the handicapped even more effective."

Ranging in age from 17 to 52, 29 disabled men and women work at various tasks at the Center for the Handicapped under the direction of the staff. The center is 12 years old and the Lions have worked with the government and private organizations in improving it and enlarging it.

According to Baldt, "Formerly all of the handicapped in our area had to go to Vienna to be helped. The building, which was donated by the city, was in terrible condition at that time. An architect who was a Lion and a member of our club designed plans for its reconstruction. The Lions contributed $50,000 at the start and overall have contributed about $100,000 in working with the project."

There are many impressive stories from the handicapped center: Andreas, who is borderline mentally handicapped, was there for seven years, from the age of 20 to 27. Now for two years he has been working in a home for the elderly as a maintenance worker and is married and has a child of his own.

Twenty-eight-year-old Karl has been a florist for six years. He was at the handicapped center for five years between the ages of 17 and 22. "At the start I had some difficulties. It wasn't easy. The people who work there were patient. I learned to concentrate on what I did and got some confidence in myself. I'd never had that before because all I did was fail. I learned to make carpets at the center and these were sold. I was proud of that. I've been a florist for six years and these are the best years of my life."

A Lion for 25 years, Fritz Baldt has been a powerful mover in the development of the Center for the Handicapped and the new home for its residents. "Our club has always worked extensively with the handicapped. We heard of the need for the workshop years ago and dug right in to raise money and get it moving. Through the years of our club's involvement with the handicapped center and the home where the workers can live, our club has contributed $200,000.

Two grants. Two success stories. Two examples of how LCIF is helping Lions worldwide provide opportunities both for children in greatest need to regain their health and to help other individuals become contributing citizens of their communities and nations.

Acapulco Lions Bring Water

"Our village has pure water for the first time in its history," said Pablo Hernandez Beiza, mayor of Las Plazuelas, a small village 25 miles from Acapulco, Mexico. "The Acapulco Lions raised money to drill a 220-foot deep well that provides clean water for our community. They began the project two years ago and just completed it. It includes a 30,000 gallon concrete reservoir on a hill to store the water."

Until the Lions arrived, the villagers drank impure water from shallow wells and open ponds. As a consequence, there was a great deal of sickness in the community. So far, the Las Plazuelas project has cost $25,000, all of it raised by Acapulco Lions.

After the Lions drilled the deep well in Las Plazuelas, they constructed a network of pipes to carry the fresh water to groups of 20 homes, making it easily accessible to the residents. The grateful villagers want to change the name of their community to Villa Lionism. "The new well completely changed our lives," pointed out 27-yar-old Maria Fernandez, a fourth-grade teacher in the Las Plazuelas school. "We have 1,000 people in our town and never knew what kind of germs we were drinking when we lifted a glass of water. Unless you've experienced it, you don't know what it's like to live without fresh, clean water."

The Acapulco Lions' ongoing commitment to the village includes teaching residents modern farming techniques in growing corn, sesame seeds, tomatoes, coconuts, limes, tobacco, cotton and other local crops. Each year the Acapulco Lions bring doctors and dentists to Las Plazuelas to treat patients for dental and general health problems. The worst cases come to Acapulco for advanced treatment.

Four years ago eight-year-old Luz Maria was brought to Acapulco for an operation on her nose. Her nose was severely disfigured and she had quit school because of self-consciousness and teasing from classmates. The Lions brought her to Acapulco for an operation by a local plastic surgeon, Dr. Georgina Lara. Results were excellent. Luz Maria's doctor transformed her appearance, attitude and future. The Acapulco lions paid for everything.

"I'm a new person," Luz Maria proudly declared, "and every day I get up knowing that my life is better than it has ever been."

The Acapulco Lions expanded and refurbished the elementary school in Las Plazuelas, providing desks and books and building an outdoor basketball court. They supply nets, basketballs and shoes for the youngsters, and all of these activities are handled by the Lions with no government money whatsoever.

Lions Clubs International came to Mexico with the Mexican City Lions Club in 1931. In 1943, Agustin M. Montano founded the Acapulco Lions Club and was an active member until his death in 1986. The club meets weekly and 13 members are Melvin Jones fellows.

A Lion for 22 years, Oscar Meza Celis was Governor of District B-13 in 1984. The District is now B-6. "I really had no choice but to become a Lion," said Meza with a smile, "because I went to Lions' parties and learned their spirit, plus the father of my future wife was the man who founded Lions in Acapulco. The wives work hard with our club, probably harder than we do, and are certainly an important part of Lions in Acapulco."

His wife, Lourdes Montano de Meza, added, "I knew about Lions almost from the day I was born. All my life I've been involved with the Lions and seen the many good things that they do. As far back as 1948, the Lions built a school here for teaching the arts, such as weaving, painting and jewelry making, and this has been an extremely important part in our city. My father was an example of Lions at its best and I'll always remember the many wonderful things he did."

In India, a Lions project started with an operation on a 12-year-old Indian girl and soon expanded into a global medical mission linking Lions clubs in India and Canada.

A moving story of international medical teamwork, it began when the Weston, Ontario, Lions Club and the Chembur, India, Lions Club arranged an operation on the girl to correct crippling scoliosis, the damaging curvature of the spine. She was flown to Toronto where Dr. John Hall, an orthopedic surgeon, implanted special steel rods in her back in a highly technical operation. The successful procedure transformed her life.

Altogether, the cost of the operation and of flying the girl to Canada totaled $8,000. With costs like those, the Lions could help only two Indian children a year on a continuing basis. After thoughtful consideration they devised an alternative. They asked Hall if he would train Indian doctors brought to Canada to do the operation. Better yet, could he himself go to India and conduct training sessions? Hall not only could but would.

Before Hall departed, Lions did extensive groundwork. They appealed successfully for donations of supplies and equipment. J.B. Watt, past president of the Weston Lions Club, approached a Canadian company and obtained five copies of a film showing a scoliosis operation. The company which made the special steel rods used in the operation provided them at half the usual cost.

One company provided body braces required for the post-surgical therapy at cost. Another firm donated an orthopedic table. A local doctor gave the Lions $450 worth of instructional slides and films.

Hall flew to India with anesthesiologist Dr. John Relton and physiotherapist Gordon Plorin. Once there, the surgical team did 15 scoliosis procedures. At each operation, Indian doctors either assisted or observed. The three Canadians also lectured at Indian universities where more Indian doctors learned about the operation.

Copies of the scoliosis film were provided to universities in Bombay, New Delhi, Lucknow, Calcutta and Madras.

The Lions had done nothing less than bring a new surgical technique to India. Now Indian doctors perform this surgical miracle on Indian patients in Indian hospitals. In the words of Past President Watt: "The success of this mission has gone beyond our most optimistic expectations in that 15 children have been cured, Indian doctors are now able to perform the technique, Indian brace makers are now able to manufacture the braces needed, and films have been left at five major universities to assist in teaching young doctors."

In remote Robinpet Village, India, 1,300 villagers now have a reliable source of pure drinking water because Lions joined in that "single purpose to help people in need" International President Wroblewski described in his inaugural speech.

Robinpet Village had made many appeals to governmental and municipal authorities for fresh, safe drinking water. When the Lions Club of Ootacamund, India, offered to help, the villagers were skeptical. If government, with all of its resources could not help, what could a single Lions club do?

The Ootacamund club asked for assistance from the Lyn Lions Club in England, which quickly provided both funds and guidance. An analysis determined that it would be possible to pump pure water from a well some distance from the village to a nearby distribution point and finally to the village itself. The idea looked good on paper and the club built a pumping station. But how could the Ootacamund club — far from the village — see that the system was maintained so that it would continue to meet the needs of the villagers?

With typical Lions zest, the club struck a deal with a nearby private school, the Lawrencewood School. The headmaster agreed to arrange for a permanent crew of workers to keep the system pumping, with the costs to be paid monthly by the Ootacamund club. So once built, through the international cooperation of two clubs and one school, pure water continues to flow to Robinpet Village.

Lionism originally came to Japan from the Philippines. Therefore, it was natural for Lions of Japan's District 334-E to decide to do something about the health needs of the men, women, and children who live on some of the 7,200 islands which make up the Philippines.

Because of inadequate medical facilities, many suffered from a variety of diseases. In 1977, District 334-E sent a medical team to four different locations for four days.

The medical mission got full support from the Filipino Health Ministry, local physicians, the governor of the state of Sulacan, and the Bulacan state hospital. Initially, many Filipinos expressed strong anti-Japanese feelings. But when local newspapers publicized the team and its purpose, hostility based on memories of World War II faded away. The free treatment offered by the team attracted some 8,000 people.

Preliminary studies indicated that the team, which included specialists in internal medicine, dentistry and ophthalmology, should place emphasis on inoculations to prevent TB. In makeshift clinics set up in warehouses and town halls, the days began with long lines of Filipinos. Physicians, dentists, pharmacists, pathologists and general assistants dispatched from District 334-E, together with doctors and nurses from local hospitals and their assistants totaled 130 people. Barely stopping for meals, the group treated 3,107 patients.

Stories about the team's work ran in newspapers and on radio and television all over the Philippines, and the Japanese press gave the story good coverage. The team capped its work by receiving keys of honorary citizenship from the mayor of Manila and letters expressing gratitude from the governor of Bulacan state and the governor of District 301-D in the Philippines. Since the initial mission, District 334-E has continued its service activities in the Philippines and even expanded them to include preventive medicine.

When a cry for help came from Singapore, the Lions Club of Northshore Pakeke, New Zealand, answered. The club is composed of retired Lions who have been answering the call to service for most of their lives. The club banner reads "As elders we serve." In the International Year of the Child, this group heard an appeal from the Lions Club of Singapore (East).

The two-year-old son of a member of the Singapore club suffered from a serious congenital heart disease and was going to Auckland, New Zealand, for an operation to be performed by Sir Brian Barrett-Boyes, a distinguished heart surgeon. Both parents, only one of whom knew English, would accompany their son, Kar Wee Tan, for a one-month stay in this unfamiliar country. Unfamiliar, but friendly, thanks to the Northshore Pakeke Lions and their wives, the Tans' home away from home was provided by Lion Syd Hewetson and his wife, Mary.

The warmth of a welcome which was to extend throughout the Tans' stay in New Zealand began at the airport where the couple and Kar Wee were greeted by President Ron Mogridge. The heart operation, performed by the Mater Hospital, was a complete success, and the Tans began to relax a little in their new household. After Kar Wee left the hospital he was even able to go for a few short trips around Auckland to shop for souvenirs. The family then flew back to Singapore, but not before Lion Tan attended a meeting of the Northshore Pakeke Lions Club. Club banners were exchanged in a simple ceremony in which Tan thanked every member who had welcomed and helped his family.

The story of the Tans is a little story — about one club reaching out to another culture to help one small boy and his family — but also on a world scale, there is a willingness among Lions to lend a hand when famine, disaster or personal distress strike.

Chapter Fifteen
The Association Today:
A World Perspective

The very first Object of Lions Clubs International challenges Lions "To create and foster a spirit of understanding among the peoples of the world." Lions have been doing precisely this for more than nine decades.

International conventions and area forums reflect the manner in which Lions and their families representing scores of languages and cultures have bonded in a true spirit of good will and mutual respect. "Our international conventions personify the global nature of this association," said 2003-2004 International President Dr. Tae-Sup Lee. "I have witnessed this common purpose during the general sessions and the quality learning experiences at seminars and, of course, amid the aura of fellowship generated at the big parade."

The historic 2004 convention was a case in point. It was the first time an international convention was held in two countries and a celebration of the year the association actually became "international." The 87th convention was held in Detroit, Michigan, USA, and Windsor, Ontario, Canada, and it brought together more than 10,000 members and their families from around the world. It was an occasion to reflect on the chartering of a Lions clubs that was the association's first step toward becoming the world's largest international service club organization. In 1920, the Detroit Lions Club sponsored the Windsor Lions Club, the first established outside the United States. This 2004 convention served as still another chapter in how Lions were answering human needs the world over. Four years later, the historic expansion that began in Canada witnessed Lions clubs having been chartered in more then 200 lands…and growing.

There are myriad examples of how Lions are promoting good will the world over. Among the most gratifying are projects that join Lions of different lands. Eye missions have already been specified, but other humanitarian activities further exemplify how Lions are giving substance to the heralded First Object. They demonstrate how the global goodwill of Lions extends far beyond national borders. Languages and cultural differences are easily bridged when Lions work together as a united force for good.

Two projects of Austrian Lions in the late 1990s highlight this ideal. The Lions of District 114-M used a US$50,000 grant to refurbish a building in Albania and convert it into a school for children 6-14 and a clinic which now offers primary medical services. A second activity took the Austrian Lions of District 114-W to the heights of the Himalayas in Tibet. Here, the Lions, thanks to LCIF funding, constructed a school, certainly, one of the most *elevated* projects in association history. "This has been the most exciting project I was ever involved in as a Lion," commented District 114-W Governor Dr. Franz Horner, a political science professor at the University of Salzburg. "It reinforced my ideals in international Lionism. My wife and I had the opportunity to meet with charming children and adults in Tibet. After learning of the crucial educational needs of Tibetan children through an international organization named Oko-Himal, located at the University of Salzburg, my home Lions club, Salzburg-Hohensalzburg, initiated the project in the Himalayan community of Basung.

Another example of this across borders cooperation involved a United States Lions club and a family in Poland. In 2000, Voytek Putz, a member of the Riverside, Illinois, Lions Club had traveled to Poland from where he immigrated to the United States 20 years earlier. His purpose was to visit his mother who was under the care of Catholic nuns in Warsaw. A nun told him of the plight of the Lagowska family, whose 13-year-old daughter, Paulina, was afflicted with severe scoliosis that required surgery to straighten and fuse the vertebrae. "Arrangements were made with the Shriner's Children Hospital in Chicago to take care of all surgical and hospital expenses," said Lion Putz. Paulina and her mother made the trip provided by Lot, the Polish national airline, at no charge. However, they needed a place to stay and this Lion Putz's family provided. It was a five-month stay during which time the girl received five operations to correct the problem, including two needed to relieve her of an E.coli infection.

Her mother's endurance was incredible," added Putz. "She had to carry Paulina everywhere, and I never heard her complain once. Also, the Lions were active from the start, offering help before I could even ask. Every dollar that was given changed the lives of Paulina and her mother." In addition to improved health and memories of visits to sites in the Chicago area, Paulina returned home with more than 100 stuffed animals for which her father, Wladyslaw, happily built shelves in their Warsaw apartment.

"It's miracle," said Paulina, "when I think of all the beautiful people I met who reached out to help. My life is better today and the future looks brighter because of all these new friends."

To further emphasize the status of Lions Clubs International in the world, the association, in 1987, was designated a "Peace Messenger" by the United Nations in recognition of making concrete contributions to the UN-designated International Year of Peace. The award was made at the world body's headquarters in New York where the UN expressed its hope that the association will continue its cooperation in working toward the realization of the long-term objectives set forth by the International Year of Peace which was observed in 1986. In accepting the award, then International President Judge Brian Stevenson remarked, "The receipt of this certificate recognizes the role which Lions are playing, in creating an atmosphere conducive to peace. Peace, after all, is the result of following our First Object."

Peace among people worldwide results from mutual respect and assistance, which is a hallmark of the work of Lions. In yet another example of this goal, the Lions banner was raised atop Mt. Kilimanjaro in Tanzania. Kilimanjaro, at 19,340 feet, is the world's tallest free-standing mountain and seven Lions led by Drs. Frank Villa of the Waterford, Pennsylvania, Club and Doug Villella of the Lynchburg (Host) Virginia, Lion Club scaled the peak in a project organized by the Volunteer Optometric Service to Humanity of Pennsylvania (VOSH/PA) which utilizes valuable Lions resources in eliminating blindness from identified regions in the world. This cooperation has implemented permanent Lions eye clinics in Honduras, Haiti, Nicaragua and Guatemala. The Mt. Kilimanjaro in 2000, in fact, raised funds for the Lions eye clinic in the Peten region of Guatemala.

It was estimated that more than 300 surgeries could be performed with the funds raised after the lofty climb.

Whether in locations the world over or in their own communities, Lions give evidence of their commitment to the ideals of *We Serve*. Donald E. Banker, 1991-1992 International President, emphasized this global perspective when he said, "Let us dedicate ourselves to extending our Lions club's identification with our local community to a similar relationship of our international association with the world community. Join with our global family of Lionism in striving to enhance the image of our emblem in every community where Lions clubs are active. Become involved in serving together so there can be no doubt whatever that Lions Clubs International is a true reflection of the world community. I ask that we re-dedicate ourselves to the principles of humanitarian concern, comradeship and personal involvement that have enabled Lions Clubs International to earn a deserved reputation for leadership in service to mankind."

This global perspective was witnessed in a joint service prospect between Lions in the West Indies island nation of Trinidad and the Florida Lions Eye Bank. The San Juan-Petit Lions Club had co-sponsored 30 cataract surgeries for residents of the Republic of Trinidad and Tobago, but, in 2004, were in need of two corneas for transplants that a local ophthalmologist had agreed to perform at no cost. Selwyn Skinner at the time was president of the Fort Lauderdale, Florida, Lions Club and had been an active Lion in Trinidad. The Lions in his former home informed him of the need and he immediately contacted the Florida Lions Eye Bank. Lion Skinner and his wife, Hulday, also a Fort Lauderdale Lion, picked up the corneas from the eye bank and boarded a flight for Trinidad. They hand-carried the two corneas to Trinidad to ensure a timely arrival. The transplant surgery was successful and news coverage was widespread, with articles appearing in Trinidad and Florida newspapers. According to a statement from the Florida Eye Bank , "Providing these corneas is a continuation of the International Gratis Project of sending excess tissue from eye banks across the United States to countries in the Caribbean and Central and South America."

Promoting international goodwill among young people has been a decades-long goal of Lions and is observed in programs such as International Youth Exchange and Youth Camps. In one example, the Lions of Germany invited young people from around the world to help observe the World Trade Fair—EXPO 2000—in Hannover. Local Lions selected the youth and paid for their trip, and after their arrival they were guests for five days in the homes of German Lions in or near Hannover. The young guests also traveled to Berlin where they stayed at a campsite opened for EXPO visitors, attended a seminar and visited with families elsewhere in the country. The purpose, according to the sponsors, was to demonstrate the interest of Lions in the young people of the world and in building a future together. Lions were convinced that these young people would carry the international contacts and friendships made through EXPO with them the rest of their lives and, in turn, bring us one step closer to world peace.

Twinning—Hands Across the Seas

Twinning, initiated after the end of World War II, has proven to be an especially popular way to promote global goodwill and understanding. Late in the 1940s, Lions in European countries were initiating a program which had as its objective person-to-person contact between people of varied languages and cultures. It was first was witnessed between clubs in Sweden and Switzerland, the first two nations hosting Lions clubs on the continent. Specifically, twinning occurs when a club in one country establishes contact with a club in another nation. Once accomplished, the clubs trade banners, relate news of their service activities and offer general information of life in their respective lands. Visits between members are common. The program caught on, and by the mid-1950s Lions clubs in nations that had been enemies only a few years earlier—France, Germany, Italy and Austria—were participating in this new concept of international friendship. The same occurred in Asia when Lions clubs in Japan began similar relationships with clubs in Korea, Multiple District 300 Taiwan, the Philippines, Australia and other countries.

The French refer to the program as Jumelage; in English, it's Twinning. But by whatever name one calls it, the program has grown dramatically as a means of generating friendship among Lions. Clubs have twinned across the oceans, with those in the United States, Japan and Canada being especially active. Twinnings result in a number of ways. For example, oftentimes when a United States club is involved, it has come about through a sister-city relationship between a U.S. city and one in another land. More than an arrangement to promote fellowship, twinned clubs often help one another in time of need, such as when natural disasters strike. Needed relief supplies have been collected by one club and sent to the Lions in the nation affected. Early in the program, twinned clubs in Texas and Israel arranged a life-saving operation for an Israeli youth in Dallas. In a different type of cooperation, the Tajami, Japan, and Terre Haute, Indiana, clubs traded a total of 164 paintings by school children as part of their cultural exchange. The paintings were publicly displayed and judged, with each club forwarding prizes to the winning young artists.

No doubt each pair of Lions clubs in the world has its own story of how the twinning has come to pass and how they work together. Each is an inspirational message of what people of various cultural, linguistic and, perhaps, racial backgrounds can accomplish when the superficial walls of national boundaries are removed. The goodwill that has come about because of these relationships has been incentives to people everywhere, Lions and non-Lions, to extend the hand of friendship to citizens of other lands.

Walking with a Humanitarian Purpose

Still another type of international goodwill was promoted by Polly Letofsky who, in 1999, left her home in Vail, Colorado, to begin what was to amount to a 1,825 day trek around the world to raise funds for breast cancer research and to raise the awareness of women to check for the killer disease. She eventually walked through part of the United States, New Zealand, Australia, Singapore, Malaysia, Thailand, India, Turkey, Canada, and nine European countries. It was in Australia that she gained some very welcome support. Lost on the outskirts of Melbourne, she obviously looked lost when a woman named Margaret approached her to ask her destination. When Polly explained her mission, Margaret exclaimed, "My goodness, we have to get involved in this." "We?" Letofsky asked. "The Lions," said Margaret. It was the beginning of a partnership that witnessed Lions helping her raise funds and calling ahead to advise other Lions of her humanitarian project. For example, the Mackay North Lions in Queensland, Australia, invited her to join their club and District 201-Q2 made her mission a district project. The Aussie Lions then contacted Malaysian Lions and when she began her walk through that nation, she had 100 people walking with her. The government also took up her cause and went on to subsidize mammograms for women aged 55-64.. The partnership with Lions continued to grow. In Thailand the Lampang Regional Cancer Center agreed to open a facility solely for breast cancer education and the Stranraer Lions in Scotland raised $150 from some generous ferry passengers. In Elk Grove, Minnesota, Lions threw a pizza party for her and donated $3 for every pizza they sold and then added another $1,000.

She said she was overwhelmed by the friendliness and hospitality of the Lions. "The people I met, especially the Lions," she commented, "formed a human chain that supported me and what I was walking for." She admits that when Margaret first approached her outside of Melbourne, she had no clue who the Lions were. "I must have been living under a rock," she said. Polly now talks to groups about her journey and adds that seldom was she alone.

And a final note, Polly Letofsky was soon inducted into the Highlands Ranch, Colorado, Lions Club.

These and countless other project that span oceans and continents give further substance to the international objectives of the association. "As members of the world's largest service club organization," observed 2004-2005 International President Dr. Clement F. Kusiak, "Lions have a responsibility to make every effort to bring people closer together in peace. To participate in programs that rise above national boundaries and differences in language, culture and politics. Our history shows this is one of the things we do best and we should recognize this special aptitude and expand our commitment to global goodwill and understanding. It is, therefore, essential," he added, "that Lions make every effort to cross borders to participate in service activities that bring citizens of different nations together, answer calls for assistance when disasters strike in distant communities and promote international understanding whenever and wherever the opportunities present themselves."

Bringing people of different cultures together was vividly displayed in projects initiated by the Paradise Valley, California, Lions Club. Beginning in 1995, members of the club, barely a year old, traveled to the Philippines on a medical mission to treat hundreds of people who were without funds and unable to seek treatment. The following year they expanded their project to include missions to India and Kenya. They raised funds through bowling tournaments and raffles and received financial support from friends and families. The results was that the Paradise Valley Lions raised $50,000 to purchase used medical equipment to take to their destinations. They also collected thousands of used eyeglasses. The team of 20 volunteers included seven physicians, two registered nurses, a pharmacist, two emergency medical technicians, two medical assistants and one surgical technicians.

In Kenya, medical camps were conducted in several orphanages where nearly 300 children were treated, many of whom were disabled and had lacked medical attention for more than three years. The team saw more than 600 people at one camp in India, including children from a nearby orphanage and at another camp, 1,500 people sought medical help, and received medicines, eyeglasses and donations of clothing and toys for children. Finally, in camps in the Philippines the team saw and treated hundreds of medical and dental patients. In each country the team received assistance from the local Lions. When the missions were completed, the Paradise Valley Lions estimated that they spent nearly 5,800 volunteer hours. Club President Art Arboleda told the Filipino local press that the "mission demonstrated what a small organization such as a Lions club can do. We can go anywhere in the world to deliver service if we want to do it."

The prestige Lions have earned and enjoy around the world is neatly summarized in an incident Past International President Kay K. Fukushima reported during his visit to Tunisia. "The Lions there showed me a newborn baby wrapped in a blanket who was left at the doorstep of the Lions New Bay Nursing Safe Hospital the night before. The child was born out of wedlock and, according to the

Lions, the mother equated the Lions logo over the doorway to a chance at life for the newborn."

Essays for Peace

The role Lions play as Citizens of the World was demonstrated in the mid-1960s in a project that pre-dated the Peace Poster Contest. The Peace Essay Contest was a highlight during the administration of 1966-1967 International President Edward M. Lindsey to help observe the Golden Anniversary of Lions Clubs International. It was a grassroots effort by the Lions. Any youngster between the ages of 14 and 21 could submit an essay to the Lions club closest to his or her home and there was no requirement that an entrant had to have a Lion in the family. Past International President Aubrey Green was the contests committee chairman and the panel consisted of individuals of international prominence from around the world. Former United States President Dwight D. Eisenhower served as Honorary Chairman.

More than one million entries were received and the winner was an 18-year-old high school student from Cranbrook, British Columbia, Canada, A. Russell Wodell. He was honored at the 1967 International Convention in Chicago. His essay was titled, "Is Peace Attainable?" and young Wodell concluded his award-winning submission with these words: "There is no easy road to peace. Only through evolution of his social, moral and intellectual values can man achieve true peace with himself."

President Lindsey's presidential theme, "Search for Peace," was also portrayed on the only U.S. postage stamp issued to recognize Lions Clubs International.

The Role of Conventions

During conventions—district, multiple district and international— Lions are able to join with other members in fellowship and the spirit of service. At the district and multiple district levels, Lions learn of one another's programs and plans and are able to formulate programs that meet local needs and to cooperate in conducting programs of mutual benefit to their communities and people in need. During the international conventions, Lions realize the true global spirit of the association and how respect for the values of others leads to further bonding in the spirit of "We Serve." The knowledge and motivation gained at these gatherings helps develop better Lions. The broadening of experience and outlooks enlarges the perspective of Lions themselves and ultimately benefits their respective club, community and nation.

The role of international conventions has grown to be one of the most effective ways to promote the programs and ideals of the association.

Thousands of Lions and their families participate in each international convention, the largest attendance thus far being the 2002 convention in Osaka, Japan, when 48,431 members of the association's family registered. Regardless of the numbers, however, each gathering enables attendees to renew old friendship, make new ones and fortify the strength the Lions Clubs International as a leader in worldwide fellowship and humanitarian action.

Every convention provides an array of attractions and learning experiences that stimulate participants to increase their personal role in club and district activities. The primary purpose of international conventions is to elect officers and directors for the upcoming year and to consider changes to the International Constitution and By-Laws. These conclaves, however, also afford the thousands of participants to enjoy the official plenary sessions, during which the presentation of the flags representing the nations of the association is a colorful highlight of the opening session. The solemn Memorial Service pays homage to Lions who have died during the previous year and guest speakers draw further attention to the international stature of Lions. Over the years, speakers have included former United States Presidents Jimmy Carter and George H.W. Bush, Dr. Henry Kissinger, General H. Norman Schwarzkopf, Cary Grant, Clair Booth Luce, U.S. Secretary of Labor Elizabeth Dole, Nobel Peace Prize winner Elie Wiesel, columnist George Will, newscasters Charles Osgood and Peter Arnett, Australian Prime Minister R.J.L. Hawke, former president of Costa Rica and Nobel Peace Prize winner Oscar Arias, U.S. Astronauts Dr. Mae Jemison, James A. Lovell and Buzz Aldrin, Mrs. Coretta Scott King, oceanographer Jacques-Yves Cousteau and the president of Iceland, Dr. Olafur Ragnar Grimsson.

And, in 1985, Ronald Reagan addressed the convention in Dallas, the only sitting U.S. President to so honor Lions Clubs International.

The hours-long convention parades demonstrate the global flavor of the association as Lions and their families, many delegations dressed in attire representing their homelands, along with bands and floats strut down the parade route. Also during convention week a variety of seminars and forums help prepare registrants to provide the leadership to help their clubs and districts more effectively serve their communities and people in need.

A highlight of every international convention is the presentation of the annual Lions Clubs International Humanitarian Award, the association's highest honor. It is presented to individuals who exemplify the objectives of Lions worldwide and is accompanied by a check for a substantial amount from the Lions Clubs International Foundation to help enable the recipients to further the work of the organization with which he or she is associated. Those receiving this prestigious award have been:

- 1973-74—Danny Kaye for his dedicated work with UNICEF
- 1974-75—Danny Thomas for his work in establishing the St. Jude Children's Hospital in Memphis, Tennessee
- 1975-76—Dr. Jules Stein, founder of Research to Prevent Blindness for his work in supporting research in the causes of visual disease
- 1976-77—Orlando Villas Boas, world-respected Brazilian anthropologist
- 1977-78—Sir John Wilson, president of the International Agency for the Prevention of Blindness
- 1978-79—Rev. Robert Rumball for his work with the Ontario Mission for the Deaf
- 1979-80—The Salesian Sisters of St. John Bosco for educating the young and providing social services, nurseries, orphanages and homes for the blind and aged
- 1980-81—Robert W. Woodruff for supporting programs to help the needy and philanthropy in expanding the eye research facilities and eye bank at Emory University in Atlanta

- 1981-82—Koki Taiho, sumo wrestling champion for his service to his fellow man and promoting volunteer participation among citizens of Japan.
- 1982-83—Art Linkletter for being a leader in the fight against drug abuse
- 1983-84—Nancy Reagan for her work in fighting drug abuse
- 1984-85—W. Clement Stone for his years of philanthropy and books on self-motivation and positive mental attitudes
- 1985-86—Mother Teresa for her dedicated life work in helping the destitute, starving, homeless and ill
- 1986-87—Robert C. Gallo, M.D. and Luc Montagnier, M.D. for their research in working toward the development of a blood-screening test to isolate the AIDS virus in donors
- 1987-88—Operation Eyesight Universal, the Canadian charity that finances sight restoration and blindness prevention programs worldwide
- 1988-89—Dr. M.C. Modi, the internationally acclaimed eye surgeon for this eye camps and touring hospital free of charge to indigent patients
- 1989-90—Dr. Newton Kara Jose for coordinating cataract-free zone projects and establishing clinics that screen for eye diseases in Latin America
- 1990-91—Dr. Douglas Coster, an ophthalmologist renowned for his work in corneal transplantation and programs to prevent blindness in Australia and Asian-Pacific regions
- 1991-92—Dr. Carl Kupfer, the director of the National Eye Institute for his long career of service in eliminating preventable and reversible blindness
- 1992-1993—Arvind N. Mafatial, eye camp and disaster relief coordinator from India for several relief and rehabilitation services following earthquakes, floods and famine conditions in his country and for organizing eye camps and providing surgery to nearly 250,000 individuals
- 1993-94—Arthur Jampolsky, M.D., founder of the Smith Kettlewell Eye Research Institute, his research having been

responsible for the prevention, detection, diagnosis and improved treatment of blinding disorders

- 1994-95—Sonia Gandhi, chairperson of the Rajiv Gandhi Foundation, the Indian Council for Child Welfare and the Jawaharlal Nehru Memorial Fund
- 1995-96—Jimmy Carter for the humanitarian work of The Carter Center which addresses national and international issues of public policy in efforts to resolves conflict, promote democracy, defend human rights and prevent disease
- 1996-97—Dr. Zilda Arns Neumann, founder of the National Children's Pastoral Home in Brazil which serves more than two million children
- 1997-98—Martha Macguffie, M.D., the founder and president of the Society for Hospital and Resources Exchange (SHARE) dedicated to the health and welfare of orphaned children in western Kenya
- 1998-99—His Majesty King Bhumipol Adulyadej for developing programs to upgrade that standard of living throughout Thailand
- 1999-2000—Jim Stovall, co-founder of the Narrative Television Network, which makes television and movies accessible to blind and visually impaired children and adults
- 2000-2001—Barbara Hendricks, acclaimed opera soprano who created her own Foundation for Peace and Reconciliation, dedicated to preventing conflicts around the world and to facilitating enduring peace
- 2001-2002—Hugh O'Brian, television's Wyatt Earp, who founded Hugh O'Brian Youth Leadership (HOBY), dedicated to the recognition and development of leadership potential in young people of high school age
- 2002-2003—Greg Smith 13-year-old college graduate founder of International Youth Advocates and the Youth Spokesperson for World Centers of Compassion for Children
- 2003-2004—Dr. Billy Jang Hwan Kim, religious leader and broadcaster in Seoul, Korea, who has brought together

individuals and groups worldwide to fight racial and ethnic conflict

- 2004-2005—Dr. Arnall Patz, former director of the Wilmer Eye Institute at Johns Hopkins University in Baltimore, Maryland
- 2005-2006—Shri Dipchard Savaraj Gardi, whose charitable trust provides generous funding each year for a variety of projects in India such as schools, hospitals, homes for the elderly and community health programs
- 2006-2007—Dr. Timothy Shriver, chairman of Special Olympics which in cooperation with the LCIF Opening Eyes Program has screened more than 100,000 Special Olympics athletes and provided prescription eyeglasses and goggles
- 2007-2008—Muhammad Yunus, micro-credit pioneer, author and Nobel Peace Prize recipient

The presentation of the Humanitarian Award has proven to be yet another example of how Lions Clubs International is helping others fund and conduct a wide range of activities to improve the lives of men, women and children around the world.

"The annual international conventions and area forums have also proven to be occasions for Lions to demonstrate that harmony and friendship among the people of the world are more than merely dreams, more than faint possibilities—they can become realities, and quite easily at that, when individuals enthusiastically join together to make it happen," said 1995-1996 International President Dr. William H. Wunder. "With this as their goal, Lions throughout the world are giving evidence, undeniable evident, that they are leaders, indeed messengers of peace as the United Nations so proclaimed, in bringing about a better, more harmonious world. As founder Melvin Jones stated, 'Lions are unflinchingly united in a strong stand for a peace that ensures freedom and justice for all people and nations.' Yes, my fellow Lions, we are united in leadership in this glorious cause on behalf of humanity."

Partnership with the United Nations

Yet another manner in which Lions are playing a central role in promoting goodwill and understanding is the association's more than half century involvement with the humanitarian missions of the United Nations. Lions Clubs International, in fact, played a key role in the formation of the world body and today maintains a partnership with a number of UN agencies.

A big step was taken in the association's expanding international role came when U.S. President Harry Truman asked Lions to help write the nongovernmental section of the United Nations Charter. "The idea of this section," explained Robert Uplinger, who served as international president and for many years as the liaison of Lions Clubs International to the UN, "was that it would be a grassroots sounding board for citizens of all nations to pass on thoughts and opinions to their representatives at the United Nations."

The initial steps, however, were taken earlier. Late in 1944 the U.S. State Department invited Lions to send representative to the Dumbarton Oaks Conference in Washington, D.C., and a few months later to the Bretton Wood Conference, both gatherings of world leader preceding the chartering of the UN. These led to the San Francisco Conference where the UN charter was drawn and Lions Clubs International was again asked to send representatives. Three were chosen, then International President D.A. Skeen, Third Vice President Fred W. Smith and Melvin Jones. As could have been expected, there was a good deal of debating and haggling in the entire American delegation, resulting in little time to confer with the non-governmental consultants. The Lions put an end to this by deciding on a course of action. They extracted a guarantee from the U.S. delegation to hold briefings on a twice-a-week basis with the consultants. A dinner was set up which turned out to be much like a Lions club meeting. The people were mixed up at the tables sitting with strangers of widely different backgrounds. After the dinner and before the meeting began, guests were asked to arise and introduce the man or woman at their left. The affair, with its fellowship and good humor, did a great deal to preserve American optimism during those formative days.

The three representatives of Lions Clubs International were soon asked to help formulate the non-governmental organization section of the United Nations Charter. Shortly after the charter was adopted on October 24, 1945, the association was granted special consultative status on the United Nations Economic and Social Council which is dedicated to humanitarian efforts throughout the world. As a result, Lions Clubs International has become affiliated with a number of UN agencies that provide assistance and hope to people in greatest need. Among these agencies are UNICEF, the World Health Organization, the Food and Agriculture Organization and the UN Committee on Narcotics and Substance Abuse. This partnership has grown to reflect the highest ideals of service and commitment of both world organizations. Upon examination, the first Object of Lions Clubs International, "to create and foster a spirit of understanding among the peoples of the world," closely parallels the second and third purposes of the United Nations which are "to develop friendly relations among nations" and "to achieve international cooperation in solving international problems of an economic, social, cultural or humanitarian character."

An outgrowth of this affiliation has been the annual Lions Day with the United Nations. Begun at UN Headquarters in New York in 1958, it now includes more than 700 attendees from the United States and other countries and is also held in additional cities around the world. Generally held in March, Lions meet with a number of UN ambassadors from various nations and guest speakers, including UN officials and the association's international president, speak of the role of United Nations agencies and the generous support of the Lions.

In commenting on the cooperative role between Lions Clubs International and the United Nations at the 2000 Lions Day, John Ruggie, special advisor to the UN Secretary-General said, "When pollsters asked what people wanted from the United Nations, the number one response was the protection of human rights. Governments know they can't accomplish their goals alone. There's a new attitude of partnerships with NGOs at the UN." Ambassador James B. Cunningham, the United States Deputy Representative, added, "You are to be congratulated for your work. Lions have built support for the UN and in programs. To achieve success, the UN needs the aid of NGOs such as Lions. I want you to know how much we appreciate the input you give us on a host of important issues such as good citizenship and health, among others."

Yesterday, Today and Tomorrow

How have Lions clubs responded to community and human needs over the years and have these patterns changed? Shortly after World War II the primary areas of the service activities of Lions were witnesses in 44 percent of the clubs involved in community betterment, 13 percent in youth programs, eight percent in vision projects, 14 percent in other service activities. Presently, 24 percent of Lions clubs were engaged in community services, 23 percent in youth activities, 17 percent in sight-related programs, 11 percent in health, eight percent in the environment, 3 percent in hearing and two percent in a variety of other services.

As 2006-2007 International President Jimmy Ross reflected, "You can see a lot of similarity and at the same time, there are many differences. My point is that as community needs have changed, so have the service projects of Lions. We've always been Lions, dedicated to service. We've always been Knights of the Blind and we will continue with this same identity. But we will also adapt and modify. From club to club, Lions help decide who they are and how they serve. That keeps our association young and fresh. No one can predict with any precision exactly how Lions will serve or what rituals and procedures will fall away and which ones will endure and grow more prominent. But I am certain clubs will not hesitate to take the steps necessary to remain vital and active."

Commenting on the importance of current and past programs, 2005-2006 International President Dr. Ashok Mehta observed, "Our success in blindness prevention programs will be a continuing story in the 21st Century. Lions have a vision to make wherever they are in the world better than it was before their arrival, and each program Lions undertake projects our unflinching determination. We have made a difference wherever we are needed, be it in sponsoring relief in the wake of natural catastrophes, youth programs, health care or global peace initiatives. Lions are a worldwide network that enable people to hold their heads high despite all challenges."

The history of Lions Clubs International demonstrates conclusively that the global goodwill generated by Lions extends far beyond national borders. The membership has given little doubt that whenever the opportunities avail themselves, language and cultural differences are easily bridged with Lions and their families working together as a united force for good.

In studying the role of Lions today, 1998-1999 International President Kajit "KJ" Habanananda emphasized, "I can't help but stress that it is people—men, women and young people dedicated to volunteerism—who eliminate the artificial boundaries between nations and cultures. It is *people* who establish good will, not governments. Treaties and official statements and agreements by political leaders have their value, of course, but it is the people of those nations who will, ultimately, establish good will and understanding, thus making mistrust and war unthinkable. *We*, the family of Lions Clubs International and the citizens of all nations committed to peace, will bring this about—we will make it happen. People of good will, who practice mutual respect and promote fellowship and harmony, will make everlasting peace not only a possibility, but, in fact, a reality."

Chapter Sixteen
The Future, and the Role of Lions Clubs International

Changes in the direction of service programs when deemed necessary at every level of the association will be decisive to the role Lions will play in the future. The consensus has always been to maintain the programs that are still popular and viable in the local and world communities, but to also institute new activities and alter directions when required by studying living conditions and the needs of the citizens residing in those communities. To achieve this requires, above all, strong and effective leadership, again at all levels of Lions Clubs International. As in the past, such leadership will play a key role on how Lions will successfully address the needs of tomorrow.

Upon assuming the office of the presidency in July 1995, Dr. William H. Wunder stated, "It is now our turn to lead, whether we have been Lions for a year or for 50 years. It is our turn to take up the challenge inherent in the Lions emblem and to stamp the future with it in our own way. The next century looms, perhaps with problems unknown, but Lions clubs and Lion leaders will be needed more than ever before." In his inaugural address at the 78th International Convention in Seoul, Republic of Korea, he stressed, "Where do we begin? Obviously, where all programs must start if they are to be a success: at the grass roots. Individual Lions in every club around the world are the basic resource which will be molded into the leadership of Lions Clubs International into the 21st Century and beyond. Leadership skills can be developed and cultivated and we of Lions Clubs International are committed to do exactly that with our global membership."

To help ensure that this leadership will be available throughout the association, a wide range of institutes, seminars and workshops are conducted. Perhaps the most well-known and certainly the most involved of these leadership training programs are the District Governors-elect Seminars conducted prior to each international convention. The incoming governors, often looked upon as occupying the most important and sensitive leadership post in the association, are both instructed in the manner in which they are charged in carrying out their responsibilities and in challenging the members of their respective districts to implement the spirit and meet the objectives of the coming year's international program. They are able to exchange ideas with their fellow incoming governors and learn about Lions programs and activities in countries around the world, thus gaining an insight into the global scope of the association. Each session of the seminar is developed to promote group discussion and includes very little in the way of lectures. The roll of DGE Seminar group leaders is crucial, each being responsible for facilitating the curriculum in his or her classroom. It is common for a district governor-elect to form a long-lasting bond with the group leader, who serves to mentor the district governor during the coming year and often, beyond.

While each DGE Seminar provides similar formats in achieving a total understanding of what will be expected of the attendees when they assume their new post and in strengthening their morale, fellowship and enthusiasm, each seminar also offers some never-before-seen theatrics.

For example, at the 2004 International Convention in Detroit/Windsor an actor portrayed Melvin Jones to give a "first-hand" account of the background of the association and where it needs to be heading. A further twist was that, in celebrating the Motor City's historic partnership with the car, the "Founder" stepped out of a vintage auto driven onto the stage of the convention center to begin his chat with the Lions. It was a performance that was repeated, albeit with some variations, at the 2007 seminar in Chicago. This time, he was accompanied by two actresses playing the roles of Helen Keller and Anne Sullivan.

The various leadership institutes also constitute learning experiences that look to the future of Lions Clubs International. Each is adapted to the areas in which they are conducted and are critiqued annually to determine how they may even better serve the needs of the participants. They are based on feedback from faculties who led institutes in the past and the views of participants from all constitutional areas with changes made in order to prepare appropriate content. The methods of the training are aimed at fostering positive attitudes and increasing understanding of major concepts of leadership through the active involvement of the participants.

There are four main categories of these institutes, all initiated and perfected in the early years of the 21st Century's first decade:

Senior Lions Leadership Institutes provide training to prepare experienced Lions for responsibilities in leadership positions at the district level. Emerging Lions Leadership Institutes prepare Lions for leadership roles at the club level. "The Emerging Lions and Senior Lions Institutes, along with training programs in districts and multiple districts, are where the future of our association leadership instruction lies," said Past International President J. Frank Moore III. "These must be nourished and sustained as we move along this important path far into the 21st Century."

The MERL Chairpersons Seminars train newly appointed multiple district and district membership, extension, retention and leadership chairpersons. The MERL program is considered to be a foundation stone of all the association's membership development and growth programs. In order to maximize the effectiveness of MERL teams, the seminars include a flexible structure, intense communication and innovative tools and resources to achieve their objectives for strengthening the future of Lions Clubs International. The Regional Institutes also serve to enhance the skills of current and future association leaders. They are based on the Emerging Lions Leadership Institutes and provide grants to multiple districts to assist in the training of vice district governors and district leadership training chairpersons.

Quality leadership development programs require proficient Lions faculty. The Faculty Development Institute is dedicated to the development and expansion of the pool of skilled Lions faculty capable of delivering quality training in an educationally sound manner. The curriculum focuses not only on presentation skills, but encompasses many of the skills and concepts that impact the quality of training delivery and ultimately the effectiveness of Lions Clubs International's leadership development programs. In all, more than

14,000 Lions have received quality training since the inception of the programs.

To further develop knowledge of the programs and potential of leadership and service activities, the Lions Learning Center was instituted early in the new century. An e-learning program, it is accessible through the association's Web site, enabling Lions to take advantage of the benefits of online training. It is available 24 hours a day and is popular for its self-paced and self-driven learning. Also providing an eye to the future is The Leader Network, a quarterly e-newsletter which is aimed at promoting a dialogue between multiple and district leadership development chairpersons and the association. Its format includes articles on the programs of Lions Clubs International, upcoming events, training tips and leadership development success stories.

As Past President Wunder, a strong advocate of leadership, observed: "We have seen changes in our family units, communities, cities and society as a whole, even some cultural changes. If Lions Clubs International is to be successful in the future, we must also be willing to change in order to address the needs of today and of tomorrow. We must prepare *now*!"

Past International President Kay K. Fukushima was also insistent on the uncompromising importance of quality leadership. "The promise for a bright future of any large and older organization is based upon its visionary, quality leadership that possesses a high degree of ethical standards, character, honesty, trust and integrity. History teaches us that all organizations, profit and non-profit, are impacted negatively whenever self-serving leaders are not sensitive to the welfare and needs of those whom they lead. Whenever an organization has outstanding leaders who are good communicators, who look after the interests of others and who are compassionate, understanding, visionary and positive, they can bring people together. That organization will do very well and will continue to grow and be relevant into the future. So long as Lions Clubs International will be served by quality leaders at all levels and stay ahead of the change curve that we all face and be ready to adapt to needed changes to improve the relevancy of what we do and how we do it, our association will have a great future."

The Need to Develop and Maintain Quality Public Relations

The ability of Lions to reach their goals is also dependent to a large degree on the support they receive from the general public. Consequently, quality public relations will also play a crucial role in the success of Lions clubs the world over.

Lions have been urged throughout the association's history to develop a close partnership with their local news media—print, radio and television—in order to inform the public of the accomplishments of their clubs and their plans for future service endeavors. Newspapers have often provided full-page coverage to a local Lions club's service project, but whether it happened to be such lengthy coverage or a photo or story of an activity, it was always because the Lions took the time and effort to make the necessary contacts to reach the public in this manner. During 2006-2007, articles appeared in more than 5,000 publications around the world and on more than 400 television stations. Public service announcements about the association and its objectives are also becoming increasingly prominent on radio and television. The Public Relations Matching grant program is also reaching new levels with districts the world over using their grants to place ads in local newspapers, rent billboard space and produce their own public service announcements.

Two examples can be cited of how Lions are gaining momentum in their efforts to inform the public. In October 2003, ESPN broadcast four 30-second commercials supplied by Lions Clubs International during an association-sponsored program entitled "Superior Beings." It was subsequently shown in 200,000 high schools around the United States. During the year, a three-minute interview with First Vice President Clement Kusiak was shown on all United Airlines flights over a two-month span, reaching a potential audience of 20 million people.

In 2006, the association released its quarterly video magazine, *Lions Quarterly*, shown on the Lions News Network. The magazine demonstrates the mission of service common to all Lions by highlighting innovative Lions projects around the world, sharing photos and providing news updates on the association. The association's Web site now averages more than 500,000 visits each month with its redesigned home page making information and materials more readily accessible and to drive traffic to sections such as member services and club resources.

"As Lions," stated 2005-2006 International President Dr. Ashok Mehta, "I know you have a passion to serve. The passion to promote is also important, and should become part of your monthly club activities. Whether through television, radio, newspapers, magazines, billboards or the Internet, the goal is to increase public awareness of the Lions."

The year 2007 was, in fact, of special importance to all Lions not only because it celebrated the association's 90th anniversary, but also that it marked the 50th anniversary of the Leo Clubs program and the 20th anniversaries of women joining Lions clubs and the Peace Poster Contest. All were duly reported to the news media and featured in THE LION Magazine and on the Web site. A common theme of these observances was that 2007 was the association's "Year of Celebrations."

"Today, we live in a world where a good public image is an indispensable asset and for this to occur, quality public relations must be in place," said 2000-2001 International President Dr. Jean Behar. "We must remember that public relations is a responsibility of each individual Lions club. Every effort must be made to alert the news media to upcoming projects and make them aware of our achievements. This is public relations of the first order and the beneficiaries will be both the individual Lions clubs and the entire association."

Vision for Tomorrow

For more than 90 years, Lions focused on serving their communities with uncompromising commitment. It has been a commitment that insists on quality and purpose in every endeavor. As historian Barbara Tuchman observed: "Quality means investment of the best skill and effort possible to produce the finest and most admirable result possible. Quality does not allow compromise with the second rate." It is witnessed in the decades-long quest Lions have demonstrated in promoting peace and goodwill, objectives emphasized by Melvin Jones when he said in proclaiming the goal of Lions to help bring about a better, more harmonious world: "Lions are unflinchingly united in a strong stand for a peace that ensures freedom and justice for all people and nations."

The spirit of service has been an identifying mark of Lions Clubs International since 1917 and shows no sign of abating. In fact, sustained accomplishment is the force that has propelled the association's explosive expansion around the world. Ever sensitive to human needs, Lions are active in the international arena with principles that dissolve all boundaries and meet basic human requirements. Indeed, Lions strive for peace where there is war, build homes for the homeless, bring food to the hungry, restore vision to the sightless and hearing to the deaf. They provide opportunities to those who have lost all hope. And Lions assure all who listen that they will continue doing these things, and more, into the future. Consider these following examples of how Lions have answered recent humanitarian needs and promoted international good will—and what they portend for tomorrow.

The Dan Paz Lions Club in Tel Aviv, Israel, is active on both the national and international levels. The word Dan Paz means "give peace" and the club is unique in that it is Spanish-speaking, most of its members having emigrated to Israel from Latin America. "Our ties with Latin America are extensive," related Touvia 'Teddy' Goldstein who arrive from Peru more than 35 years ago. "Therefore, increasing connections with our countries of origin is part of the long-term agenda of the Dan Paz Lions Club, as well as serving communities in our home country." His club twinned with the Istanbul (Levent) Lions Club in Turkey and in collaboration with its Israeli district helped to alleviate the suffering in Turkey following a disastrous earthquake. A number of distinguished guests have visited the Dan Paz Club to speak at meetings, including former ambassadors to Israel from Colombia, Peru and Argentina who addressed relationships between Israel and their nations.

Giving further evidence of the ability of Lions to reach across borders, The Brussels (Heraldic), Belgium, Lions Club, an English-speaking club, demonstrated that on a continent of many languages and cultures, community spirit recognizes no boundaries. In 2001, these Lions partnered with the Timisoara Lions Club in Romania by providing a 12-seat minibus to be used for transporting children to schools and hospitals. The Brussels Lions drove the bus, along with a backup vehicle for the drive back, in non-stop shifts and made the trip in two days. They were met at the Romanian border by a member of the Timisoara Club who facilitated the customs processing. The pre- Christmas holiday arrival of the minibus was doubly welcome because it was filled with school and art supplies, toys and games for the children, simple items which could be hard to find at that time in Romania. The Heraldic Lions have also been involved in other projects of an international nature, including the purchase of a bus for an orphanage in Warsaw, Poland, and helping a school in South Africa rebuild its facilities.

To answer a crucial need that will have a far-reaching impact on the future health of individuals, the Bursa Yesil Lions Club in Turkey sponsored a panel on menopause and osteoporosis. The District 118-K public health service committee was involved in its planning and a large culture center was chosen as its venue. Hundreds of posters were hung in public buses and trains, local hospitals, shopping malls, area drug stores and other locations of high visibility; billboards were erected and educational brochures were printed for distribution to participants. Ads were published in local newspapers and public service announcements were broadcast on the radio. The club president even was a guest on radio talk shows to publicize the event. In all, more than 700 people, most of then women attended the panel discussion, which consisted of professors from Uludag University who were experts in obstetrics, gynecology, medicine and orthopedics. A question and answer session followed. Free bone density tests were also administered to more than 100 women.

In the Peoples Republic of China, voluntary action was new, but it didn't take the Lions long to become involved in responding to community needs. The Shenzhen Xiang Mi Xu Lions Club, for example, immediately began working to provide housing and other necessities for orphans and autistic children. They constructed a playground at the orphanage and were instrumental in establishing the first rehabilitation and therapy center of its kind where children receive speech, behavioral, occupational and music therapy at no cost to their parents. The therapy is done on a one-to-one setting with the Shenzhen Lions acting as companions for the children. Shenzhen

Lion Danny Chen, who was named Lions of the Year during the 2005 Academy Awards of Lions Clubs International at the International Convention in Hong Kong for his efforts at the orphanage said, "The government cannot fill all the needs of people, so as Lions it is our responsibility to help. We are proud to do these things. I view these orphans as my own children and want them to live a happy life, the same as my daughter."

Chen continued, "As a member, I know it's not only myself helping others, but that there are people all over the world helping others. The more Lions, the more help to society and the world, making it a better place."

During 2005, 2,000 children in Shenzhen were screened through the Sight for Kids program. LCIF and Johnson & Johnson have teamed up with local Lions in this ambitious project to offer free eye screenings and eye health education to children. Johnson & Johnson committed $835,000 over four years to help fund Sight for Kids in China as well as the Republic of Korea, Hong Kong, Multiple District 300 Taiwan, India, Malaysia and Thailand.

Still another example of how Lions today can envision how they can serve people in distant communities and expand services into the future is found in Canada where the Alberta Shock Trauma Air Rescue Society (STARS) celebrated its "20 years of Care in the Air" in 2005. Lions of Multiple District 37 in Alberta have helped fund the program since the beginning when it provided a $100,000 donation to, as the Lions said, "get the program off the ground." STARS provides specialized emergency transport by helicopter for critically ill patients in Alberta and British Columbia. To date, MD37 Lions have contributed more than $1.2 million to STARS.

Activities such as these have been multiplied thousands and thousands of times around the world and are a firm prediction of how Lions will be personally involved in their communities in the years to come. How may the membership approach their responsibilities? Will their commitment differ from what has happened in the past? For example, meetings have always been a constant source of inspiration and fellowship since 1917. But will they be as relevant for a club's success and motivation for individual members in the future? Obviously, it will depend upon the perspective of the club and the individual member. "The goal of Lions is to serve their communities and people in need," said 2008-2009 International President Albert F. Brandel. "This doesn't necessitate that the members attend every meeting. What is necessary is that each Lion is dedicated to the principles of 'We Serve.' " He also observed that "while check writing is necessary in such cases as support of LCIF and generosity when such disasters as Hurricane Katrina, 9/11 and the tsunami occur, it is vital for Lions to take a hands-on approach in their service activities. This direct contact with people in need in their communities will inspire Lions to increase their direct involvement."

A special activity of Lions worldwide in promoting goodwill and understanding is the Lions International Stamp Club (LISC). The club took its first steps in 1942 when President Franklin Delano Roosevelt, an avid stamp collector himself, founded a rehabilitation program for World War II veterans called Stamps for the Wounded. Lions began supervising collection points for the stamps, eventually assuming its direction. LISC was officially established by the association in 1951. It is now recognized by Lions Clubs International as a means for stamp collectors to organize educational, recreational and therapeutic activities in rehabilitation programs for veterans. More than 500 million stamps are collected each year and eventually shipped to VA hospitals serving thousands of patients and homebound veterans. Members of LISC have built their own collections and quite naturally focus on stamps that highlight Lions Clubs International. Nations throughout the world have issued such stamps and many Lions can boast full collections. There are presently thousands of Lions who are members of LISC and the club even operates a booth at international conventions. Lasting international friendships are made through membership in the stamp club, friendships that will multiply and extend into the future.

To be sure, scientific and technical developments predictably means that Lions clubs will be undertaking different kinds if projects in tomorrow's world. But in many ways, Lions Clubs International will remain profoundly the same. While it has been said that our next neighbors may be extra-terrestrial, the goal of Lions in the future will definitely remain down to earth. Lions clubs will continue to work on projects that change lives which otherwise might be without hope. Lions will do these things because they find, stated 1989-1990 International President William L. Woolard in his inaugural address, "that in helping others, we find happiness for ourselves, and if we help more today than we did yesterday, then each tomorrow will hold greater promise for everyone."

This is a vision that enjoys a global perspective. For example, some years ago a journalist was interviewing El Salvador's President Alfredo Cristiani in the presidential home in San Salvador, the nation's capital. In responding to a question about the work of local Lions, President Cristiani remarked, "For nearly 50 years, the Lions of my country have developed effective programs that meet the needs of the less fortunate. They have extensive projects involving health as well as promoting education and fostering activities for the needy, The Lions of El Salvador are a positive force in making lives better for everyone."

How may Lions be involved in answering future needs? SightFirst and LCIF are, of course, two prime examples. Other activities, however, will also demand attention. The environment could well be among the most important. While Lions worldwide are known as builders, they also stand firm on helping to preserve what is vital. Consequently, many Lions clubs have turned their attention to projects aimed at preserving the natural environment with the world's rain forests being a centerpiece of this concern. Consider this: Tropical forests exist on only about six percent of the Earth's land surface. However, they support more than 50 percent of all living species, protect water supplies, help regulate global climate and prevent soil erosion. They contain many of the plants that have important medical uses for such ailments as arthritis, heart disease and cancer. But humans are relentlessly destroying these areas at the rate of 50 acres a minute; even faster in some places.

Trees change carbon dioxide into oxygen and help preserve the planets breathable air. The world's forests are critical factors in the world's climate and the nursery for a least half the world's plants and animal species. The widely-publicized "greenhouse effect" and global warming are among the deadly results of the destruction of our forests.

The Amazon rain forest is a case in point. It is home to at least 60 million species of life. An incredibly complex natural laboratory, it is a place to study anything from evolution to global warming to the medical uses of plants. With more than 2.5 million square miles of green carpet, fertile valleys and savannah, the Amazon rain forest is two-thirds the size of the 48 contiguous U.S. states. Seventy percent of it lies within Brazil; the rest occupying areas of Peru, Ecuador, Bolivia, Colombia, Venezuela, Guyana and Surinam.

A long-time student of the destruction of the fragile rain forest is Past International Director Zander Campos da Silva of Goiania, Brazil, in the central part of the country near the capital city of Brasilia. A Lion since 1965, he is also the editor of one of the Portuguese language editions of THE LION Magazine. "Saving the Amazon rain forest is an issue that has excited Lions throughout the world," he said. "Lions club were first organized in my country in 1956 and many of our clubs are hard at work on projects that protect the forest. Preserving the world's forests," he insisted, "is one of the most important goals for us and for everyone in the world because of the danger of global warming."

Lions will agree that international cooperation in protecting our ravaged environment is long overdue. The problem cuts across all national boundaries, a fact that makes the Lions of the world natural allies in halting this savage destruction.

Together in Future Service Activities

Every service program in which Lions are involved, be it at the club, district or international levels, demands cohesiveness in approach and conduct. Only in this manner will success be assured. Where precisely will Lions Clubs International be in the years to come? Past President Jimmy Ross put it this way in the association's preparation for the world of tomorrow:

"I am certain of exactly where Lions are headed in the future," he said. "We will be where we are needed most, as we have been throughout our 90-year history. There is no other option for us. If we fail to move in the right direction, we will have outlived our usefulness. But that won't happen. It has not happened in 90 years and it won't happen in the next 90."

Sight programs, through SightFirst and individual club and district projects, will continue to be among the most extensive humanitarian objectives of Lions worldwide. Focusing on this, Lions worldwide will maintain their commitment to support the mission of SightFirst and, with the new funds generated through Campaign SightFirst II, the association is optimistic that preventable and reversible blindness will be conquered. Indeed, what greater challenge could Lions face than to reverse the course of blindness in the 21st Century?

It is frustrating for Lions and those in the field of blindness prevention to realize that most blindness is preventable—or reversible once it occurs. Eye care specialists estimate that 80 percent of those who are blind today would not be if proper health measures had been taken. Significantly, 90 percent of those with vision loss live in developing countries—countries with resources too meager to train people to answer this medical need, buy equipment and set in place programs which would prevent and cure blindness.

Because most blindness is either preventable of treatable, the global attack of Lions on blindness has an excellent chance of eradicating the disease.

It is estimated that fully 50 percent of the world's blind are blind from cataracts with the result that many SightFirst projects will be devoted to providing teams of ophthalmologists and other medical specialists to perform cataract surgery. SightFirst will continue, in the future, to target other devastating eyesight conditions such as diabetic retinopathy, trachoma, onchocerciasis and xerophthalmia.

As we move further into the 21st Century, Lions will maintain and, whenever necessary, enhance their action as "knights of the blind in the crusade against darkness." And SightFirst will maintain its drive as the global thrust that will dramatically reduce the odds of the spread of blindness. The battle is not over, nor has it only begun, but with continually renewed dedication, vigilance and generosity in funding and hands-on involvement, the end to this human tragedy could be in sight.

"Ever since SightFirst became a central element of our association's obligation to the health well-being of humanity, countless innovative activities have taken root and flourished," observed Past International President Dr. Tae-Sup Lee. "Indeed, it has grown to exemplify all that can be achieved when Lions commit themselves to tasks that perhaps have never before been attempted, at least never on such a grand scale. SightFirst has demonstrated without a doubt how innovative project can open gateways to the future for millions of people who were blind or were potentially among those who could well have suffered permanent vision loss."

Again, new technology and medical advances will multiply the sight conservation efforts of Lions. As Lions move further into the 21st Century they will be able to do more to prevent blindness and restore sight to greater numbers of people than at any time in the past.

"The expansion of our humanitarian services is governed by community needs in all parts of the world," observed Past International President Dr. Ashok Mehta. "Volunteerism has always been identified with our programs, and now growing professional expertise is becoming a greater part and parcel of our activities. Planned and focused programs are always poised for success. Funds have always been made generously available. Lions believe that if we have a purpose, means are bound to follow."

Whatever the technological and material advance the world of tomorrow will boast, however, there will always be a need, a crucial need, for the voluntary involvement of men, women and young people. The need for community service will never diminish; it will only grow, and the millions of Lions and young people around the world who are part of this association will find still greater opportunities for putting their ideals and active concern into practice to help improve the human condition in communities spanning the globe.

The emblem of Lions Clubs International—proud of past achievements and looking to the future with unbounded confidence— will be increasingly visible as our membership accepts the challenges of the 21st Century.

The association has come a long way since those first days in Chicago and Dallas. Through war, depression, the atomic age and the space age, The International Association of Lions Clubs has grown to be the largest and most active service club organization in the world. Members of Lions clubs are known and respected around the world for their unselfish work in building their communities and in alleviating human misery. They have demonstrated by their actions that people do care about each other and that, properly motivated, will seek to make their own communities and the world community better places in which to live. Such involvement is needed if the world is to be united someday in peace and harmony—and this association will stand ready to provide opportunities for individuals to give generously of themselves in creating such a world.

This will demand investigation of all that is truly required, intense planning and then putting these plans into action. For more than 90 years, Lions have given solid evidence that half-way measures are not acceptable. They have gone the distance in implementing their countless community projects and the far-reaching programs of the association such as LCIF, SightFirst and all activities that bring the Lions of the world together in service and in fellowship. They have, indeed, heeded the call of Daniel Burnham, the architect who, among other widely acclaimed accomplishments, drafted Chicago's magnificent Lake Front Plan in 1909 when he wrote, "Make no little plans. They have no magic to stir men's blood and probably themselves will not be realized. Make big plans: aim high in hope and work..."

Born during the fury of World War I, Lions Clubs International came of age in the peace following World War II. With undiminished vigor, it has moved into the 21st Century with 1.3 million members in over 44,000 Lions clubs. The number of countries and geographical areas in the association's family are currently in excess of 200, and growing, bringing service and hope with practical designs for effective action. The 800 members at the end of 1917 have been multiplied countless times.

How will Lions Clubs International meet the challenges of the future? In what manner will Lions extend their reach to answer needs in their own communities and throughout the world? How will they draw upon the association's proud legacy of achievement and enhance their stature as members of the world's largest service club organization? If the past is any prediction, it is certain that they will face the future with courage and determination. Melvin Jones was optimistic that the enduring principles of "We Serve" will ensure continued growth and progress when he stated:

"I hope there will always be a land of beyond for Lions Clubs International; a goal that will keep growing larger and larger as we approach it, yet will keep just out of reach, challenging us to run faster, work harder, think bigger, give more."

Appendices

Acknowledgments

Writing a book detailing historical events, the author or authors are indebted to a great many individuals for their collaboration and assistance. In the preparation of this book on the history of The International Association of Lions Clubs, this is most assuredly the case. There are so very many individuals who provided us with the information and support without which this book would never have made it to press.

Past and present international officers and directors were generous with their thoughts and observations on the history, goals and aspirations of Lions worldwide. Some of these leaders who are quoted have passed on, but their legacy is an inspiration to those who are dedicated to carrying on the spirit of "We Serve."

We are also indebted to key members of the International Headquarters staff who provided information and assistance during the two years of this endeavor: Dane La Joye, manager, Public Relations and Communications Division; Jay Copp, Senior Editor, THE LION Magazine; Pamela Mohr, Associate Editor, THE LION Magazine; Brett Rush, Assistant Editor, THE LION Magazine; Patti Repenn, manager, Leadership Division; Melitta Cutright, manager, Public Relations Department; Connie Schuler, manager, Christy Jacobs and Jim Sinclair, Graphic Arts Department; Nicole Brown, LCIF communications manager; Mindy Marks, manager, and Becca Pietrini, New Clubs Department; Sue Haney, manager, Membership Programs Department; Sue Crosson-Knutson, manager, Program Development Department; Deborah O'Malley, coordinator, Health and Children Services Department; Caryn Adolph, manager, International Activities and Program Planning Division; Kristopher Kempski, Michelle Blomeke, Christina Cygan and Joyce Truby of the Public Relations staff and Kevin Cherep and the staff of Campaign SightFirst II.

Each of these individuals are providing the professional expertise in helping Lions Clubs International maintain its stature as the world's largest and most active service club organization.

And, of paramount importance, we thank the men, women and young people who for more than 90 years have given so very generously of themselves to enhance the proud image reflected in the emblem of this association.

International Presidents

(1) 1917-18 Dr. W.P. Woods, Evansville, Indiana, U.S.A.

(2) 1918-19 L.H. Lewis, Dallas, Texas. U.S.A.

(3) 1919-20 Jesse Robinson, Oakland, California, U.S.A.

(4) 1920-21 Dr. C.C. Reid, Denver, Colorado, U.S.A.

(5) 1921-22 Ewen W. Cameron, Minneapolis, Minnesota, U.S.A.

(6) 1922-23 Ed S. Vaught, Oklahoma City, Oklahoma, U.S.A.

(7) 1923-24 John S. Noel, Grand Rapids, Michigan, U.S.A.

(8) 1924-25 Harry A. Newman, Q.C., Toronto, Ontario, Canada

(9) 1925-26 Benjamin F. Jones, Newark, New Jersey, U.S.A.

(10) 1926-27 William A. Westfall, Mason City, Iowa, U.S.A.

(11) 1927-28 Irving L. Camp, Johnstown, Pennsylvania, U.S.A.

(12) 1928-29 Ben A. Ruffin, Richmond, Virginia, U.S.A.

(13) 1929-30 Ray L. Riley, San Francisco, California, U.S.A

(14) 1930-31 Earle W. Hodges, New York, New York, U.S.A.

(15) 1931-32 Julien C. Hyer, Fort Worth, Texas, U.S.A.

(16) 1932-33 Charles H. Hatton, Wichita, Kansas, U.S.A.

(17) 1933-34 Roderick Beddow, Birmingham, Alabama, U.S.A.

(18) 1934-35 Vincent C. Hascall, Omaha, Nebraska, U.S.A.

(19) 1935-36 Richard J. Osenbaugh, Denver, Colorado U.S.A.

(20) 1936-37 Edwin R. Kingsley, Parkersburg, West Virginia, U.S.A.

(21) 1937-38 Frank V. Birch, Milwaukee, Wisconsin, U.S.A.

(22) 1938-39 Walter F. Dexter, Sacramento, California, U.S.A.

(23) 1939-40 Alexander T. Wells, New York, New York, U.S.A.

(24) 1940-41 Karl M. Sorrick, Springport, Michigan, U.S.A.

(25) 1941-42 George R. Jordan, Dallas, Texas, U.S.A.

(26) 1942-43 Edward H. Paine, Michigan City, Indiana, U.S.A.

(27) 1943-44 Dr. E.G. Gill, Roanoke, Virginia, U.S.A.

(28) 1944-45 D.A. Skeen, Salt Lake City, Utah, U.S.A.

(29) 1945-46 Dr. Ramiro Collazo, Marianao, Habana, Cuba

(30) 1946-47 Clifford D. Pierce, Memphis, Tennessee, U.S.A.

(31) 1947-48 Fred W. Smith, Ventura, California, U.S.A.

(32) 1948-49 Dr. Eugene S. Briggs, Edmond, Oklahoma, U.S.A.

(33) 1949-50 Walter C. Fisher, St. Catharines, Ontario, Canada

(34) 1950-51 H.C. Petry Jr. Carrizo Springs, Texas, U.S.A.

(35) 1951-52 Harold P. Nutter, Oaklyn, New Jersey, U.S.A.

(36) 1952-53 Edgar M. Elbert, Maywood, Illinois, U.S.A.

(37) 1953-54 S.A. Dodge, Bloomfield Hills, Michigan, U.S.A.

(38) 1954-55 Monroe L. Nute, Kennett Square, Pennsylvania, U.S.A.

(39) 1955-56 Humberto Valenzuela G., Santiago, Chile

(40) 1956-57 John L. Stickley, Charlotte, North Carolina, U.S.A.

(41) 1957-58 Edward G. Barry, Little Rock, Arkansas, U.S.A.

(42) 1958-59 Dudley L. Simms, Charleston, West Virginia, U.S.A.

(43) 1959-60 Clarence L. Sturm, Manawa, Wisconsin, U.S.A.

(44) 1960-61 Finis E. Davis, Louisville, Kentucky, U.S.A.

(45) 1961-62 Per Stahl, Eskilstuna, Sweden

(46) 1962-63 Curtis D. Lovill, Gardiner, Maine, U.S.A.

(47) 1963-64 Aubrey D. Green, York, Alabama, U.S.A.

(48) 1964-65 Claude M. De Vorss, Wichita, Kansas, U.S.A.

(49) 1965-66 Dr. Walter H. Campbell, Miami Beach, Florida, U.S.A.

(50) 1966-67 Edward M. Lindsey, Lawrenceburg, Tennessee, U.S.A.

(51) 1967-68 Jorge Bird, Rio Piedras, Puerto Rico

(52) 1968-69 David A. Evans, Galveston, Texas, U.S.A.

(53) 1969-70 W.R. Bryan, Doylestown, Ohio, U.S.A.

(54) 1970-71 Dr. Robert D. McCullough, Tulsa, Oklahoma, U.S.A.

(55) 1971-72 Robert J. Uplinger, Syracuse, New York, U.S.A.

(56) 1972-73 George Friedrichs, Annecy, France

(57) 1973-74 Tris Coffin, Rosemere, Quebec, Canada

(58) 1974-75 Johnny Balbo, LaGrange, Illinois, U.S.A.

(59) 1975-76 Harry J. Aslan, Kingsburg, California, U.S.A.

(60) 1976-77 Prof. Joao Fernando Sobral, Sao Paulo, S.P., Brazil

(61) 1977-78 Joseph M. McLoughlin, Stamford, Connecticut, U.S.A.

(62) 1978-79 Ralph A. Lynam, St. John, Michigan, U.S.A.

(63) 1979-80 Lloyd Morgan, Taupo, New Zealand

(64) 1980-81 William C. Chandler, Montgomery, Alabama, U.S.A.

(65) 1981-82 Kaoru Murakami, Kyoto, Japan

(66) 1982-83 Everett J. Grindstaff, Ballinger, Texas, U.S.A.

(67) 1983-84 Dr. James M. Fowler, Hot Springs, Arkansas, U.S.A.

(68) 1984-85 Bert Mason, Donaghadee, Northern Ireland

(69) 1985-86 Joseph L. Wroblewski, Forty Fort, Pennsylvania, U.S.A.

(70) 1986-87 Sten A. Akestam, Stockholm, Sweden

(71) 1987-88 Judge Brian Stevenson, Calgary, Alberta, Canada

(72) 1988-89 Austin P. Jennings, Woodbury, Tennessee, U.S.A.

(73) 1989-90 William L. Woolard, Charlotte, North Carolina, U.S.A.

(74) 1990-91 William L. Biggs, Omaha, Nebraska, U.S.A.

(75) 1991-92 Donald E. Banker, Rolling Hills, California, U.S.A.

(76) 1992-93 Rohit C. Mehta, Ahmedabad, India

(77) 1993-94 James T. Coffey, Toronto, Ohio, U.S.A.

(78) 1994-95 Prof. Dr. Giuseppe Grimaldi, Enna, Italy

(79) 1995-96 Dr. William H. Wunder, Wichita, Kansas, U.S.A.

(80) 1996-97 Augustin Soliva, Sao Jose dos Campos, Brazil

(81) 1997-98 Judge Howard L. Patterson, Hattiesburg, Mississippi, U.S.A.

(82) 1998-99 Kajit "KJ" Habanananda, Bangkok, Thailand

(83) 1999-2000 James E. "Jim" Ervin, Albany, Georgia, U.S.A.

(84) 2000-01 Dr. Jean Behar, Sainte-Adresse, France

(85) 2001-02 J. Frank Moore III, Daleville, Alabama, U.S.A.

(86) 2002-03 Kay K. Fukushima, Sacramento, California, U.S.A.

(87) 2003-04 Dr. Tae-Sup "TS" Lee, Seoul, Republic of Korea

(88) 2004-05 Dr. Clement F. Kusiak, Linthicum, Maryland, U.S.A.

(89) 2005-06 Dr. Ashok Mehta, Mumbai, India

(90) 2006-07 Jimmy M. Ross, Quitaque, Texas, U.S.A.

(91) 2007-2008 Mahendra Amarasuriya, Colombo, Sri Lanka

(92) 2008-2009 Al Brandel, Melville, New York, U.S.A.

ANNUAL INTERNATIONAL CONVENTIONS

No.	Year	Place	Date
1	1917	Dallas, Texas	October 8-10
2	1918	St. Louis, Missouri	August 19-21
3	1919	Chicago, Illinois	July 9-11
4	1920	Denver, Colorado	July 13-16
5	1921	Oakland, California	July 19-22
6	1922	Hot Springs, Arkansas	June 19-24
7	1923	Atlantic City, New Jersey	June 26-29
8	1924	Omaha, Nebraska	June 23-26
9	1925	Cedar Point, Ohio	June 29-July 2
10	1926	San Francisco, California	July 21-24
11	1927	Miami, Florida	June 25-18
12	1928	Des Moines, Iowa	July 10-13
13	1929	Louisville, Kentucky	June 18-21
14	1930	Denver, Colorado	July 15-18
15	1931	Toronto, Canada	July 14-17
16	1932	Los Angeles, California	July 19-22
17	1933	St. Louis, Missouri	July 11-14
18	1934	Grand Rapids, Michigan	July 23-25
19	1935	Mexico City, Mexico	July-23-25
20	1936	Providence, Rhode Island	July 21-24
21	1937	Chicago, Illinois	July 20-23
22	1938	Oakland, California	July 19-22
23	1939	Pittsburgh, Pennsylvania	July 18-21
24	1940	Havana, Cuba	July 23-25
25	1941	New Orleans, Louisiana	July 22-25
26	1942	Toronto, Canada	July 21-24
27	1943	Cleveland, Ohio	July 20-22
28	1944	Chicago, Illinois	August 1-3
	1945	NONE HELD	

29	1946	Philadelphia, Pennsylvania	July 16-19
30	1947	San Francisco, California	July 28-31
31	1948	New York, New York	July 18-21
32	1949	New York, New York	July 16-20
33	1950	Chicago, Illinois	July 16-20
34	1951	Atlantic City, New Jersey	June 24-28
35	1952	Mexico City, Mexico	June 25-28
36	1953	Chicago, Illinois	July 8-11
37	1954	New York, New York	July 7-10
38	1955	Atlantic City, New Jersey	June 22-25
39	1956	Miami, Florida	June 27-30
40	1957	San Francisco, California	June 26-29
41	1958	Chicago, Illinois	July 9-12
42	1959	New York, New York	June 30-July 3
43	1960	Chicago, Illinois	July 6-9
44	1961	Atlantic City, New Jersey	June 21-24
45	1962	Nice, France	June 20-23
46	1963	Miami, Florida	June 19-22
47	1964	Toronto, Canada	July 8-11
48	1965	Los Angeles, California	July 7-10
49	1966	New York, New York	July 6-9
50	1967	Chicago, Illinois	July 5-8
51	1968	Dallas, Texas	June 26-29
52	1969	Tokyo, Japan	July 2-5
53	1970	Atlantic City, New Jersey	July 1-4
54	1971	Las Vegas, Nevada	June 22-25
55	1972	Mexico City, Mexico	June 28-July1
56	1973	Miami, Florida	June 27-30
57	1974	San Francisco, California	July 3-6
58	1975	Dallas, Texas	June 25-28
59	1976	Honolulu, Hawaii	June 23-26
60	1977	New Orleans, Louisiana	June 29-July 2
61	1978	Tokyo, Japan	June 21-24

62	1979	Montreal, Canada	June 20-23
63	1980	Chicago, Illinois	July 2-5
64	1981	Phoenix, Arizona	June 27-20
65	1982	Atlanta, Georgia	June 30-July 3
66	1983	Honolulu, Hawaii	June 22-25
67	1984	San Francisco, California	July 4-7
68	1985	Dallas, Texas	June 19-22
69	1986	New Orleans, Louisiana	July 9-12
70	1987	Taipei, Taiwan, ROC	July 1-4
71	1988	Denver, Colorado	June 28-July 2
72	1989	Miami/Miami Beach, Florida	June 20-24
73	1990	St. Louis, Missouri	July 11-14
74	1991	Brisbane, Australia	June 19-22
75	1992	Hong Kong	June 22-26
76	1993	Minneapolis/St. Paul/ Bloomington, Minnesota	July 6-9
77	1994	Phoenix, Arizona	July 12-15
78	1995	Seoul, Republic of Korea	July 4-7
79	1996	Montreal, Canada	July 9-12
80	1997	Philadelphia, Pennsylvania	June 30-July 5
81	1998	Birmingham, England	June 29-July 3
82	1999	San Diego, California	June 28-July 2
83	2000	Honolulu, Hawaii	June 19-23
84	2001	Indianapolis, Indiana	July 2-6
85	2002	Osaka, Japan	July 8-12
86	2003	Denver, Colorado	June 30-July 4
87	2004	Detroit, Michigan/Windsor, Canada	July 5-9
88	2005	Hong Kong, China	June 27-July 1
89	2006	Boston, Massachusetts	June 30-July 4
90	2007	Chicago, Illinois	July 2-6
91	2008	Bangkok, Thailand	June 23-27

Index

Fujhou, China 38
Fukushima, Kay K. 80, 112, 153, 167, 332, 346, 365
Funabashi Higashi, Japan, Lions Club 18
Fusco, Tina 102

G

Galimberti, Maurizio 64
Gambill, Shauna 268
Gandhi, Mahatma 24
Gangstad, Lowell 251
Ganlose, Denmark, Lions Club 98
Garcia, Maria 309–310
Garcia de Paez, Yolima 174
Gargurevich, Rosa 99
Georgia Lions Eye Bank 50
Gill, Barney 148
Give the Gift of Sight Foundation 56
Glasser, William, M.D. 277
Glaucoma 1, 48, 50, 52–55, 73–75, 77, 132, 260, 264
Glenside, Pennsylvania, Lions Club 257, 259, 262
Goff, Dr. Charles Ray 147
Goldberg, Dr. Morton I. 48
Golden Anniversary 147
Goldstein, Touvia 'Teddy' 349
Golembek-Peltier, Dr. Sarah 49
Goncz, Arpad 23
Gonzales, Manuel J. 144
Goodwill Children's Village, India 116
Goulds Leo Club, Newfoundland, Canada 271
Grand Prize Winners - Peace Poster Contest 254
Grant-Higgins, Susan 270–271
Graver, Bill 257–258
Green, Jack 313

Green, Marilyn 61
Greer, Dr. H. Courtney 47
Gresham Breakfast, Oregon, Lions Club 100
Griese, Dr. Wolfgang 299, 302
Grimaldi, Dr. Giuseppe 75, 156, 267, 365
Grindstaff, Everett J. "Ebb" 24
Guatemala Central Lions Club 115–116
Gujarat, India, earthquake 126

H

Haas, Dr. Oskar 316
Habanananda, Kajit "KJ" 158, 342, 365
Habitat for Humanity 128–129, 246
Habyaramana, Juvenal 302
Hachicho, Lisa 178
Hadley, William Allen 36
Hadley School for the Blind 37–38, 149
Haidar-Akbar 51
Haley's Comet 43
Hall, Dr. John 320
Hall, Jerry 50
Hall, Mike 258
Hansen's Disease Center, Carville, Louisiana 275–277
Hartford, Connecticut, Lions Club 137
Hasbun, Lorenzo 116
Havre du Fjord 277–279
Heart Foundation of Jamaica 291, 293
Helen Keller 27–32, 35–36, 38, 42–43, 45, 52, 62, 67, 73, 86, 92, 104, 108, 145, 149, 344
Helen Keller International 73, 86

Rubl, Wolfgang 317
Ruffin, Ben 32
Rugarama Health Center, Uganda
41
Ruggie, John 340
Ryan, Peter 251

S

"Search for Peace" Contest 147
"Search for Peace" postage stamp
333
Sagrai, Tomoko 231
Saito, Joseph 247
Samana City, India, Leo Club 271
San Diego, Callifornia, Lions Club
265
San Diego (Host), California,
Lions Club 283, 284
San Francisco Conference - United
Nations 339
San Juan-Petit Juan, Trinidad &
Tobago, Lions Club 40
San Juan Zacatepeque Children's
Hospital, Guatemala 115
San Lorenzo, Argentina, Lions
Club 98
Sarajevo, Bosnia, First Ladies
Lions Club 58
Savio House, Colorado 234
Schafer, Dr. Herbert 280
Schaumburg-Hoffman, Illinois,
Lions Club 160
Schweitzer, Dr. Albert 145
Seal Beach, California, Leo Club
274
Seberang Jaya, Malaysia, Lions
Club 57
Second International Convention,
St. Louis, Missouri 366
Seidensticker, Thomas 300
Seki, Japan, Leo Club 267

Selby, Elmer 37
Seno, Kazuhiro 120
Sheahan, A.F. 3
Shenzhen, China, Lions Club 42
Sheppard, Morris 35
Shriver, Dr. Timothy 133, 338
Shriver, Eunice Kennedy 132
SightFirst 43, 46, 55, 57, 59,
67–68, 70–87, 89–104,
106–110, 112, 119, 134, 155,
166, 353, 355–357, 361
SightFirst Advisory Committee
77, 80, 85–86
SightFirst China Action 55,
78–81, 166
SightFirst China Action, Phase II
79–80
SightFirst Fundraising Committee
89
Sight for Kids 56
Siliguri Greater, India, Lions Club
107
Singapore (East) Lions Club 322
Sivamani 116
Skeen, D.A. 339, 363
Skills for Action 129, 131
Skills for Adolescence 129, 131
Skills for Growing 129, 131
Skinner, Selwyn 40
Slattery, Tom 62
SmileTrain 243–245
Smith, Dr. Goodrich T. 39
Smith, Fred W. 142, 339, 363
SMK Batu Lintang, Malaysia, Leo
Club 271
Sobral, Joao Fernando 21
Soliva, Augustin 158, 365
South Asia Tsunami Disaster Fund
123
South Pole Antarctica Lions Club
138, 145

Spartanburg, South Carolina, Lions Club 105
Special Olympics 131–133, 164, 171, 173, 176, 260, 338
Sri Lankan Lions 57
St. Albert Host, Alberta, Canada, Lions Club 65
St. Augustine, Florida 33
St. Petersburg, Florida, Lions Club 248
STARS 351
Steffes, Ron 244
Stevenson, D.A. 144
Stevenson, Judge Brian 89, 92, 95, 98, 101, 327, 365
Stickley, John L. 24
Stoner, Sara 235
Strauss, Marty 245–246
Sturcken, Ann 173
Sturrock, John 38
Sudbury, Ontario, Canada, Lions Club 33
Sullivan, Anne 28, 32, 92, 344
Swakopund, Namibia, Lions Club 56
Sweeny, Texas, Lions Club 160

T

Tableview, South Africa, Leo Club 269
Tacke, Hans-Dieter 316
Tajami, Japan, Lions Club 330
Tallinn, Estonia, Leo Club 267
Tamaqua, Pennsylvania, Leo Club 257
Tan, Kar Wee 322
Tasmania, Australia 281
Taveira, Rui 305
Taylor, Austin 63
Taylor University, Indiana, Campus Lions Club 165

Templeton, Clarence 262
Terre Haute, Indiana, Lions Club 330
Thatcher, Margaret 93
The Business Circle, Chicago 2
The Carter Center 68–69, 81–83, 85–86, 103, 128, 337
the International Association of Lions Clubs 1–2, 106
THE LION Magazine 6, 10, 15, 18, 28, 33, 40, 108, 136, 150, 257–258, 348, 354, 361
THE LION Magazine - language editions 150, 354
The Netherlands Embassy in Jamaica 292
The New York Times 83
Thompson, Major A.G. 145
Three-member membership committee 154
Tibet 42, 80, 326
Tientsin, China, Lions Club 138
Tillman, Arthur 264
Timisoara, Romania, Lions Club 349–350
Timmerman, Robert D., M.D. 286
Tingo Maria, Peru, Leo Club 263
Toft, Judy 176
Tomkins, Dennis 240
TOUCH 41
Trachoma 68
Trafford, Pennsylvania, Leo Club 273
Trautman, Dr. John 276
Tremblay, Jacques 278
Trick, Dr. Gary L. 59
Tropical Ophthalmology Institute of Africa (IOTA) 83
Trujillo, Cesar Gaviria 97
Truman, Harry 339
Truro Episcopal Church 41

137–138, 357
World War II 34–35, 64, 141–143,
231, 322, 329, 341, 352, 357
Wroblewski, Joseph L. 48, 365
Wunder, Dr. William H. 76, 79,
157, 338, 343, 365
Wyatt, Jack 283–284
Wyndham, Col. Edward 143

X

Xerophthalmia 69

Y

Year of Campaign SightFirst
90–93, 95–96
Year of Inspiration and Motivation
107
Year of Organization and Motiva-
tion 90
Year of Planning and Preparation
89
Yngvadottir, Gudrun 173
York, Sergeant Alvin 138
Young, Andrew 267
Yung, Dicken 133

Z

Zamboanga City La Bella, Philip-
pines, Lions Club 7
Zamboanga Preciosa, Philippines,
Lions Club 183
Zaragoza, Spain, Lions Club
307–309
Zaumschirm, Dr. Andrew 315–
316
Zemin, Jiang 80
Zirm, Dr. Eduard 48
Zithromax 69
Zvishavane, Zimbabwe, Lions
Club 282